A Century of
London
Murders and
Executions

A CENTURY OF
LONDON
MURDERS AND
EXECUTIONS

JOHN J. EDDLESTON

The
History
Press

First published in the United Kingdom in 2008 by
Sutton Publishing, an imprint of The History Press Limited
Cirencester Road · Chalford · Stroud · Gloucestershire · GL6 8PE

British Library Cataloguing in Publication Data
A catalogue record for this book is available from the British
Library.

ISBN 978 0 7509 5040 4

Typesetting and origination by
The History Press Limited.
Printed and bound in England by Ashford Colour Press Ltd., Gosport, Hants.

CONTENTS

INTRODUCTION

This book is divided into four sections. The first two sections cover Greater London itself and is thus split into north and south of the River Thames. The third section lists those crimes which took place outside the capital but still ended in an execution at a London prison.

These three sections would not, however, include every single London execution. Thus, the fourth and final section lists those crimes other than murder which still ended in an execution within London. In this way, the book details every single London murder, and also lists every single London execution – making it the definitive work on capital murder in London in the twentieth century.

Unless otherwise stated, all illustrations are from my own collection.

John J. Eddleston, 2008

NORTH LONDON

Louisa Josephine Jemima Masset, 1900

At 6.19 p.m., on Friday, 27 October 1899, two ladies alighted from a train at Dalston Junction station. Mary Teahan and her friend, Margaret Biggs were going to a lecture in Tottenham Road, Kingsland, but first Miss Teahan needed to attend to a call of nature.

The ladies' rest room was on platform three and Margaret waited there while her companion walked to the lavatory, which was situated at the end of the same platform.

There were just two cubicles inside the lavatory and Miss Teahan decided to use the first one. Unfortunately, some bundle behind the partly closed door was blocking her way. Looking down, Miss Teahan saw what looked like a face. Assuming that some other lady might have been taken ill, Miss Teahan returned to Miss Biggs and the two then found a porter, Joseph John Standing, and reported what they had discovered.

In his turn, Joseph took the story to his foreman, Mr Cotterell and these two gentlemen then went to investigate. Sure enough, there was something behind the cubicle door and closer inspection revealed the dead body of a small child. Without further delay, the police were called in to investigate.

The body of the young boy was naked except for a black shawl covering his midriff. There was a good deal of blood about the child's face and close to his head lay a broken clinker brick which looked like the murder weapon. In fact, according to Dr James Patrick Fennell, who was called to the scene and later did the post-mortem, the child had indeed been battered but had also been suffocated, and the time of death was placed between 3.55 p.m., and 4.55 p.m.

The body bore no marks of identification so the police allowed a detailed description of the child to be published in the local newspapers on Monday, 30 October. It was this that led Helen Eliza Gentle to come forward. Helen, a children's nurse, lived with her mother at 210 Clyde Road, Tottenham. She explained that a young boy fitting the published description had been in her care until the previous Friday; the very day the body had been found. Miss Gentle was escorted to the mortuary and there made a positive identification. The dead child was 3½-year-old Manfred Louis Masset.

Manfred Masset had been born on 24 April 1896 and almost from that time, his mother, Louisa Masset, had placed him in Miss Gentle's care. Louisa was unmarried and lived with her sister at 29 Bethune Road, Stoke Newington. Every fortnight she visted her son and took him out to the local park. This situation had continued without any problems until very recently when Louisa had written

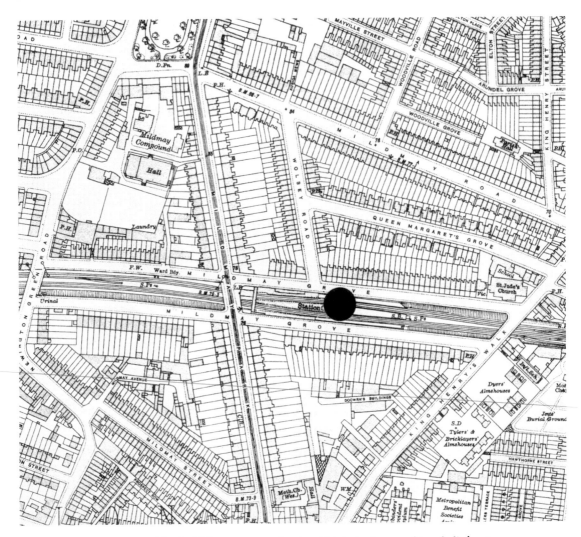

The station where Manfred Masset was murdered and his body discovered in a ladies' rest room.
(Reproduced with the permission of Alan Godfrey Maps)

to Helen stating that the boy's father, who lived in France, wanted the boy sent to him. As a result, on Friday, 27 October, Helen had handed Manfred over to his mother outside the Birdcage public house on Stamford Hill. The handover had taken place at 12.45 p.m. The next move for the police was to find Louisa Masset.

The house at Bethune Road was actually owned by Richard Cadisch who was married to Louisa's older sister, Leonie. They both confirmed the story that Manfred had been taken to his father in France. Louisa left the house at 12.30 p.m. on 27 October and had not returned until 9 p.m. on the Sunday, 29 October. Since her return she had behaved no differently and was now out, attending to some of the pupils she taught music and French. The police now waited outside for Louisa to return.

In the early hours of Tuesday, 31 October, a man was seen to arrive at 29 Bethune Road. Within a minute or two, that man left again, with Richard Cadisch. The police decided to follow the two men. Eventually, they were seen to enter a house in Streatham Road, Croydon. The police knocked on the door.

The house at Croydon was owned by George Symes, who was married to Louisa's other sister, Mathilde. Entering the house, the police found a distressed Louisa Masset. George explained that Louisa had arrived there at 11 p.m. saying that she had seen a newspaper report stating that Manfred's body had been found and she was now being sought by the police. She denied any involvement in his death but was asked to explain what had happened.

Louisa admitted that the story of taking the child to France was a lie. She had been concerned that he was not being taught properly by Miss Gentle and had discussed moving him to another tutor. On 4 October, she had visited Manfred as usual and taken him to the park. There she met two

Part of the letter that Louisa Masset wrote to Helen Gentle, asking for her son to be returned to her. (Public Record Office)

ladies, one of whom was named Browning, and they fell into conversation. Miss Browning told her of a new school they were starting and asked her if she would like Manfred to attend. After some discussion, Louisa agreed terms and arrangements were made to hand the boy over on 27 October.

The plan was to take the child to London Bridge station where Louisa would meet Miss Browning and her companion. Once the exchange had taken place, Louisa would then travel down to Brighton to enjoy a short break. The police found the story hard to believe and took Louisa into custody. In due course, she was charged with the murder of her son.

Louisa Masset appeared before Mr Justice Bruce at the Old Bailey on 13 December 1899. The proceedings would last until 18 December.

Louisa said that she had taken Manfred to London Bridge station. She was seen by Helen Gentle getting onto an omnibus outside the Birdcage. Thomas Bonner was the conductor of that bus and he testified that his vehicle had left Stamford Hill at 12.48 p.m. He noticed Louisa and Manfred and said that they alighted at the station at around 1.35 p.m.

Georgina Worley was an attendant in the ladies' waiting room at London Bridge and she remembered a woman and child at around 1.42 p.m. The couple remained until around 2.30 p.m. Georgina had spoken to the woman who said she was waiting for someone to arrive.

In fact, there were two waiting rooms at the station. Ellen Rees was the attendant at the other and on the day in question she came on duty at 2.30 p.m. Soon afterwards, at perhaps 2.40 p.m., a woman and child had come into the room. She remembered them particularly because the child was crying. This was certainly Manfred, as the two women fell into discussion and the woman confirmed that they boy would turn 4 next April and was crying now because he was missing his nurse. She last saw them at around 3 p.m.

According to Louisa's story, she had been supposed to meet the two ladies who were setting up the new school at 2 p.m. They did not turn up until about 3.55 p.m. and after handing Manfred over to them, Louisa was just in time to catch the 4.07 p.m. train to Brighton. Unfortunately, three witnesses were to count heavily against Louisa.

To begin with, Ellen Rees claimed that she had seen Louisa again at 6.50 p.m. and by now she was alone. She asked Ellen the time of the next Brighton train and was told it was due to leave at 7.20 p.m. If true, this meant that Louisa had lied about the earlier train, implying that she was also lying about the two ladies who took Manfred.

The second witness was Annie Shears, an attendant at Brighton station. On Saturday, 28 October, she had found a brown paper parcel in the waiting room. When it was eventually opened it was found to contain Manfred's clothing, suggesting that Louisa had dumped it at the station while she was in Brighton.

The final witness was a young Frenchman named Eudor Lucas who lived next door to Louisa in Bethune Road. He confirmed that he and Louisa had become close and they had spent that weekend together, in Brighton. This outraged the morality of the time and probably destroyed any sympathy for Louisa in the minds of the jury.

In the event, after a deliberation of just thirty minutes, Louisa was adjudged to be guilty and sentenced to death. She was hanged at Newgate on Tuesday, 9 January 1900, by James Billington and William Warbrick. It was the very first execution of the new century.

Henry Grove, 1900

Henry Smith was brutally murdered over a debt of 1s.

Thirty-four-year-old Henry owned a sweetshop in Enfield, and at the back of his shop was a yard and stable which he rented out to individuals at the princely sum of six pence per week. One of the other traders who took advantage of this arrangement was a 26-year-old hawker named Henry Grove. By Saturday, 24 February 1900, Henry Grove hadn't paid his rent for two weeks, putting his total debt at 1s. As a result, Smith told Grove that he would not be allowed to stable his horse there again until he paid off the outstanding amount. That same night, a somewhat drunken Henry Grove returned from his day's trading, ignored what he had been told and started to stable his horse.

Seeing what was happening, Smith came out of his shop and tried to prevent Grove from entering his yard. An argument started and at one stage Grove was heard to announce that he would kill both Smith and his wife. Mrs Smith had also come outside and, in an effort to maintain the peace, told her husband to come away and let Grove do as he wished. Smith listened to his wife, thought she might well be correct in what she said, and returned to his shop. Grove, however, was not prepared to let the matter rest. He followed Smith inside and struck him twice.

For a time it looked as though that might be the end of the matter. Grove left the shop, found a couple of rusty old scythes in the yard and took them back to his own garden. A few minutes later, though, Grove returned to the yard, still carrying one of the scythes. Finding Henry Smith there, Grove then battered him to the ground, using both the handle and the flat of the blade. When Mrs Smith tried to intervene, she too was struck but her cries caused neighbours to call for the police. Grove was duly arrested.

Grove was originally charged with assault but Henry Smith had been very badly hurt. His right arm and leg were both fractured. His left leg was broken, as was a rib, and he had received severe injuries to the back of his head.

Smith held on to life for another few weeks but finally succumbed to his injuries on Tuesday, 20 March. Grove was now charged with wilful murder and appeared at the Old Bailey before Mr Justice Lawrance on 3 May.

Grove's defence was that Smith had started the fight by striking the first blow and he had merely acted in self-defence. He also denied using the scythe, or indeed any other weapon, and had only used his fists. This was refuted by a statement Smith himself had made in hospital before he died. As a result, the jury took only one hour to decide that Grove was guilty as charged, though they did add a recommendation to mercy. It did nothing to save Henry Grove, who was hanged at Newgate by James Billington on Tuesday, 22 May 1900. He was the first man executed in the twentieth century.

Alfred Highfield, 1900

Twenty-two-year-old Alfred Highfield and 19-year-old Edith Margaret Poole seemed to be such a devoted couple. By 1900 they had been seeing each other for some six years and had now set a provisional wedding date for August of that year.

On Easter Monday, though, the couple argued. Alfred, it seemed, blamed Edith for losing him his job as a labourer at the Westminster Brewery Company, but whatever the truth, Edith announced that she didn't want anything more to do with him. The relationship was over and even when Alfred wrote to her and apologised for his behaviour, Edith was not to be moved.

Alfred was still on good terms with Edith's family and on Sunday, 13 May, Edith's brother invited Alfred to tea. This may have been an attempt to get the couple to talk and possibly sort out their differences and if so, Alfred was certainly willing. At one stage he asked Edith if they could start seeing each other again but Edith would only confirm that as far as she was concerned, the relationship was well and truly over. It was a quiet and subdued Alfred who later agreed to accompany the entire family on a brisk walk after they had finished their tea.

As the group walked, Alfred and Edith fell a little way behind the rest. Then, as they strolled down Great Queen Street near Lincoln's Inn Fields, the family heard a cry. Turning around, they saw Alfred kneeling over the prone figure of Edith.

Running back to where they were, Edith's brother managed to pull Alfred off his sister, but it was too late. Alfred had cut Edith's throat. She was rushed to hospital but despite the best of treatment, she died from her injuries nine days later, on Tuesday, 22 May. Alfred was charged with murder.

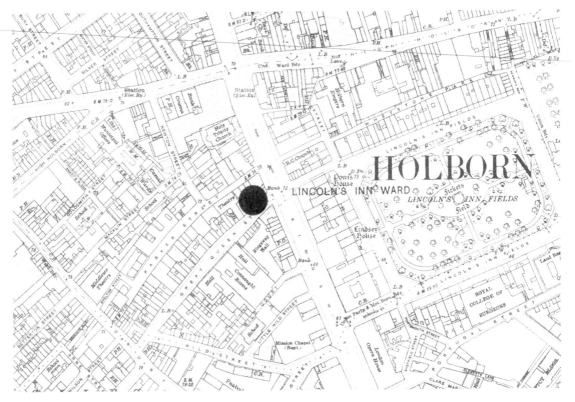

The spot where Alfred Highfield murdered Edith Margaret Poole.
(Reproduced with the permission of Alan Godfrey Maps)

Alfred Highfield appeared at the Old Bailey before Mr Justice Ridley on 27 June 1900. His defence was that this was only a case of manslaughter, not murder.

Alfred said that he had asked Edith, once again, to go out with him. When she had refused he had taken out a razor he habitually carried with him and held it to his throat intending to take his own life. Edith had tried to stop him and in the ensuing struggle he had accidentally cut her throat. However, this defence was largely negated by a statement Alfred made immediately after the attack when he had said, 'I know what I have done. I don't care if I die for it.'

After some deliberation, the jury filed back into court to announce that they could not agree on a verdict. Eleven had voted one way but one juror did not agree. After some discussion with the judge, the jury returned to their deliberations and subsequently returned to say that they had found Highfield guilty but wished to add a recommendation to mercy on account of his youth and previous good character.

Alfred Highfield did not escape the noose, though. On Tuesday, 17 July, he was hanged at Newgate by James Billington. It was exactly eight weeks since Edith Poole had died.

William James Irwin, 1900

Catherine Amelia Irwin was William's second wife. Their relationship was not all it should have been, but even so, before they finally parted in May 1899, four children had been born to the union, the last in February of that same year.

The parting was a civilised one and the couple still saw each other quite often. William was unemployed and Catherine helped him out with gifts of money whenever she could. There was, however, one problem. Catherine had become rather friendly with a gentleman named Sexton and this made William very jealous indeed.

There can be little doubt that this jealousy was a major factor in the break-up of Catherine and William's marriage. It had been Sexton who had visited Catherine in hospital when she was confined with her fourth child, and it was Sexton who had found her somewhere to live once she left. William took to keeping watch outside Catherine's home and on the night of 20 June 1900, he saw that Sexton only left the house at 11.30 p.m.

The following evening, William asked Catherine if she could lend him some more money but she said that she had none to spare. An argument took place and William was heard to say that she had just 'driven the last nail into her coffin.'

The following morning, Friday, 22 June, at 8 a.m., Catherine left home to go to her work as a draper's assistant at Messrs Peter Robinsons of Oxford Street. She was in the company of a fellow worker, Emily Wright. As the two women walked down Great Titchfield Street, William Irwin came up behind them. He demanded to speak to Catherine but she told him she would be late for work. At that, William took out a knife and plunged it into Catherine's breast.

While Catherine was taken to the Middlesex Hospital, William was arrested and charged with attempted murder. Later that same day, Catherine passed away and the charge was amended to one of murder.

William Irwin faced his trial at the Old Bailey on 27 July, before Mr Justice Bigham. Here, a deposition given by Catherine while she was in hospital was read out. In part it stated that when she had said that she didn't have time to talk to him, William had replied, 'Take that then' and had stabbed her.

For the defence, William's barrister argued that this was a crime of passion. He was insanely jealous over the supposed relationship that Catherine had with Sexton and this provocation meant that he could only be guilty of manslaughter. The jury, however, did not agree, though they did add a recommendation to mercy.

Less than three weeks later, on Tuesday, 14 August, William Irwin was hanged at Newgate by James Billington.

John Charles Parr, 1900

Of all the places to commit a murder, none could be more foolish than right outside a police station. Nevertheless, that is precisely what 19-year-old John Parr managed to do.

Parr was engaged to Sarah Willett, but in the summer of 1900 she broke it off. She discovered that Parr had been imprisoned for theft and he had also lied about being in regular employment. Sarah said that she simply couldn't trust such a man and wanted nothing more to do with him. This decision affected Parr badly and he began to display some very strange behaviour.

On 25 August, Parr was in a public house with three female friends. At one stage he drew out a small revolver and said that he was going to use it to kill Sarah and then himself. As if to emphasis the point he then fired the gun into the street shouting, 'Instead of a marriage you will hear of a burial.' Somewhat surprisingly, no one who saw this thought it worth reporting to the police!

On Saturday, 27 August, Sarah and two girlfriends visited the Forester's Music Hall in the West End. Parr had heard of this arrangement and also turned up. He asked Sarah to buy him a drink and when she refused he simply picked up her glass and drained the contents. Seeking to avoid a confrontation, Sarah and her friends, Emily Samson and Kate Burgess, left the music hall. Parr followed behind.

As the three girls walked down Bethnal Green Road, Parr caught up with them and demanded to know if Sarah would take him back. She replied, 'I don't want you. All I want is an honest, hard-working fellow – not one who robs others.' She then pulled away from Parr and threatened to go and report him at the police station, which was directly opposite where they were standing.

Parr told Sarah to go ahead and she turned on her heel intending to do so. At that moment Parr drew out the small revolver and shot Sarah in the head. A police officer, hearing the shot, ran out of the station and found Parr with the gun still in his hand, shouting, 'I have done it! I have done it!'

Parr appeared at the Old Bailey, before Mr Justice Bucknill on 13 September. The defence was one of insanity and testimony was given that there was a history of madness within the family and Parr himself had received a severe blow to the head some years ago, which might have affected his mental balance.

The jury was not swayed but they did add a recommendation to mercy on account of Parr's youth. Despite this, he was hanged at Newgate by James Billington on Tuesday, 2 October.

William Burrett, 1900

William and Ada Gubb Burrett were married in July 1900, and from that moment on he lived off her earnings as a prostitute. It was not a state of affairs that Ada relished and she repeatedly begged William to get a job so that she could give up her profession. William refused to listen.

In mid-July, the Burretts took a room in Alexandra Road, Plaistow, but still William did no work while Ada earned her living on the streets. The truth was that the relationship was strained, to say the least.

On the morning of Saturday, 25 August, Mrs Fitzpatrick, the landlady of the house, heard the front door slam shut. Very soon afterwards a young boy delivering newspapers looked in at the open door of the house and saw what he took to be a bundle of rags at the foot of the stairs. The bundle was, in fact, the body of Ada Burrett and she had been stabbed a number of times. The same paper-boy would later report that he had seen a man leave the house with a large knife sticking out of his pocket.

Although very badly injured, Ada was not actually dead. She was taken to hospital where she was able to make a statement outlining the attack her husband had made upon her. She had been stabbed nine times in all with the crucial wound being a deep one in her stomach. Later that same evening, Ada died from her injuries.

William Burrett was facing a charge of murder, but had it not been for the inept behaviour of the doctor called to the scene he might have been facing a much lesser charge. Dr James Parker had been called to the scene and he later gave evidence that he had refused to attend to the poor woman until the police arrived as he had wanted them to see precisely what state she was in.

Burrett appeared at the Old Bailey before Mr Justice Bucknill on 14 September. Besides Ada's deposition, witnesses were called who had heard William threaten more than once that he would kill his wife. For his part, William said that he had stabbed Ada in the heat of an argument and so should only be guilty of manslaughter.

Not surprisingly, he was found guilty of murder and was hanged at Chelmsford on Wednesday, 3 October by James Billington.

Samson Silas Salmon, 1901

Constable John Bensted would certainly remember this particular day. There lay 32-year-old Lucy Smith, in the kitchen of her house at 23 Venour Road, Bow, her head almost hacked from her body. On the floor were two bloodstained knives, and sitting on a chair nearby was Samson Salmon, the man who admitted to killing her.

Salmon had lived with his cousin, Lucy and her husband, Samuel, since early in 1899 and had paid then 23s per week for his lodgings. In due course, however, Salmon lost his job at the chemical works but was allowed to stay on, even though he could no longer afford to pay. Things would have been fine but, depressed at being unemployed, Salmon took to drink and his personality changed.

On 10 December 1900, Salmon struck Lucy, Samuel and a neighbour, Mr Baker, who tried to intervene. Salmon also brandished a knife and it was with some difficulty that Samuel and the neighbour disarmed him and evicted him from the house. Later that same day, though, Salmon returned, climbed a wall at the back of the house and announced that it was his intention to sleep in the cellar. Rather surprisingly, Samuel Smith said that Salmon could return to his old room on condition that he behaved himself. Salmon agreed.

The following day, Salmon was again very troublesome and threatened to kill the Smiths and their daughter. He later apologised, left the house and said that he was going to look for work away from London. Once again, the house was quiet.

On Saturday, 15 December, Samuel Smith returned home from work at 8 a.m. to find Salmon waiting for him in the hallway. Smith demanded to know what he was doing there but Salmon would only say that he should go and fetch a policeman. Samuel then went into the kitchen and found his wife's body on the floor.

Salmon appeared before Mr Justice Wills at the Old Bailey on 28 January 1901. The proceedings lasted for two days and Salmon admitted that on the day in question he had again climbed over the wall at the rear of the house. He had then hidden in the yard until Lucy finally came out with some ashes from the fire. As she returned to the kitchen, Salmon followed her and, after an argument, hit out at her and then slashed her throat – his defence being that he was drunk at the time and so was not responsible for his actions.

This defence was largely negated by the evidence of Constable Bensted, who said that when first spoken to, Salmon had said, 'I did it and I will swing for it.' On that score he was correct, being hanged at Newgate by James Billington on Tuesday, 19 February.

Marcel Fougeron, 1901

Marcel Fougeron was a Frenchman who spoke very little English and had arrived in Britain some time in July 1901. Somewhat down on his luck and recently thrown out of his lodgings in Whitfield Street, Fougeron needed assistance. Fortunately, he knew just where he could find it. Hermann Francis Jung ran a jeweller's shop at 4 Lower Charles Street, Clerkenwell. He was a member of the Swiss Benevolent Society and was known to help foreigners in need of employment or a place to stay.

On Tuesday, 3 September Mrs Jung saw Fougeron come into her husband's shop. The two gentlemen began to chat, quite amicably, in French, so she went downstairs to get on with her own work.

At 3.40 p.m., Mrs Jung heard some kind of commotion coming from the shop upstairs. Going to investigate, she found her husband lying on the floor in an ever widening pool of blood, a knife sticking out of his chest. Fougeron was just dashing out of the front door and, bravely, Mrs Jung gave chase, calling for help. Fortunately, Constable Troughton was nearby and he ran after Fougeron, blowing his whistle as he did so. Fougeron turned into Bydon Crescent as a second officer, Constable Bevan, joined in the chase. Very soon, the fugitive was captured and taken back to the jeweller's shop.

Mrs Jung immediately identified Fougeron as the man who had attacked her husband. The poor man was clearly dead and this was now a case of murder.

Fougeron appeared before Mr Justice Bigham at the Old Bailey on 28 October, the proceedings lasting over two days. The defence was startling to say the least.

Fougeron claimed that Hermann Jung was, in fact, an anarchist and had been busily recruiting people to his cause. He went on to say that they had met up a few times and Jung had given him money, but then, on the day in question, Jung had suggested that he assassinate the Colonial Secretary, Mr Chamberlain. Fougeron had refused and tried to leave the shop, whereupon Jung had blocked his way and demanded repayment of the monies he had given him in the past.

A struggle had broken out and at one stage Jung threw a heavy piece of iron at Fougeron, who had then drawn his knife and stabbed the man in self-defence. There was, however, one major problem with this scenario. The piece of iron had indeed been found in the shop but it was covered in a thick layer of dust, showing that it had not been touched for some considerable time. The jury found little difficulty in returning a guilty verdict.

Fougeron was hanged at Newgate by James Billington and Henry Pierrepoint on Tuesday, 19 November 1901.

George Woolfe, 1902

Depending perhaps on one's affiliations, the name Tottenham is synonymous with football. It was that very game that, on Sunday, 26 January 1902, took a group of schoolboys to Tottenham Marshes for a quick kickabout.

After some minutes of play, an erratic shot fired the ball into a ditch and one of the lads went to retrieve it. As he moved down into the ditch, the boy discovered the battered body of a young woman. All thoughts of football were forgotten and the players ran off to fetch the police.

The body was soon identified as 22-year-old Charlotte Cheeseman and, from the crime scene, it looked as if she had been taken to the spot where a struggle had then taken place. In fact, Charlotte had also been stabbed, possibly by a chisel, as well as being badly beaten and her body then rolled down an embankment into the ditch.

Charlotte's family were traced and they were able to inform the investigating officers that she had been walking out with 21-year-old George Woolfe, an ex-soldier. The relationship had been rather strained of late and many arguments had been overheard. Indeed, only recently Woolfe had been heard to say that he intended to '…get shot of her.'

Further investigations revealed that on the night she was killed, Saturday the 25th, Charlotte and Woolfe had been seen drinking together in the Rosemary Branch public house. Later still, they were in the Park Hotel where customers described Charlotte as being slightly the worse for drink and Woolfe as looking very angry indeed.

When officers visited Woolfe's home at 20 Eagle Wharf Road, Hoxton, they found that he was no longer there. The only other facts they could discover was that at around midnight on the 25th, Woolfe had been in the company of three men, in yet another pub. He had argued with one of them, a man named Sapsford, who had struck Woolfe. Finally, the last sighting of Woolfe had been on the 26th when he had called at Charlotte's house and asked her mother if she had come home the previous night.

Since Woolfe was an ex-soldier, it was suggested that he might well have re-enlisted. Upon checking, it was found that no-one named Woolfe had signed up around that time but a man named Slater had just joined the Surrey Militia and was now stationed at St George's Barracks. When he was interviewed, Slater turned out to be none other than George Woolfe and he was promptly arrested and charged with murder.

Woolfe appeared before Mr Justice Grantham at the Old Bailey on 14 April. The proceedings would last until 16 April.

Woolfe readily admitted being with Charlotte on the night she died. He claimed, however, that she was still alive when they parted at around 7.30 p.m. Witnesses were then called from the Rosemary Branch and the Park Hotel to show that they had been together long after this time. There was also the fact that Woolfe was badly scratched when he called at Charlotte's house on the 26th and he claimed that these were injuries from the altercation with Sapsford. Unfortunately for Woolfe, the three men he had been drinking with all swore that no blood had been drawn when the punch was thrown.

Found guilty after a deliberation of less than one hour, Woolfe was hanged at Newgate by William and John Billington on Tuesday, 6 May 1902. He earned his place in history by being the last person to be executed at the infamous prison.

George Woolfe became the last man to ever suffer death by hanging at Newgate Prison.

John MacDonald, 1902

Henry Groves, who was known by the nickname 'Soldier', was murdered because of a debt of 5s.

In late 1902, 5s had been stolen from 24-year-old John MacDonald while he slept at the Salvation Army Hostel in Middlesex Street, Spitalfields. Though it couldn't be proved who had taken the cash, MacDonald blamed Groves, and on 21 August MacDonald was seen sharpening a knife and threatening to kill Groves.

Exactly one week later, on Thursday, 28 August, MacDonald was walking past a crockery shop in Old Castle Street when he noticed Groves inside. MacDonald went into the shop and an argument broke out between the two men. After some minutes of heated discussion Groves left the shop, followed by MacDonald.

Groves turned into Wentworth Street where, at the gateway to a school at the top of the street, MacDonald caught up with him, grabbed him, spun him around and hit him. Groves might have been much older than his assailant but he was a fit enough man and he hit back, knocking MacDonald to the ground before walking off.

MacDonald picked himself up and went after Groves again. A passer-by, one Samuel Dodds, tried to break the two men up but even as he intervened he noticed that MacDonald had drawn out a knife. Once again Groves was spun around by his attacker, but this time MacDonald plunged the knife deep into the front of his neck.

As Groves staggered off up the street, bleeding from his throat, Dodds bravely leapt on top of MacDonald and held him until the police arrived. A few minutes later, Henry Groves breathed his last, the knife having penetrated an artery.

MacDonald was put on trial at the Old Bailey on 11 September, before Mr Justice Walton. His defence was that he was so drunk he had not known what he was doing and had had no intention of killing Groves. This was countered by his threats of the previous week and the fact that just forty-five minutes before the attack he had shown someone the weapon and said that he intended to stick it into Groves.

On Tuesday, 30 September 1902, MacDonald became the first man to be executed at Pentonville when William Billington, assisted by John Billington and Henry Pierrepoint, hanged him.

Henry Williams, 1902

Henry Williams had been seeing Ellen Andrews since 1893. The couple never married but were soon living together and, in 1897, she gave birth to a daughter, Margaret Anne. Henry was besotted by his daughter and loved her with all his heart. That same year, Henry went off to fight in South Africa and did not return to England until July 1902. By now, his beloved daughter was 5 years old.

There was, however, one major problem. Henry had managed to convince himself that while he had been away fighting for his country, Ellen had been having an affair with a sailor. Ellen tried her best to convince him that nothing had happened but he would not be persuaded. He decided that he had to hurt Ellen just as much as she had hurt him.

There was one other factor playing on Henry's mind. If he left his daughter with such a woman then perhaps she might grow up to be cast in the same mould and break some other man's heart. How could he hurt Ellen and at the same time ensure that his daughter never turned out to be the same sort of person as her mother?

That autumn, Ellen and Margaret were enjoying a short break in Worthing, Sussex. Henry went down to see them, argued with Ellen and told her that he would never hurt her but he was going to break her heart. He returned to London that same day, taking his daughter home with him to Waterford Road, Fulham. It was Wednesday, 10 September.

That same evening, Henry entered the Lord Palmerston public house on King's Road. Speaking to a friend of his, Henry said that with Ellen being as she was, he could never allow Margaret to call him 'daddy'. He went on to say that he had solved his problem. He had murdered his precious daughter.

Henry had put his daughter to bed, laying her favourite doll by her side. Then, with tears clouding his eyes, he had told her that they were going to play a game. He gently covered her eyes with a handkerchief then took a sharp knife from his pocket and cut her throat. He then covered her body with a union flag.

Henry appeared before Mr Justice Jelf at the Old Bailey on 23 October. His defence tried to claim that he had been insane at the time he killed Margaret, but the jury had little difficulty in deciding that he was guilty of murder, though they did add a strong recommendation to mercy.

It did nothing to save Henry's life and on Tuesday, 11 November he was hanged at Pentonville by William Billington and Henry Pierrepoint.

Thomas Fairclough Barrow, 1902

Although they were not actually married, 49-year-old Thomas Barrow and 32-year-old Emily Coates had lived together as man and wife for almost fifteen years. Indeed, Emily was also Barrow's stepdaughter, and by 1902 they were living at 17 Red Lion Street, Wapping.

In due course, the relationship became strained and arguments more frequent. They also became physical as Barrow had become violent towards Emily. Finally, she decided that it was time to move out and call it a day. She had one, final parting shot. Emily served Thomas with a warrant for assaulting her. It was presented to Thomas on 16 October and was to be answered by him on Saturday, 18 October.

On the Friday, Thomas visited Emily at her lodgings and demanded to know what she was up to. She refused to speak to him and slammed the door in his face. Thomas then crouched down, pushed open the letterbox and shouted that she would hear more from him before noon the following day.

The next morning, Emily set off to work and as she turned into Glamis Road, Shadwell, a figure ran up behind her. It was Thomas, and before Emily could say a word, he drew out a knife and stabbed her five times. One of those wounds penetrated her heart and Emily died immediately. Thomas then calmly waited for a policeman and, when the officer arrived, announced, 'This will end it all; now all I want is a rope around my neck.'

Thomas Barrow appeared before Mr Justice Bigham at the Old Bailey on 19 November. At the trial, Dr Scott, the medical officer of Brixton Prison, testified that Barrow had complained of pains in his head. Family history showed that he had once attempted suicide and, as a result, his defence claimed that he was insane at the time of the attack. Dr Scott did not agree and said that the prisoner was perfectly sane. The jury did not even bother to leave the box before announcing their guilty verdict.

On Tuesday, 9 December 1902, Thomas Barrow was hanged at Pentonville by William and John Billington.

Amelia Sach & Annie Walters, 1903

For some time, 29-year-old Amelia Sach had run a small home for unmarried mothers in East Finchley. For a reasonable fee she would assist the women as they gave birth and then find a nice home for the newborn infant. Occasionally, however, there might be a problem finding such a home. In such cases, Amelia would call upon her friend and colleague, 54-year-old Annie Walters.

Annie was perhaps rather simple-minded, but she had a reliable method of dealing with hard to place babies. She would simply take the child, administer a few drops of a morphine-based sedative called chlorodyne, and eventually the poor child would die from asphyxia. If the drug failed to work, then Annie would help things along by smothering the baby.

In August 1903, a Miss Galley gave birth to a boy at the home run by Amelia. She was told that a new home had already been found and she had no need to worry; the child would be well looked after. The fee for this service was the not inconsiderable sum of £30.

The activities of the two ladies had already come to the attention of the police, who were curious to discover what exactly was happening to the many children who passed through the establishment. So, when Annie Walters was seen leaving the home on Tuesday, 18 November 1902, carrying a small bundle, she was followed by officers.

Annie was trailed to South Kensington and stopped at the railway station. The bundle was examined and found to contain the dead body of Miss Galley's son. A later medical examination would confirm the cause of death as asphyxiation.

Annie said that she had been asked to take the boy to Kensington, to meet a potential foster mother. The child had been somewhat raucous and so to quieten it she had administered two drops of chlorodyne. She had not known that the child had died until she was stopped by the police. At worst, this was a case of manslaughter.

When Amelia was interviewed, she denied handing the child to her partner. As a matter of routine, the home was then searched and more than 300 articles of baby clothing discovered. It was estimated that as many as twenty young victims might be placed at the door of the two women.

The two defendants took their place before Mr Justice Darling at the Old Bailey on 15 January. The proceedings lasted two days and again the defence was one of manslaughter. However, after listening to all the evidence, the judge in his summing up said that the only possible verdicts were not guilty or guilty of wilful murder. The jury took just forty minutes to decide that the latter was the correct conclusion.

On Tuesday, 1 February 1903, Sach and Walters were hanged together by William Billington and Henry Pierrepoint. They were the first executions to be carried out at Holloway.

George Joseph Chapman (Severiano Antoniovitch Klosowski), 1903

At 12.30 p.m. on Wednesday, 22 October 1902, Maud Eliza Marsh died at The Crown public house on High Street, Islington. Dr Stoker, the medical practitioner in attendance, refused to issue a death certificate. The reason for this was that the good doctor had attended another woman who had displayed identical symptoms. He believed he was almost certainly looking at a case of poisoning.

The doctor believed that the cause of death had been arsenic, but the subsequent post-mortem showed only minute traces of that element. A tissue sample was therefore sent to two colleagues who both deduced that another substance, tartar emetic, an antimony-based poison, had been responsible for the death of Maud Marsh. As a result, three days after her death, Maud's paramour, 37-year-old George Chapman was arrested, under his real name of Klosowski.

Klosowski had certainly led an interesting life. Born in Poland, he had first set foot in England in 1888 and taken employment as a barber's assistant in a shop underneath the White Hart public house at 89 Whitechapel High Street. The following year he married Lucy Baderski in Walthamstow, and a son was born to the union soon afterwards. The relationship did not last, however, for just a few weeks after giving birth, Lucy was dismayed to see another woman appear, from Poland, claiming to be Klosowski's legal wife.

The woman was sent packing and in 1891, Klosowski, Lucy and their child emigrated to America where the boy died. Lucy returned to England, to be followed a few weeks later by Klosowski. On 12 May 1891, Lucy gave birth to a daughter, but one year later she decided that she had had enough of her husband's womanising ways and left him for good, taking her daughter with her.

At the end of 1893, Klosowski became involved with a woman named Annie Chapman and they soon started living together. The relationship lasted until the end of 1894, by which time Klosowski had taken to calling himself George Chapman, a name he kept for the rest of his life.

Once George and Annie had split up, he moved in with John Ward, an old friend. Another lodger there was Isabella Mary Spink. A relationship developed and soon the couple were announcing their intention to marry. They moved to Hastings in March 1896 and Chapman opened a new barber's shop, which was, by all accounts, a great success. For a time at least, all seemed to be well.

Unfortunately for Isabella, though, Chapman soon tired of her and wished to move on to pastures new. On 3 April 1897, he purchased one ounce of tartar emetic from Davidson's Chemist, in Hastings. A fatal dose of the substance was estimated to be around 15 grains. The ounce Chapman had purchased was equivalent to over 400 grains.

In the autumn of that same year, September to be precise, Chapman and Isabella moved back to London. He had by now decided on a change of career and took the lease on the Prince of Wales pub in Bartholomew Square, Finsbury. It was at that establishment, on Saturday, 25 December 1897, that Isabella passed away after a short illness. The cause of death was given as a consumptive disorder.

By Easter of 1898, Chapman had decided that he needed a new barmaid. So it was that one Elizabeth Taylor, known as Bessie, started work at the pub, and very soon she and Chapman became lovers. There might well have been some local gossip over how soon after Isabella's death the new relationship had started because the couple soon left the Prince and Wales and took a lease on The Grapes in Bishop's Stortford. They didn't stay there long though, and returned to London in 1899.

On 2 March 1899, Chapman took over The Monument pub in Union Street, Islington, and it was there, on Wednesday, 13 February 1901, that Bessie Taylor died after a period of illness. Dr Stoker attended and gave the cause of death as an intestinal obstruction. Once again, Chapman didn't wait too long before finding a replacement, and by August, Maud Marsh was the new barmaid and Chapman's new lover.

It was soon time to move on again because, by June 1903, the lease on The Monument was about to expire. Before it did, however, the place caught fire. Luckily, Chapman and Maud were out at the time and simply claimed on the insurance. However, the insurance company suspected arson and refused to pay. Chapman simply moved on and took over The Crown in High Street, Islington.

No sooner had the move taken place than Chapman found himself falling for yet another young, attractive barmaid. This time the object of his desire was Florence Rayner. He asked her to go to America with him but she refused and quit her job. It didn't change how Chapman felt about Maud though. He had grown tired of her. It was time for her to go.

Once again there was a short period of illness, during which Maud was fussed over by an attentive Chapman. His ministrations did no good though, so she was moved into Guy's Hospital on 28 July. Maud stayed there until 28 August, during which time her condition gradually improved. Once she returned to Chapman, the old symptoms returned and Maud finally expired on 22 October.

The findings of the doctors were now taken to the police and Chapman was arrested and charged with Maud's murder. The bodies of his two previous lovers were exhumed and tests showed 3.83 grains of tartar emetic in Isabella and 29.12 grains in Bessie. On the last day of 1902, Chapman was charged with two further counts of murder.

Chapman appeared before Mr Justice Grantham at the Old Bailey on 16 March 1903. The proceedings lasted until 19 March. No witnesses were called for the defence, his barrister relying instead on the apparent absence of motive. Also, there was no hard evidence to show that it was Chapman who had actually administered the poison. The jury looked at the circumstantial evidence though, and deliberated for just ten minutes before returning a guilty verdict.

On Tuesday, 7 April 1903, Chapman was hanged at Wandsworth by William Billington and Henry Pierrepoint. In subsequent years, Chapman was named as a possible suspect for the Jack the Ripper murders of 1888. The only evidence is that he did live in the area of the crimes in that year, and of course he later became a convicted multiple murderer. It is, however, highly unlikely that someone who butchered prostitutes as the Ripper did would later turn to poison as a weapon.

Charles Jeremiah Slowe, 1903

Being a barmaid means that, occasionally, a customer might come on just a little too strong and overstep the mark. Of course, most barmaids are more than capable of coping with such unwelcome attention and this was certainly true of 20-year-old Martha Jane Hardwick.

Martha lived with her sister, Jane Starkey, who was the landlady of the Lord Nelson public house on Whitechapel Road. In return for her keep, Martha would help out behind the bar. She was certainly very popular with the customers, especially one in particular, Charles Jeremiah Slowe.

Slowe constantly asked Martha to go out with him, and she just as constantly refused. He persisted though, and became such a nuisance that Martha began avoiding him. When Slowe walked into one of the bars, Martha would leave and go into the other. Slowe soon picked up on this behaviour; it angered him and he was heard to issue threats against her. These threats came to the ears of Martha herself and this made her avoid him even more. It was a circle of behaviour that would lead to tragedy.

On the evening of Wednesday, 23 September 1903, Slowe walked into one of the bars at the Lord Nelson and saw Martha leave and go into the other. It would be the last time she ever slighted him. He finished his drink and left without speaking. It was then around 10 p.m.

By the time the pub closed and the last customers had been turned out into the night it was just after midnight. Martha stood in one of the doorways bidding her good nights to the last of the drinkers and did not see Slowe creep up behind her. The next thing anyone knew, Slowe was apparently hitting her in the side and shouting, 'I've got you now!'

In fact, Slowe had a knife in his hand and was stabbing Martha repeatedly. As she sank to the floor, Slowe ran off, bravely chased by Jane Starkey who managed to get a passer-by to assist her. Slowe was captured and held until the police arrived to take him into custody.

Slowe's subsequent trial took place before Mr Justice Bigham at the Old Bailey on 21 October. The defence was that Slowe had acted in a fit of insane jealousy and that the crime had not been premeditated. This was largely negated by the fact that Slowe had left the pub at 10 p.m. and returned just after midnight in order to carry out his attack. As a result, the jury found little difficulty in returning a guilty verdict.

On Tuesday, 10 November 1903, Slowe was hanged at Pentonville by William and John Billington.

Chalres Wade & Joseph Potter, 1904

At 6.30 a.m. on Wednesday, 12 October 1904, an errand boy arrived at Matilda Emily Farmer's newsagency at 478 Commercial Road, Stepney. To his surprise, the shop was open but there was no sign of the owner.

An hour passed and still there was no sign of 65-year-old Miss Farmer. In due course, the concerns of the errand boy and various potential customers were passed on to the police, and when an officer attended and entered the shop he immediately spotted a set of false teeth and a single boot lying near the counter. Going into the back of the shop, the officer also found a pair of spectacles on the stairs and, on going upstairs, found Matilda lying face down on the bed. She had not simply fallen ill, though, for her hands were tied behind her back and a towel was around her mouth. The officer did find a faint pulse, but by the time Dr Grant had been called out Matilda had passed away, the cause of death later being given as asphyxiation.

The bedroom where the body was found was in a state of disarray. It looked like the shopkeeper had been tied up during a robbery and her death had probably been accidental, the towel being forced into her mouth to prevent her calling for help. However, she had died as a result of a robbery and that still made this a case of murder.

An appeal for anyone with information brought forward Richard Barnes. He said that late on 11 October he had seen two men standing close by the shop, behaving somewhat suspiciously. Further, he could name one of the men as 22-year-old Charles Wade.

Another witness described two men he had seen leaving the shop at around 6.20 a.m. on the day Matilda had been found. One of the descriptions he gave fitted Charles Wade, while the other described Wade's half-brother, Joseph Potter, who was also known as Conrad Donovan. Both men, who had previous convictions for robbery, were arrested on 16 October.

In fact, what might have looked like an open and shut case was anything of the sort. None of the missing property was traced to either man; one witness admitted that he had seen pictures of the two men in the newspapers before he identified them and two other witnesses failed to pick out either man. However, both men were still put on trial for murder.

The trial opened before Mr Justice Grantham at the Old Bailey on 18 November and lasted until 21 November. Despite problems with the evidence, the jury still only took ten minutes to return guilty verdicts on both men.

On Tuesday, 13 December 1904, Potter and Wade were hanged together at Pentonville by William Billington and Henry Pierrepoint. It was said that shortly before they were hanged, Potter said to the chaplain, 'No murder was intended.' Those four words confirmed that the verdict had been correct.

Alfred Bridgeman, 1905

At Christmas 1904, 22-year-old Alfred Bridgeman and his fiancée broke off their engagement. They remained on excellent terms though, and he would often visit her home in Compton Street, St Pancras. Bridgeman did not, however, enjoy the same warm relationship with the woman who would have become his mother-in-law, 48-year-old Catherina Balhard.

On Friday, 3 March 1905, Bridgeman created something of a disturbance at Mrs Balhard's house. He had perhaps had a little too much to drink so nothing much was made of this lapse in his behaviour. The following day, Saturday, Bridgeman was drinking again with his ex-fiancée, in a pub close to Compton Street. In due course, the couple left to walk back to her house.

Mrs Shadbolt was a lodger at Mrs Balhard's house and she saw Bridgeman leaving his girlfriend's room later that same day. Some minutes later she heard his footsteps returning up the stairs, followed by the sounds of an argument and then a terrible scream.

Mrs Shadbolt dashed out of her room in time to see Bridgeman running down the stairs and out of the house. Further investigation revealed Catherina Balhard lying dead, her throat cut savagely. Mrs Shadbolt immediately called for the police and told them what she had seen.

Bridgeman was not arrested until Monday, 6 March, in Hunter Street and was found to be still carrying the bloodstained razor he had used. Further, when interviewed by the police he readily admitted his guilt, saying that Mrs Balhard had ben saying bad things about him and he was, 'ready to swing' for what he had done.

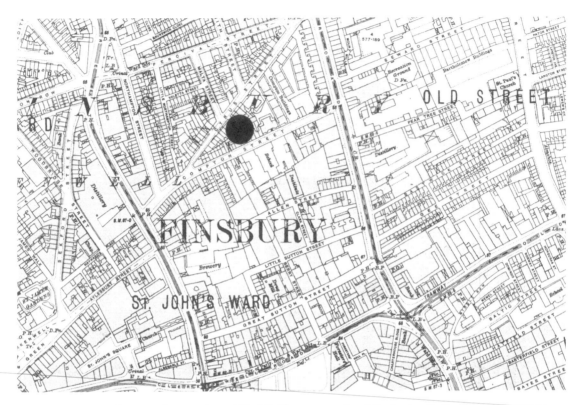

Compton Street, where Alfred Bridgeman murdered Catherina Balhard.
(Reproduced with the permission of Alan Godfrey Maps)

Alfred Bridgeman appeared before Mr Justice Jelf at the Old Bailey on 5 April, the defence being one of drink and insanity. Bridgeman claimed that he had not known what he was doing owing to being very drunk at the time, and also referred to an incident some years before in South Africa, when a large piece of iron had fallen onto his head. None of this convinced the jury who returned a guilty verdict after just a few minutes of deliberation.

On Wednesday, 26 April 1905, Bridgeman was hanged at Pentonville by John Billington and Henry Pierrepoint.

Arthur Devereux, 1905

Ellen Gregory hadn't seen her married daughter, Beatrice Devereux, or her three grandchildren for the best part of three weeks – not since Saturday, 28 January 1905. Since then, Ellen had been away but it was unusual for Beatrice not to write to her. Now, in February, Ellen knocked on the door of her daughter's house at 60 Milton Avenue, Harlesden, but there was no answer. While she was still trying to gain admittance, a neighbour told her that the family had moved out on 7 February.

Ellen was not one to be put off lightly, and by talking to other neighbours she discovered that a removal firm named Bannister's had taken the furniture. Their offices in Kensal Rise was the next port of call. It was there that Ellen determined that the new address was 92 Harrow Road and that a large trunk had been left in storage at the firm's depot.

The owner of 92 Harrow Road was John Tabboth and he confirmed that on 6 February, Arthur Devereux, Ellen's son-in-law, had taken on the property for himself and his son. This puzzled Ellen, for there were five people in the family: Arthur and Beatrice, Stanley, who was almost 6, and 2-year-old twin boys, Laurence Rowland and Evelyn Lancelot. The tenacious Ellen Gregory then discovered that Arthur and his son had moved on again, this time on 20 February, apparently for a new position in Coventry.

It was not until April that Ellen felt that all of her own avenues of investigation were now exhausted, so she took her suspicions to the police. The first step for them, naturally, was to investigate the trunk left at Bannister's. This was taken out of storage by officers on 13 April.

The trunk was padlocked, strapped and sealed with red wax. When it was forced open, a layer of carefully fitted wooden planks was found inside, sealed with glue. Once this had been breached, some clothing was seen and below this, finally, the bodies of a woman and two small boys were found. They were identified as Beatrice and the twins. An examination would show that all three had been poisoned with morphine.

It was a very simple matter to trace Arthur Devereux, for he had written to Mr Tabboth giving a return address of 156 Spon Street, Coventry; the business premises of a chemist, Mr Bird. Devereux had taken employment with that gentleman and was arrested at that address on the evening of 13 April. His eldest son, Stanley, was found safe and well. Taken back to London, Devereux was then charged with three murders.

Devereux's trial opened before Mr Justice Ridley at the Old Bailey on 26 July. The proceedings were to last for three days and Devereux's defence was simply that he was not the killer, though he admitted he had hidden the bodies.

Devereux explained that he had been a chemist, employed at a shop in Kilburn, but business was bad and it was clear that he was going to lose his job. He started to apply for new positions and wrote off to Mr Bird in Coventry on 13 January, describing himself as a widower with one child. This statement was, in fact, most useful to the prosecution as it seemed to show premeditation since Beatrice and the twins were certainly alive at that time.

Continuing his testimony, Devereux said that his wife had last seen her mother on 28 January, and when he had returned home from work on that date he found the house smelling strongly of chloroform. Going upstairs, he had found his wife and the twins lying dead in their beds. It was clear that Beatrice had killed herself and the twins, no doubt due to financial concerns over him losing his job and having to move to the Midlands. In a panic, he had believed that the only thing to do was to hide the bodies, which is precisely what he did.

Further evidence was given that Beatrice might well have been unstable enough to commit such a crime. In July 1903, her brother Sidney had vanished. His clothing was found on Plymouth Hoe and it was presumed he had drowned himself. A Mrs Harries, who had known Beatrice for many years, testified that in 1899 she had heard Beatrice threaten to do away with herself and Stanley. Even Ellen Gregory herself admitted that her daughter had suffered badly from depression.

Devereux himself was not exactly mentally stable. In the past he had made outlandish claims; once posing as a millionaire, claiming also that he had helped God to create the world and had written all the books in the world. Wouldn't a man of this type have behaved precisely as he had said if faced with three dead bodies?

The jury were not convinced and deliberated for just ten minutes before returning their guilty verdict. Just over two weeks later, on Tuesday, 15 August, Devereux was hanged at Pentonville by Henry Pierrepoint and John Ellis.

George William Butler, 1905

Mary Allen had twice been married but both relationships had ended and, by 1902, she was involved with 50-year-old George William Butler, living with him in Union Street, Marylebone. Things were fine between them until, in the summer of 1905, Mary's son, George Melhuish, went to live with her and Butler. From the outset, the two men did not get on.

Towards the end of July, the antipathy between the two finally spilled over into violence with Butler coming off worst. Indeed, Butler needed hospital treatment for injuries to his jaw and he was still in great pain when he was discharged and returned home.

On 17 September, Butler argued with Mary and later that same day, while talking to a neighbour, complained that Mary and Melhuish were conspiring against him. He ended by threatening to 'do for the two of them.'

Exactly one week later, on 24 September, Butler was visited by his own son and the two went out drinking together. Butler's jaw was still causing him trouble and he had to drink his beer through a straw. He told his son the details of what had happened and again threatened Melhuish and Mary, saying he would get a gun and blow their brains out. Butler's son took little notice, assuming it was simply the beer talking.

On the afternoon of the next day, Monday, 25 September, Mary Allen was heard calling for help. George rushed into her room to see what the problem was, only to find that Butler had stabbed Mary four times. Butler was arrested and charged with attempted murder, but when Mary died two days later the charge was amended to one of wilful murder.

Butler appeared before Mr Justice Jelf at the Old Bailey on 19 October. He claimed that he had not known what he was doing due to effects of alcohol, but his previous threats to injure Mary and her son were well documented and showed that the crime was premeditated. Found guilty, Butler was hanged at Pentonville by Henry Pierrepoint and John Ellis on Tuesday, 7 November.

John Esmond Murphy, 1909

It was just before noon on Saturday, 7 November 1908 and people were going about their business as normal in Shaftesbury Avenue, when all of a sudden all hell broke loose.

The window of no. 84 shattered as a piece of metal was hurled through it from within. As the glass tumbled to the pavement, people looked inside to see two men grappling with each other. The taller man was coming off worst, though, as the shorter one was stabbing him repeatedly with a dagger.

Number 84 Shaftesbury Avenue was the office of Carnell and Schlitte, bankers and money changers, and the man being stabbed was none other than Frederick George Wilhelm Maria Julius Schlitte, one of the partners. The man attacking him was 21-year-old John Esmond Murphy, who also used the name James McDonald.

Murphy finally got to his feet and tried to run from the scene. A cabman, George Thomas Carter, bravely blocked his way and was rewarded with a deep stab wound to his left hand. Next a policeman, Constable Albert Allen Howe, moved to intercept the fleeing man but he was stabbed in the shoulder. It was not until a number of other men leapt upon Murphy and pinned him down that the injured policeman was able to make his arrest.

Murphy was put on trial at the Old Bailey on 14 December. The proceedings lasted two days and were heard by Mr Justice Pickford.

One of the most damning pieces of evidence was a statement made by Schlitte before he passed away. He explained that he had looked up from his desk to see Murphy standing before him with a gun levelled at him. Without saying a word, Murphy had fired once, the bullet hitting Schlitte who had then thrown himself at his attacker, knocking the gun to the floor. Murphy had then drawn a knife and began to stab Schlitte, who threw something through the window to attract attention.

Murphy claimed to have no memory of the attack and said he must have suffered some sort of mental seizure, but other witnesses showed that he had been practising his shooting at a range in Oxenden Street and it was surmised that this was nothing more than an attempted robbery which had ended in murder.

Found guilty, Murphy was hanged at Pentonville on Wednesday, 6 January 1909 by Henry Pierrepoint and William Willis.

Morris Reuben & Marks Reuben, 1909

The plan was simple enough. Emily Allen, the girlfriend of 23-year-old Morris Reuben, along with Ellen Stevens, a friend of hers, would find some unsuspecting stranger who might have a few shillings on him. The two girls would then allow the man to buy them a few drinks before taking him back to 3 Rupert Street, Whitechapel, where Morris and his younger brother Marks would waylay him and take his cash.

Thirty-six-year-old William Sproull was a sailor and on the evening of Tuesday, 16 March 1909, he and his shipmate Charles McEachran were in the Three Nuns Hotel when, at around 11 p.m., the two women walked over to them. After a couple of drinks and some discussion, the two men agreed to go back to Rupert Street.

Later still, just as the two men were leaving the house, they were attacked. McEachran was struck over the head and rendered unconscious almost immediately but Sproull proved to be made of sterner stuff. He fought back and the struggle spilled out into Rupert Street itself when suddenly Marks Reuben settled matters by stabbing Sproull.

In due course, McEachran recovered to find himself leaning against a wall with a police inspector standing over him. Close by lay Sproull's body and a trail of blood led straight back into no. 3. Inside the house, the police found Ellen Stevens in bed and Morris Reuben dressing himself. He readily admitted that he had robbed Sproull but said that the two sailors had started the fight and he had simply defended himself. The police took no chances, arrested all four occupants of the house and charged them all with murder.

In the event, only the Reuben brothers faced trial before Mr Justice Jelf at the Old Bailey on 22 April. By now, both of the women had had their charges dropped and Emily Allen had even agreed to give evidence for the prosecution. The hearing lasted two days and at the end, the jury took just ten minutes to return two guilty verdicts.

An appeal was entered and an attempt made to save the life of Morris Reuben. He had not struck the fatal blow and his defence argued that as such, he should only be found guilty of manslaughter. The judge pointed out that both brothers had a common purpose in robbing Sproull, were partners in the venture and so were equally guilty. Both appeals were then dismissed.

On Thursday, 20 May 1909 the Reuben brothers were executed at Pentonville by the Pierrepoint brothers, Henry and Thomas.

Madar Lal Dhingra, 1909

It had been a most pleasant evening. The concert at the Imperial Institute in South Kensington had been enjoyed by all. Now, as the crowd began to disperse at around 11 p.m. on Thursday, 1 July, one of the more distinguished guests, Sir William Hutt Curzon-Wylie, the Aide-de-Camp to the Secretary of State for India, chatted to a young Indian close by the entrance. Then, without warning, that same Indian drew out a revolver and fired five shots at Sir William's head. Four of those shots hit home and Sir William was dead before his body hit the floor.

People began to scream and run for cover but the man closest to the scene, Dr Cawas Lalcaca, bravely moved forward to try to grab the assassin. The young Indian turned to face him and two more shots were fired. Both bullets hit the doctor and he would later die from his wounds. The killer now calmly turned the gun towards himself, put the muzzle against his head and pulled the trigger. There was a hollow click. The chamber was empty. Now, at last, he could be overpowered and taken into custody.

The Indian happily identified himself as 25-year-old Madar Lal Dhingra and said that he had been living in England since 1906 and was a student at University College. He lived in Ledbury Road, Bayswater, and had come to believe that his homeland should be freed from the yoke of British rule. That was why he had chosen to carry out a political assassination.

There could be no doubt that the crime was premeditated. Madar had obtained a gun licence in January 1909 and had then practised assiduously. He had discovered that Sir William, his intended target, was to attend the concert and had obtained a ticket for himself. Madar had arrived at the hall at 9 p.m., listened to the concert and made his move just two hours later.

The Imperial Institute, where Madar Lal Dhingra shot two men dead on 1 July 1909.

Put on trial at the Old Bailey before the Lord Chief Justice, Lord Alverstone, on 23 July, Madar refused to be represented, saying that he did not recognise the court. He regretted the death of Dr Lalcaca but felt that he had committed no crime when it came to Sir William.

The jury did not even bother to leave the court before returning their guilty verdict, and just over three weeks later, on Tuesday, 17 August 1909, Madar was hanged at Pentonville by Henry and Thomas Pierrepoint.

George Henry Perry, 1910

In 1908, George Perry left the army but found it very difficult to find a job. As a result, money was a problem and under normal circumstances it would have been very hard to find lodgings. Luckily for George, his girlfriend's parents, the Covells, allowed him to stay with them in Ealing until he got back on his feet.

The problem was that George wasn't exactly conscientious in his search for suitable employment. Two years passed, and by 1910 George had only actually done nine weeks' paid work. The Covells had had enough and, on Sunday, 9 January 1910, George was told to find somewhere else to live.

The following day, George left the house as instructed but returned later and asked to see his girlfriend, 27-year-old Annie Covell. Annie's mother saw nothing wrong with this request and allowed George back into the house, where she left the two lovers alone.

A few minutes later a terrible scream sounded. Going to investigate, Mrs Covell found Annie lying on the floor with George kneeling over her and apparently hitting her repeatedly. It took a few seconds for her to realise that in fact George held a large bread knife and was stabbing Annie in her side. As Mrs Covell ran outside to find a policeman, George finished his attack by slashing Annie's throat.

George Perry appeared before Mr Justice Coleridge at the Old Bailey on 9 February, where he pleaded guilty to the charge of murder. The judge suggested that George should discuss this with his counsel and matters were then adjourned. Two days later, on 11 February, George was back in court and changed his plea to one of not guilty. The jury, however, had little trouble in returning their verdict and George was sentenced to death.

On Tuesday, 1 March 1910, George Perry was hanged at Pentonville by Henry Pierrepoint and William Willis.

Hawley Harvey Crippen, 1910

In 1893, Hawley Harvey Crippen married his second wife, Cora Turner, in Jersey City, America. Seven years later, in 1900, they moved to London. He was employed as a representative for Munyon's Remedies, a company making homeopathic remedies while Cora, using the name Belle Elmore, had aspirations to be a music hall artist. Unfortunately, Belle had no talent whatsoever.

In fact, neither Belle nor Cora was the real name of Mrs Crippen. She had been born Kunigunde Mackamotzki and was the daughter of a Russian-Polish father and a German mother. She was also a most overbearing and dominant character. Her long-suffering husband supported her ambitions to be first an opera singer and, when that didn't work out, a singer in the music hall but she had very little success. All she did manage to get out of her 'career' was a few showbusiness friends and the position of Treasurer of the Music Hall Ladies Guild in London.

In September 1905, Crippen and his wife took a lease on 39 Hilldrop Crescent in Holloway. Part of the thinking behind this move was that the pair could now have separate bedrooms. Belle had never really been a sexual person and according to what Crippen would later say, all physical relations between them ceased in 1907. Crippen, meanwhile, had fallen in love.

The object of his desire was Ethel Le Neve, a typist who worked for him. At about the same time that Crippen stopped having sex with Belle, he and Ethel became lovers. This situation continued until 1910.

On the evening of Monday, 31 January 1910, the Crippens threw a dinner party for two close friends of Belle's: Paul and Clara Martinetti. The meal passed pleasantly enough, except for one incident. Paul Martinetti had asked to use the toilet and because Crippen didn't escort him upstairs to show him where it was, Belle berated him. By the time the Martinettis finally left, it was around 1 a.m. on Monday, 1 February. It would be the last time that anyone saw Belle Elmore alive.

Over the next week or so people began to ask where Belle was. Crippen said that she had gone to America. As the days passed, this story was amended and now she had fallen ill. Finally, Crippen told people that his wife had passed away. There was, however, one problem with this. Ethel Le Neve had started wearing some of Belle's jewellery and, by the end of February, she had moved in with Crippen at Hilldrop Crescent. Friends grew suspicious and in due course those suspicions were passed on to the police.

On 8 July, Chief Inspector Walter Dew called at Hilldrop Crescent where he found Ethel alone. Crippen, it seems, was at work, so Dew visited him there and the two returned together to Hilldrop Crescent where Crippen happily showed the officer around the house. He also told Dew a different story. Belle had left him for another man, almost certainly Bruce Miller, an American she had met in late 1903. Dew told Crippen that it would be better if Belle contacted him to confirm this story and Crippen said that he would place an advertisement in certain newspapers, asking for her to make contact.

Things now moved very quickly. The next day, 9 July, Crippen shaved off his distinctive moustache and with Ethel Le Neve disguised as a boy, travelled to Brussels. There they bought tickets for passage to Canada, travelled on to Antwerp and there boarded the SS *Montrose*, travelling as father and son.

At about the same time, Chief Inspector Dew returned to Hilldrop Crescent. He was surprised to find Crippen and Ethel missing and decided to make another routine search of the house. In the cellar he noticed some loose bricks in the floor. Officers were ordered in to make a more thorough search and beneath those bricks they found the remains of a body. The body was headless, limbless and boneless – little more than pieces of flesh, but it was female. It was time to find Crippen.

Aboard the *Montrose*, the father and son were watched with interest. They seemed to be unduly affectionate and were constantly holding hands. Added to that, the boy's clothing seemed to be very ill-fitting. Captain Kendall had his suspicions and telegraphed a message to Scotland Yard. Dew, now determined to intercept the 'father and son', boarded a faster ship, the SS *Laurentic*, and the hunt was on.

On Sunday, 31 July, Dew and other officers boarded the *Montrose* as it sailed up the St Lawrence. The father and son were identified as Crippen and Ethel Le Neve, both were arrested and, after three weeks, were escorted back to England to face trial.

It was decided that the pair should not be tried together. Crippen would face his trial first and, once that verdict had been determined, Ethel Le Neve would take her turn in the dock, to be tried as an accessory. So it was that on 18 October, Crippen stood alone in the dock at the Old Bailey before the Lord Chief Justice of England, Lord Alverstone. The proceedings would last until 22 October.

Crippen's defence was simple. The body found in the cellar of his home was not Belle's. The body must have been of some poor unknown woman and been placed there before he and Belle had moved in. It was, therefore, crucial to the prosecution to prove that the body was Belle's.

One piece of the flesh found in the shallow grave had borne a scar and medical records showed that Belle had such a scar on her lower abdomen. More conclusive was the fact that the remains had been wrapped in a pyjama jacket and a tag inside that jacket led to the manufacturers: Jones Brothers. They confirmed that this particular cloth and pattern were not issued until late 1908, proving that the body must have been placed there after that date. This, and the scar, was consistent with the body being that of Belle Elmore.

Medical tests had shown that the flesh contained traces of hyoscine, a poison, and it was known that Crippen had purchased five grains of that substance on 17 January, two weeks before Belle had vanished. It was enough for the jury, who took just under thirty minutes to find Crippen guilty of his wife's murder.

On 25 October, Ethel Le Neve was put on trial as an accessory to murder and found not guilty. A subsequent appeal on behalf of Crippen was dismissed and his death sentence was confirmed.

On Wednesday, 23 November 1910, 48-year-old Crippen was hanged at Pentonville by John Ellis and William Willis. Crippen's last request had been for a photograph of Ethel and some of her letters to be buried with him in his unmarked grave. The request was granted.

Noah Woolf, 1910

Sometimes it can be hard for the police to find the perpetrator of a crime, but in the case of the murder of Andrew Simon it was simple, for the killer walked into the police station and gave himself up.

It was Friday, 28 October 1910 when 58-year-old Noah Woolf stepped inside the station on Upper Holloway Road, handed over a bloodstained knife, confessed to murder and then offered to take the officers back to the Home for Aged Hebrew Christians in Upper Holloway, where the body of his victim would be found.

Andrew Simon was a resident at that home and until fairly recently, Woolf had been too. The latter was, however, somewhat argumentative and was creating something of an atmosphere. As a result, some residents complained about his behaviour to the matron, Amelia Young, and the Revd Michael Machim, who ran a mission there.

As a result of those complaints, Machim called a meeting at the Home at which Andrew Simon had spoken. He claimed that Woolf was obviously not a believer in the words of the Bible and was making life a misery there for the rest of the residents. The meeting decided that Woolf had to go, and so, on 4 July, he was given 10s and a weekly grant and told to leave.

On 27 October, Woolf returned to the Home and was seen talking to Simon. The next day, 28 October, Woolf was back at around 10.30 a.m., when he was seen by Amelia Young going up to Simon's room. She also saw him leaving half an hour later. The next sighting of Woolf was at the police station when he confessed to Simon's murder.

Andrew Simon was indeed dead. Woolf said that he had gone to the Home to get Simon to change his testimony in the hope that he might be readmitted. When Simon refused, Woolf had stabbed him a number of times and then, when Simon fell to the floor, stabbed him again to make sure he was dead. In all, Andrew Simon had been stabbed eight times.

Woolf faced his trial before Mr Justice Darling at the Old Bailey on 18 November. With his own confession, the verdict was a foregone conclusion and just over a month later, on Wednesday, 21 December, Woolf was hanged at Pentonville by John Ellis and William Willis.

George Newton, 1911

George Newton and Ada Roker had been seeing each other for three years and had been engaged for six months, but all was not well with their relationship.

At the beginning of December 1910, for example, the couple had been alone in the sitting room of Ada's house at 10 Biggerstaff Road, Stratford, when Annie Roker, Ada's mother, entered. To her surprise she found her daughter bleeding from a wound in her mouth but neither she nor George would say what had taken place.

George was also behaving somewhat curiously on Christmas Eve, 24 December 1910, again at Ada's house. At one stage Ada had said she would iron George's handkerchief for him. Rather than thanking her as might be expected, George replied that he, 'might as bloody well go home.' This was heard by Eliza Roker, Ada's sister-in-law, and her husband, Charles, who managed to calm things down a little. The couple were then left alone in the house.

At 7 p.m. that same night, Ada's sister, Elizabeth, returned home to find George standing on the stairs. As Elizabeth entered, George pushed past her, ran out into the street and vanished from sight. The reason why he had behaved like this was easy to determine, for upon opening the door to the kitchen, Elizabeth found Ada lying in a pool of blood. Her arms had been fastened to the side of her body by means of a strap and her throat had been cut.

The family and the police now began looking for George Newton. The first port of call was his home at 42 Lett Road, but George's brother-in-law, Henry Allan, said he wasn't there. In fact, Henry was lying and George was in the house. He had gone there directly after killing Ada and admitted his crime to his sister and her husband and even showed Henry the razor he had used. Very soon after this, there was a second knock on Henry Allan's door. This time it was Constable Sidney Mills and finally George Newton came downstairs and gave himself up.

Nineteen-year-old George Newton appeared before Mr Justice Grantham at the Old Bailey on 13 January 1911. An attempt was made to suggest that George was insane at the time of the attack. Medical evidence was given that his sister was in an asylum and an aunt had also been confined some years before but the medical officer at Brixton Prison stated that George was sane, though admittedly he did have a quick temper.

The jury decided that George was sane and guilty of murder and on Tuesday, 31 January 1911, he was hanged at Chelmsford by John Ellis and William Conduit.

Michael Collins, 1911

In August 1910, Elizabeth Anne Kempster's husband died, leaving her alone with a 6-year-old son. Luckily for Elizabeth, she soon found someone new to take care of her and just before Christmas of that same year she moved in with 26-year-old Michael Collins at 42 A-Block, Peabody Buildings, Glasshouse Street. What started out as a happy enough relationship changed early in 1911.

On 19 March, Elizabeth seemed to be acting rather coldly towards Collins. She wouldn't tell him what the problem was. Even so, they went out together for a drink that evening and when they returned home, Collins again tried to find out what was wrong. Elizabeth would only say that she wished he would go.

By the next day, Elizabeth wasn't even speaking to Collins. Yet again she refused to elaborate beyond saying that she wished he would leave her and adding that she would face whatever trouble she was in by herself. Things did not improve during the rest of that week.

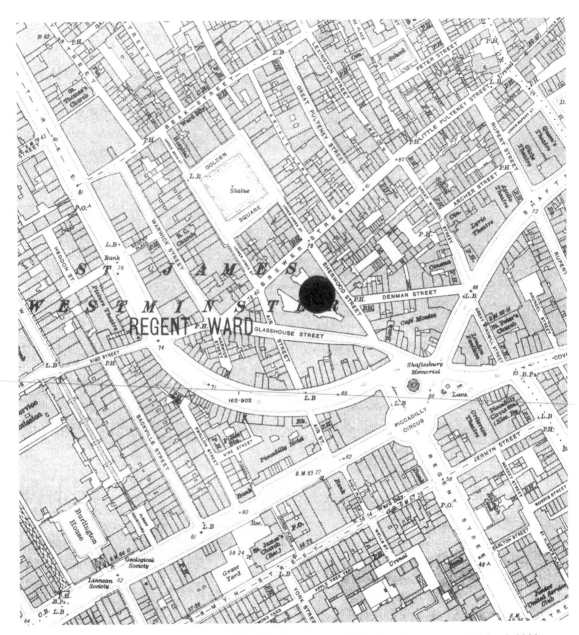

The spot in Glasshouse Street where Michael Collins murdered Elizabeth Kempster on 25 March 1911.
(Reproduced with the permission of Alan Godfrey Maps)

On Saturday, 25 March, Collins purchased a new razor from a stall in Whitechapel. Earlier that same day Collins had spoken to a friend and neighbour, George Crease, to whom he confided that he had argued with Elizabeth again and now thought that it might be best if he did away with her and himself.

At 6 p.m. that same day, George Crease was talking to another neighbour, James Rowley, when Collins approached them. His hands were wet with blood and he admitted that he had just killed Elizabeth and was about to hand himself over to the police. Around forty-five minutes later Collins did just that, walking into Leman Street police station and admitting what he had done.

At his trial at the Old Bailey on 28 April, Collins said that he had asked Elizabeth to make a final decision on whether they should live together or apart. After just a few seconds of deliberation, Elizabeth replied, 'Apart.' Collins had then shouted, 'Nothing but death shall part us!', took up a hammer and battered her with it. Then, while Elizabeth was on the floor, Collins took his new razor and cut her throat.

That confession was more than enough for the jury and Mr Justice Grantham then sentenced Collins to death. One month later, on Wednesday, 24 May, Collins was hanged at Pentonville by John Ellis and Thomas Pierrepoint.

Edward Hill, 1911

On 11 July 1911, Edward Hill married Mary Jane. Just nine days later she was dead at the hands of her new husband.

After they had married, the newlyweds took rooms on the top floor of 22 Caledonia Street, King's Cross. It was during that move that Mary noticed that 22s she had borrowed from her mother-in-law was missing. Surely the only person who could have taken it was Edward, but he denied all knowledge. Nevertheless, even at this early stage, Elizabeth found that she no longer trusted her new husband.

Things went from bad to worse. Two days after the move to Caledonia Street, a friend of Mary's, Mrs Miller, called on her to find bits of flock all over the floor. The couple had argued and in a fit of temper Hill had slashed open their bed and scattered the contents of the mattress around the room. He then went on a drinking spree and it was not until 2 a.m. on Tuesday, 25 July, that he returned home. His landlady, Mrs Barton, saw Mary Jane letting him in.

At 10 a.m. Mary Jane visted Mrs Barton and gave her some money, asking her to hold it in safe keeping for her. After all, she believed she had already had money taken by her husband once before and she wasn't going to take any chances. Very soon after this, Mrs Barton heard someone running down the stairs and, looking out of her window, saw Hill leaving the house.

At around 11 a.m., a fire was discovered on the top floor of the house. The flames were very soon brought under control but it was too late for Mary Jane. She lay on the floor of her bedroom, her face covered by two pillows and a bandage tied tightly around her neck. As for the blaze, that had been caused when someone had placed a paraffin lamp underneath the bed, which had subsequently caught fire.

The police soon traced Hill. He was found drinking in a pub close to his mother's house in Southwark. He claimed to know nothing of the fire, or his wife's death, saying that he had been in his mother's house at the time, but this was soon shown to be a lie.

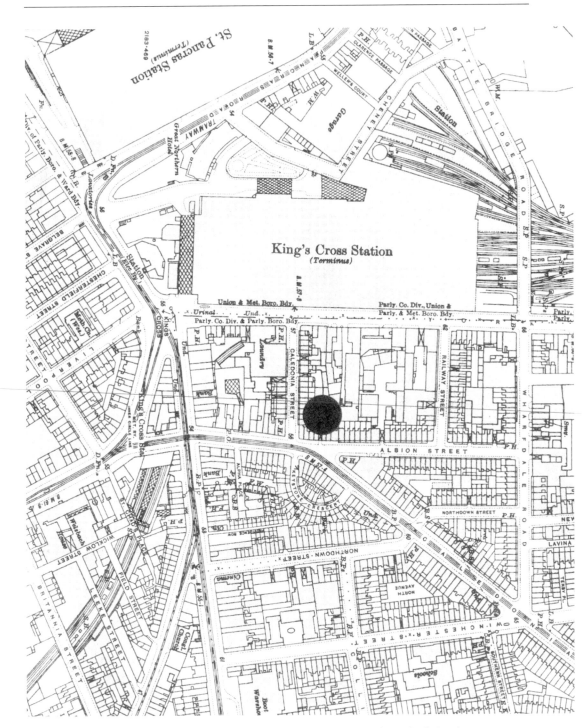

The house where Edward Hill murdered Mary Jane, his wife of nine days.
(Reproduced with the permission of Alan Godfrey Maps)

On 11 September, Edward Hill appeared before Mr Justice Avory at the Old Bailey, the trial lasting two days. Only after he had been judged to be guilty was it possible to reveal that in 1903, Hill had been jailed for setting fire to a house.

On Tuesday, 17 October, 41-year-old Edward Hill was hanged at Pentonville by John Ellis and his two assistants, William Conduit and Albert Lumb.

Myer Abramovitch, 1912

In the year 1888, one of the brutal murders committed by Jack the Ripper took place in Hanbury Street, Spitalfields. It was in 1911 in that same street, at no. 62, that Solomon Milstein and his wife, Annie, ran a small restaurant.

By November of that year, business had begun to drop off somewhat so Solomon came up with an idea for making some extra cash. He turned the basement of the premises into an illegal gambling den, in partnership with Joe Goldstein. The concept was simple. The usual game was faro and every deal of the cards meant three pence for the proprietors. Although it didn't sound much, the takings soon mounted up.

In time, another way of earning extra money was put forward. If a customer gambled a little too heavily and ran out of funds, a loan could be provided against the pledge of a little personal property such as a watch or ring. So, for example, one punter named Lazarus Rickman handed over a silver watch and chain on 24 December 1911, for which he received a sovereign. He promptly lost that money too!

Although a good deal of money was being made, Annie Milstein had some moral objections to this source of income. She didn't object to people playing cards in the cellar but didn't like money changing hands. She spoke to her husband about her qualms and he said that he would stop the gambling there and then. So it was that on Tuesday, 26 December the punters were told that this would be the last night they would be able to play cards for money.

At around 11 p.m. Joe Goldstein divided up the takings for the last time. Each of the three partners: Goldstein, Solomon and Annie, received 4s 6d with Solomon taking his share in copper coins. Later still, one of the gamblers had made one of the last pledges of property when Hermann Leferron had handed over a silver watch and a gold chain for which he received £2 10s. Hermann and four other men were the last gamblers to leave the premises, at around 12.45 a.m. on Wednesday, 27 December.

The restaurant had a flat above the premises, where one Marks Verbloot lived. At 2.30 a.m. he heard a loud groaning. The noise continued for about thirty minutes, by which time Marks could also smell burning. Going to the window to investigate, he saw a warm glow coming from the restaurant. The entire place was on fire. Marks called for the police and went down to investigate.

The door to the Milsteins' living quarters was locked and, when it was forced, the room was found to be on fire. The flames were doused but it was too late for Solomon and Annie. They lay next to each other in bed, battered to death, and whoever had killed them had then poured paraffin onto the bed and placed hot irons on top of it.

The police began by tracing all the card players from the previous night. Various players gave the names of others they had seen on the premises and soon all had been interviewed, except for one man who had not come forward of his own accord. That man was 28-year-old Myer Abramovitch, a costermonger who worked in a local market.

Further enquiries led to Lazarus Rickman, who had pledged his property on Christmas Eve. He stated that on the night before the murders he had seen Abramovitch wearing a distinctive silk neckerchief – this fitted the description of one found by police in the restaurant. Finding Abramovitch now became a priority.

On 28 December, Henry Seychur, another of the gamblers, was standing on the corner of Leman Street and Commercial Road when he saw Abramovitch at a coffee stall. Seychur went over and asked the wanted man why he had not yet spoken to the police. Abramovitch did not reply so Seychur said he would accompany him. Somewhat reluctantly, Abramovitch fell in beside Seychur and walked to the police station.

At the station, the neckerchief was shown to Abramovitch who admitted it was his. He was then searched and the watches pledged by Rickman and Leferron were discovered. Further, Abramovitch was wearing two sets of clothes, one of which was bloodstained and shown to have belonged to Solomon Milstein.

The trial opened before Mr Justice Ridley at the Old Bailey on 7 February, and despite lasting two days, was little more than a formality. There, and at a subsequent appeal, an attempt was made to show that the prisoner was insane, but both of these avenues failed and on Wednesday, 6 March 1912, Abramovitch was hanged at Pentonville by John Ellis and Albert Lumb.

Frederick Henry Seddon, 1912

It was, to say the least, something of a shock. On the evening of Wednesday, 20 September 1911, Frank Ernest Vonderahe called at 63 Tollington Park, Islington, to see his cousin, Eliza Mary Barrow, only to be told that she was dead and buried.

Eliza had lived with the Vonderahe family at 31 Eversholt Road until 27 July 1910, but following a disagreement had expressed a desire to find new lodgings for herself. It was shortly afterwards that she had moved in with Frederick Seddon and his family at Tollington Park.

In fact, Eliza had moved into Seddon's house with something of an entourage. Accompanying her had been Robert Dennis Hook, his wife and their nephew, 10-year-old Ernest Grant. After a short time, Eliza had argued with the Hooks too, and, after complaining to Frederick Seddon, they had been told to move out. This state of affairs had continued until Thursday, 14 September when Eliza had died. She had been buried just two days later, on 16 September, four days before Frank Vonderahe's visit.

The matter seemed to be most curious and, if anything, the curiosity increased once Mr Vonderahe heard about Eliza's will. She had been a woman of property and the will left her estate to little Ernest Grant and his sister, Hilda, but unfortunately, all the property appeared to have gone. She had sold most of it in order to buy herself an annuity. Now that she was dead, that annuity died too and the only person who seemed to have made any money out of this situation was none other than her new landlord, Frederick Henry Seddon.

The Vonderahe family were far from satisfied. Acting on their behalf, Frank Vonderahe wrote to the Director of Public Prosecutions. That letter was then passed on to the police who, having examined Eliza's various financial dealings, thought that there might indeed be more to this than met the eye. Consequently, on 15 November, Eliza's body was exhumed for further examination.

That examination, performed by Sir Bernard Spilsbury, led to the conclusion that Eliza Barrow had been killed by arsenical poisoning. On 4 December, Detective Chief Inspector Alfred Ward was back at Tollington Park where he arrested Seddon and charged him with murder. Further investigations showed, however, that most of Eliza's food had been prepared by Seddon's wife, Margaret Ann, so on 15 January 1912 she too was arrested and charged with murder.

The trial of Margaret and Frederick Seddon opened before Mr Justice Bucknill at the Old Bailey on 4 March. The proceedings would last until 14 March.

Details of Miss Barrow's property were given in court. She had owned the lease on the Buck's Head public house and the barber's shop next door. She had also held £1,600 of India Stock and had a large lockable chest in which she had kept various bags of gold coin. The most reasonable estimate was that the chest held some £400. What had happened to all of this wealth?

In a transaction dated 14 October 1910, the India Stock had been transferred to Henry Seddon. He in turn had sold the stock on 25 January 1911, for which he received just over £1,519. Shortly before this, on 11 January to be precise, the transfer of the Buck's Head and the barber's shop to Seddon had also been authorised. For all this property, Miss Barrow was to receive a lifetime annuity of £3 per week.

The inference was clear. According to the prosecution, Seddon had appropriated all of Miss Barrow's assets in return for the annuity. The longer she lived, the longer Seddon would have to pay out. If, however, she died soon afterwards, then Seddon would have made a very tidy profit for himself.

When she died, Eliza Barrow had been just 50 years old and her state of health was an important point. According to Seddon, Miss Barrow had become ill at the beginning of September 1911. Dr Henry George Sworn had attended her and he found her suffering from general sickness and diarrhoea for which he prescribed bismuth carbonate and morphia. Things did not improve and Dr Sworn called again on 3 September and again every day up to 9 September. He last saw her on the 13th, and on the following morning heard that she had died. Without bothering to return to the house, he then issued a death certificate giving the cause of death as epidemic diarrhoea and exhaustion.

Where had the arsenic used on Eliza Barrow come from? Evidence was given that there had been arsenical fly-papers found in the house and these were of the kind that had to be soaked in water before they became effective. Margaret Seddon admitted that these had been scattered about Eliza's room and that just before she had died, they had all been placed in one large bowl, close to Eliza's bed. Was she suggesting that Eliza Barrow might have drunk this liquid by accident?

When all the evidence had been heard, the jury were out for one hour before returning their verdicts. Margaret Seddon was found innocent but Frederick was judged to be guilty. He was then sentenced to death. A subsequent appeal failed and on Thursday, 18 April 1912, Frederick Seddon was hanged at Pentonville by John Ellis and Thomas Pierrepoint.

In his final letter to his wife, Seddon affirmed that he would die an innocent man.

William Charles Adolphus Beal, 1912

Thursday, 12 September 1912 was a very pleasant evening and Ethel King and her friend, Mrs Walford, were enjoying a walk together. The two ladies turned into Abbey Lane, West Ham, and as they passed one of the quieter parts of the street, they noticed a young couple together. They assumed at first that they were watching a courting couple and turned away. It was then that a blood-curdling scream rang out.

Turning back towards the couple, Ethel King saw that the young woman was now lying on the ground and the man she was with was himself just falling to the ground. Close by the woman's body lay something shiny. As the man crawled slowly towards his companion, Ethel and her friend noticed, for the first time, that he had a gaping wound in his throat. The two women had just witnessed a murder and an attempted suicide.

The young woman was 17-year-old Clara Elizabeth Carter and the man who had just slashed her throat was 20-year-old William Beal. He was later rushed to hospital where, slowly, he began to recover from his wounds, and it was there that he was interviewed by the police on 2 October.

Beal's story was that Clara, his girlfriend, had attacked him. They had been walking together when Clara had taken his cut-throat razor from the pocket where he habitually kept it. She had cut his throat, turned the weapon upon herself and taken her own life. In order to convince the officers, he then told of two earlier attempts; once when she had attacked him with a ginger beer bottle and once when she had stabbed him with a hatpin.

The trouble was that the evidence of both Ethel King and Mrs Walford did not back up Beal's story. When they had first turned around, Clara was already on the ground and Beal was just collapsing near her. Surely, if Clara had attacked him then Beal would have fallen first. Beal was arrested and charged with murder.

The trial took place before Mr Justice Phillimore at the Old Bailey on 11 November. It was here that telling medical evidence was given. Dr Montgomery Paton, who had attended the scene and examined both Clara and Beal, testified that it was highly improbable that Clara's wound could be self-inflicted. Further, it was almost certain that Beal's wound was. The defence collapsed and as a result, the jury took just one hour to decide on Beal's guilt, though they did add a strong recommendation to mercy on account of the prisoner's age. It did nothing to save Beal who was hanged at Chelmsford on Tuesday, 10 December 1912 by John Ellis.

Edward Hopwood, 1913

Charles Matthews was a cab driver and, as such, probably had lots of stories about some of the passengers he had carried. Nothing could have prepared him, though, for the couple he picked up on Saturday, 28 September 1912.

They were quiet enough but as the cab travelled down Fenchurch Street, three loud bangs rang out. Matthews assumed he had suffered a burst tyre and pulled over to the kerb. Almost immediately,

Mr Justice Phillimore, who sentenced William Beal to death for the murder of Clara Elizabeth Carter.

the cab door burst open and the female passenger fell out into Matthews's arms, crying that she had been shot.

A couple of people walking past dashed forward to offer assistance but even as they helped Matthews to minister to the woman, two more shots rang out from inside the cab. The male passenger had shot himself in the head.

Police enquiries showed that the female passenger was 34-year-old Florence Alice Bernadette Silles, a music hall artiste who performed under the stage name of Flo Dudley. She had been married but her husband had died in 1907. In May 1912 she had become involved with the male passenger of the cab, 45-year-old Edward Hopwood, who did not approve of Florence's choice of career.

Possibly in order to get Florence to give up the stage, he had told her that he owned his own company, had plenty of money in the bank, was a single man and was happy to support his new love. In fact, these were all lies. In reality he was married, had three children and was in severe financial difficulties.

The lies came to a head on 13 September. Hopwood had used 65 Balfour Road, Ilford, the address of Florence's sister, Annie Bland, as a mail drop, ostensibly for his 'business', but on the 13th an official looking letter from a solicitor arrived. A rather curious Annie opened the letter and found, to her dismay, that Hopwood had been issuing bad cheques and was now being chased for payment. When questioned about this by Florence and Annie four days later, Hopwood claimed that it was all a mistake.

On 26 September, Hopwood travelled down to Brighton and purchased a revolver. It seemed to him that there was no other way out of his troubles now and so, two days later, on the 28th, he had shot Florence and himself in the back of the cab. He was only half successful though. Florence was indeed dead but Hopwood recovered to face a murder charge.

The trial opened before Mr Justice Avory at the Old Bailey on 9 December, and was to last until 11 December. It was here that all the events of the fateful day were reconstructed.

At 10.20 p.m., Hopwood had met Florence in the Holborn Viaduct Hotel. A waiter there, George Alfred Warren, overheard Hopwood say at one point that he, 'had done it for the best.' Leaving soon afterwards, Hopwood had hailed a cab and asked that it take him and his friend to Fenchurch Street, and it was as they approached the station that the first shots rang out.

The defence claimed that the shooting of Florence had been an accident. As the cab turned into Fenchurch Street, Hopwood had asked Florence if she wanted them to part. She replied that she thought that it would be for the best and he then took the gun out in order to shoot himself. Florence tried to stop him and in the ensuing struggle, the gun went off and a bullet hit Florence in the head. Expert opinion agreed that the wound Florence suffered was consistent with such a scenario, but she had been shot more than once, the fatal shot being one to her lungs. Hopwood explained this by saying that the gun had continued to fire as they struggled.

The jury did not accept this story and Hopwood was found guilty. On Wednesday, 29 January 1913 he paid the penalty for his crime when he was hanged at Pentonville by Thomas Pierrepoint and Albert Lumb.

Henry Longden, 1913

Henry Longden and Alice Catlow More had been living together for some time, but of late the relationship had become rather strained. Henry had started to find fault with everything Alice did. The final straw came on 16 March 1913 when he came home from work and complained because she had not lit the fire. Alice had had enough. The next day, 17 March, she left Longden and moved into new lodgings.

The basic problem was that Longden was jealous. Alice worked for a company called the East and West Society of China, an organisation whose aim was to stimulate trade between England and the Far East. One of the customers Alice dealt with was a man named Silva who owned a business supplying crockery, and Longden had managed to convince himself that their relationship was not a purely business one.

Three weeks after Alice had left him, on 9 April to be precise, Longden saw her with Silva and marched up to them intending to sort matters out. He accused Silva of inducing Alice to leave him. When both he and Alice vehemently denied this, Longden turned to her and said that very soon he would deal with her. It was a promise he was to keep.

At 2 p.m. the very next day, Thursday, 10 April, Alice was seen staggering down Taviton Street, Gordon Square, with a gaping wound in her throat. Walking a few steps behind her and following her erratic progress was Henry Longden, carrying a butcher's knife. As Alice finally fell to the ground, Longden turned the knife upon himself and slashed his own throat.

Alice was dead but prompt medical attention managed to save Longden's life. Charged with murder, he appeared before Mr Justice Rowlatt at the Old Bailey on 2 June. The defence tried to suggest that Longden had suffered provocation and that the crime was not premeditated, but the jury had little trouble in deciding his guilt.

Just over a month later, on Tuesday, 8 July, Longden was hanged at Pentonville by John Ellis and William Willis.

Frederick Albert Robertson, 1913

There was nothing else he could do. Mr Bradforth just had to complain to his landlord. He couldn't stand the smell any longer.

Bradforth occupied the top floor room at 12 Saratoga Road, Clapton, and now, in July 1912, he had put up with the offensive smell for long enough. It seemed to be emanating from the rooms below his but was more likely to be the drains. Bradforth made his complaint and the landlord called in Joseph Lidden who made a thorough inspection of the drains but found nothing wrong with them. Perhaps the smell was coming from the rooms below Bradforth's after all.

The rooms were vacant but the smell was stronger in there. Further investigations led to one particular room and when a floorboard was lifted, the cause of the smell was finally determined. There, in the recess beneath, lay the decomposing body of a child. The police were called in without delay.

In fact, there were three bodies buried beneath these floorboards and it was a simple matter to identify them. Some six weeks before the first floorboard had been lifted, 26-year-old Frederick Robertson had moved into the rooms with his wife Lily and three children. Very soon afterwards, on 24 June 1913, Lily had been admitted to hospital where she still remained. The father, Frederick, had left the flat on 12 July and hadn't been seen since. It looked like the bodies were those of the three children; 2-year-old twins Nellie Kathleen and Frederick Ernest and 10-month-old Beatrice Maud.

Police investigations revealed that when Lily had been taken into hospital, the children had initially been cared for by a family friend. In due course they had been returned to their father who immediately tried to put them into care. On Saturday, 28 June, he had visited the Salvation Army to see if they could take the children. He was told that the Army did not have the space, yet that very same day Robertson told a fellow tenant, Phoebe Isabella Smith, that the children had been accepted. The inference was that Robertson had killed his children on that date and hidden their bodies beneath the floorboards.

Robertson's description was circulated and since he had a wooden leg, he was relatively easy to spot and was soon arrested in City Road. He claimed that he had abandoned his children near the workhouse in Homerton but failed to explain how they then found their way back to his rooms in Saratoga Road where they were killed.

Robertson faced his trial before Mr Justice Lush at the Old Bailey on 22 October, the proceedings lasting three days. Here it was shown that Robertson had found himself a new woman, one Gertrude Flude, and the prosecution's suggestion was that he needed to dispose of his children to start a new life with her. Understandably perhaps, Robertson was found guilty and sentenced to death.

An appeal was submitted and here Robertson changed his story. Now he claimed that the children had all died from natural causes and he had simply hidden the bodies as he knew he would be suspected. The appeal court judges gave the idea little credence and the sentence was confirmed. The sentence was carried out at Pentonville on Thursday, 27 November 1913 by John Ellis and William Willis.

Charles Frembd, 1914

Charles Frembd and his wife, Louisa, ran a small grocery business at 44 Harrow Road, Leytonstone, and lived above the premises. By August 1914, they had been married for just fifteen months but the relationship was far from happy. There were constant arguments and many of these were witnessed by Dorothy Woolmore, a domestic servant they employed. Dorothy had been with the Frembds since October 1913 and lived with them at no. 44.

On the evening of Thursday, 27 August, Dorothy retired for the night at 11 p.m. At that time Charles and Louisa were sitting downstairs together. Some twenty minutes later, Dorothy heard Louisa going to bed. She heard no other noises during the night.

On Friday, 28 August, Dorothy rose at 8.20 a.m. She was late. Normally it was Louisa who was up first and she was in the habit of waking Dorothy at 7.30 a.m. Why had she not done the same this morning?

Going downstairs, Dorothy saw that there was still no sign of Louisa. Thinking that she might have been taken ill in the night, Dorothy went to her bedroom door and knocked. There was no reply. Dorothy knocked again but still getting no reply, she went back downstairs and busied herself with her morning duties.

After an hour or so, with still no sign of Louisa or Charles, Dorothy returned to the bedroom and knocked again. Again there was no answer, but now a very concerned Dorothy slowly pushed the door open. Louisa lay on the bed, covered in blood. Charles Frembd was lying next to her and also appeared to be bleeding from a nasty wound in his chest. Dorothy ran for the police.

Louisa Frembd was dead, her throat having been cut from ear to ear. Charles slowly recovered from his injuries and when interviewed by the police said that after he and Louisa had gone to bed, they had argued again and she had started nagging him. He let this go on until 2 a.m. when he decided enough was enough. He had then cut her throat and stabbed himself.

Frembd's trial took place before Mr Justice Rowlatt at the Old Bailey on 15 October. The defence was one of insanity and evidence was given by Dr Sidney Dyer, the Medical Officer at Brixton Prison. He agreed that Frembd was showing signs of senile mental decay but also stated that in his opinion the prisoner was perfectly sane. Frembd's last hope was gone and he was duly found guilty and sentenced to death.

On Wednesday, 4 November, Charles Frembd was hanged at Chelmsford by John Ellis. At 71 years of age, he became the oldest man to be executed in the UK in the twentieth century.

George Joseph Smith, 1915

The terrible tragedy was reported not just in the local London newspapers but also in many of the national papers. Thirty-eight-year-old Margaret Elizabeth Lofty had married John Lloyd on 17 December 1914 at Bath. The happy couple had then travelled to London where they took rooms at 14 Bismarck Road, Highgate, with Louisa Blatch, but the very next day, Friday, 18 December, poor Elizabeth had had some sort of fit while in her bath and had subsequently drowned. Most people who read the news in their morning papers would have had nothing but sympathy for the unfortunate Mr Lloyd.

Two people who did read those reports and who did not feel sympathy for the husband were Joseph Crossley of Blackpool and Mr Burnham of Southsea. All they felt was suspicion because something very similar had happened almost exactly one year ago.

In October 1913, 25-year-old Alice Burnham had met a man and fallen in love with him. A relationship developed and on 4 November, the couple married in Portsmouth and took a belated honeymoon in Blackpool, staying at Joseph Crossley's hotel at 16 Regents Road, where they arrived on 10 December 1913.

Almost as soon as the couple had unpacked their suitcases, the husband took his new bride to see Dr George Billing at 121 Church Street South. The husband did most of the talking and he explained that his wife was suffering from a very bad headache. Though the doctor could find nothing wrong with Alice, he did prescribe some tablets.

Two days later, on Friday, 12 December, the couple went for a walk and, upon their return, Alice went to have a bath. Soon afterwards, the husband came down to tell Mrs Crossley that his wife was unable to speak to him, something was wrong and could she please call the doctor. Dr Billing attended and found that Alice was dead. She had apparently had a fit of some kind and had fallen under the water where she had drowned.

Once details of the death of Margaret Lofty were published, both Mr Crossley and Mr Burnham, Alice's father, took their suspicions to the police. Ladies did not drown in the bath every day and surely the matter deserved further investigation. The only real doubt both gentlemen had was that the husband in Alice's case had not been named John Lloyd. No, the man Alice had married was one George Joseph Smith.

Police investigations soon showed that Smith had a string of convictions for theft, deception and other crimes and that at the time of his marriage to both Alice and Margaret, he had already been legally married to someone else. They also showed that the latest bride, Alice Burnham, had been insured for £500 and that this matter was being handled by Smith's solictor, Mr Davies of 60 Uxbridge Road. Apparently, Smith had already been to see Mr Davies, on 4 January 1915, and asked him to prove the will as soon as possible. He was due to return for a progress report on 1 February. When he did, Smith was arrested on a charge of bigamy, though this would only be a holding charge while more serious matters were investigated.

George Joseph Smith had certainly led a busy criminal life. Born in Bethnal Green in 1872, he already had a string of convictions by the time he was 10 years old, when he was sent to a reformatory. That establishment did not change him. Two prison sentences for theft followed and then, in 1891, he joined the army where he served for three years. By July 1896 he was back in prison for theft and receiving stolen goods, which he served under the false name of George Baker.

Following his release, Smith embarked on a career of theft and deception using one false name after another. He was attractive and charming to women and used these abilities to obtain money from them. If he needed to marry them in order to get what he wanted, then so be it.

On 17 January 1898 he married Caroline Beatrice Thornhill, his first and only legal wife, but used the name Oliver Love. They moved to various towns around the country including London, Brighton and Hastings, and 'Love' wrote false references for his wife so that she could obtain domestic positions and then help herself to valuables which he then sold. Caroline was arrested for those offences in 1899 and sent to prison. Her husband was more fortunate; he had already left her and could not be found by the police.

Caroline was released from prison in 1900 and soon afterwards, by a remarkable coincidence, saw her fugitive husband in Oxford Street, London. Anxious that he should get his own just reward, she reported him to the police and as a result, on 9 January 1901, Smith – aka Love – was sent back to prison for two years.

Released in 1903, Smith was soon back to his old ways. In 1908, for instance, he met Florence Wilson in Brighton, and after a whirlwind romance, asked her to marry him. She agreed and he then persuaded her to draw her savings out of the post office and give them to him for safekeeping. Needless to say, on 3 July, Smith and the money vanished together. There were other women too, some of whom he married, all of whom he stole from, but then, in 1910, things changed.

In the summer of 1910, Smith was in Clifton when he met 33-year-old Beatrice Constance Annie Mundy, known as Bessie. He discovered that she had a large bank balance of £2,500. He wooed her and as a result, they married in Weymouth on 26 August 1910, with Smith using the name Henry Williams. Now all he had to do was appropriate her money and be on his way. There was, however, a problem.

Bessie's money was held in a trust and all she received was a relatively small monthly allowance. Since there appeared to be no way Smith could get his hands on the capital, Bessie was of no use to him, so after a few weeks he left her, leaving her a letter implying that she had given him venereal disease.

Smith returned to his usual ways of womanising and theft and in March 1912, was at Weston-super-Mare. By coincidence, Bessie Mundy was taking a holiday there and she bumped into her estranged husband. A reconciliation was arranged and the couple got back together. In May that same year they moved to Herne Bay where they rented 80 High Street.

Oxford Street where Caroline Thornhill, the first and only legal wife of bigamist George Joseph Smith, had him arrested for theft in 1900.

In the meantime, Smith had discovered a possible solution to the problem of Bessie's unbreakable trust fund. If she made a will, naming him as beneficiary, and then died, then all the capital would come to him. So it was that on 8 July 1912, the couple made wills in favour of each other.

The next day, 9 July, Smith obtained a new bath. On 10 July, Bessie was taken to see Dr French who was told that she had had a fit. A mild sedative was prescribed. On Saturday, 13 July, Dr French was called to Smith's house but he could do nothing for Bessie. She had drowned while taking a bath after suffering a fit.

The next few years have already been outlined. The second bride to suffer drowning in the bath was Alice Burnham and the third was Margaret Lofty. All the pieces were now being put together. The bodies of the three women were all exhumed and finally, on 23 March 1915, George Joseph Smith was charged with three murders.

Smith appeared before Mr Justice Scrutton at the Old Bailey on 22 June, the proceedings lasting until 1 July. In many ways, the proceedings were little short of a fiasco. Smith interrupted constantly, abused and insulted witnesses and refused to be quiet. He even interrupted the judge's summing up, but despite all his efforts, the jury took just twenty minutes to find him guilty of the murder of Bessie Smith, the only charge that had been proceeded with.

The charge that had been heard had been that of a Kent murder and so Smith was now transferred to that county to await his fate. On Friday, 13 August 1915, Smith was hanged at Maidstone Prison by John Ellis and Thomas Pierrepoint. The following day, 14 August, Smith's first wife, Caroline Thornhill, married Thomas Davies, a soldier.

Lee Kun, 1916

Clara Thomas was not, it seemed, very lucky with men. Although she was married, she had split from her husband some years back. After that she had lived with a Chinese gentleman, Lee Kun, in Pennyfields, Poplar, but now that relationship too was struggling and Clara had moved yet again, and was now living with a friend, Harriett Wheaton, also in Pennyfields.

On Saturday, 16 October 1915, Clara and Harriett were in the front room when there was a knock on the front door. It was Kun, who politely asked Clara if he might speak to her. Clara went to see Kun who took her by the arm and led her into the yard at the back of the house. Minutes later, Harriett heard what sounded like a scuffle taking place and, going outside to check, found Kun stabbing Clara repeatedly.

Taking up a heavy broom handle, Harriett bravely tried to beat Kun off. To her horror, Kun then turned towards her and advanced slowly, brandishing the knife. Harriett continued beating the attacker and her loud screams soon brought help from her neighbours, who managed to subdue Kun and hold him until the police arrived. But it was too late too save Clara.

Interviewed by officers, Kun's story was that Clara had stolen some money from him while they had been living together. He had gone to see her in order to get the money back but once they were in the yard, she had suddenly produced a knife and started to stab herself. He had tried to stop her and that was what Harriett must have seen. The story was unlikely, to say the least, and Kun was arrested and charged with murder.

Twenty-seven-year-old Lee Kun appeared before Mr Justice Darling at the Old Bailey on 17 November 1915. There he told the same story which was again given little credence, and was found guilty of murder.

An appeal was entered and here an interesting point of law was raised. The defence argued that Kun spoke little English and the evidence at his trial had not been properly translated for him. He had not, therefore, fully understood the proceedings, could not enter a proper defence and so had not had a fair trial. The judges considered their verdict and announced that all the evidence had been translated at the earlier police court hearings and the trial itself had not been significantly different. Kun was fully aware of the charge and the evidence and the appeal was consequently dismissed.

Kun did manage to see the New Year, but only just. He was hanged at Pentonville on New Year's Day: Saturday, 1 January 1916, by John Ellis.

William James Robinson, 1917

Sunday, 26 November 1916, had been a fairly quiet night in the Sussex Stores public house on Upper St Martins Lane, and Walter Henry Rhodes was just draining his glass as the landlord announced that it was closing time. As Walter took the last sip of his beer, he noticed a young Canadian soldier leaving the bar in the company of an attractive young woman. He also noticed two men follow them out.

Even as Walter placed his empty glass on the table, there came sounds of a scuffle from outside. Walter and a few stragglers from the bar went outside to see what was going on.

The soldier was now lying on the ground, dying from a stab wound. The young girl was leaning over him, trying to cradle him in her arms. Of the two men who had followed them out, there was no sign.

The dead soldier was soon identified as 35-year-old Alfred Williams and descriptions of his two assailants soon led to the arrest of William Robinson and John Henry Gray. Both men were charged with murder and appeared at the Old Bailey, before the Lord Chief Justice, Lord Coleridge, on 5 March 1917. The proceedings would last for three days.

The young woman who had been with Williams was Maggie Harding and she was a valuable witness for the prosecution. She testified that as they reached the street directly outside the Sussex Stores, the two defendants had come up to them and started to pick a fight. It was Robinson who suddenly drew out a knife and plunged it deep into Williams.

Both Gray and Robinson had put forward the defence that this was just a case of mistaken identity. There was no doubt that two men had assaulted Williams and stabbed him, but they were not the ones. Unfortunately, this story was destroyed by Walter Rhodes. In the end, Robinson was found guilty of murder and sentenced to death while Gray was adjudged to be guilty of manslaughter and received three years.

Then there came an astounding development. While waiting for his appeal to be heard, Robinson wrote to Maggie Harding, confessing his guilt and that he had been correctly sentenced. She destroyed the letter, which then actually formed the basis of Robinson's appeal!

The letter had also said that before going to the Sussex Stores, Robinson had been in a different pub where he had argued with a gang of Canadian soldiers. When he saw Williams later, he mistook him for one of his assailants and had attacked him on the spur of the moment. Since there had been no intention to kill, he too should only be guilty of manslaughter.

The appeal court judges gave that argument no support and the death sentence was confirmed. On Tuesday, 17 April, Robinson was hanged at Pentonville by John Ellis and Robert Baxter.

Louis Marie Joseph Voisin, 1918

The morning of 2 November 1917 started off as a perfectly normal one for Thomas Geoffrey Henry. At 8.30 a.m. he left his home at 17 Regent Square, Bloomsbury, in order to go to work. In the centre of the square was a small garden area surrounded by railings, and as he walked by, Thomas saw that some vandal had dumped a parcel in those gardens.

Climbing over the railings to retrieve the parcel, Thomas found that it was rather heavy. Curious, he unfastened the string and to his horror saw that he had found the torso of a woman. Only now did he notice a second parcel which, when examined later, would be found to contain a pair of legs.

It was Sir Bernard Spilsbury, the pathologist, who examined the remains. Without the rest of the body, it was impossible to determine the exact cause of death but the parts had been drained of blood and he surmised that some sort of injury to the head or neck was the most likely cause. It was time now to examine the wrapping paper itself. Parts of the body had been fastened with strips of white fabric, each of which bore the words 'Argentine La Plata, cold storage'. Fabric like this was used to wrap meats and, since the body had apparently been dissected with some degree of skill, it was reasonable to assume that the perpetrator was a butcher or someone who had worked in that trade. Also inside the parcel was another piece of fabric with a laundry mark. The final clue was a piece of brown paper on which some had written the misspelt message, 'Blodie Belgium'.

The first breakthrough was due to the laundry mark. This was traced and determined to have been on clothing belonging to 31-year-old Emilienne Gerard, who lived at 50 Munster Square, near Regent's Park. Officers now called at that address. Miss Gerard was not at home so the police spoke to her landlady, Mary Elizabeth Rouse, who lived next door at no. 48.

Mary Rouse stated that on 3 April 1916, she had rented no. 50 to Paul and Emilienne Gerard. Paul had since joined the French Army and was now fighting in the trenches, but Emilienne should be at home. Luckily, Mary had a spare key, which she handed over to the police.

Once inside no. 50, a number of interesting clues were discovered. There were some bloodstains in the bedroom but Spilsbury did not think the murder had taken place there. A more likely scenario was that the killer had visited the flat in order to find bits of clothing or fabric that he might use to wrap the body parts.

Of more value was a piece of paper on the table in the lounge. This turned out to be an IOU for £50, dated 15 August and due for payment on 15 November. It was signed Louis Voisin and bore the address 101 Charlotte Street, London. Another talk with Mary Rouse elicited the fact that Emilienne had been a housekeeper for Voisin and that his occupation was that of a butcher.

The last time that Emilienne Gerard had been seen alive was on the night of Wednesday, 31 October 1917. That same night there had been a German Zeppelin raid on the capital. It was now time to determine Voisin's movements on that night.

When interviewed, Voisin said he certainly remembered that night because of the raid, and had not left his home all night. This was confirmed by the woman he lived with, Berthe Roche. Officers now spoke to some of Voisin's neighbours. One reported that on the morning following the Zeppelin raid, Berthe had been seen outside in the yard washing blood out of one of Voisin's shirts.

The police now changed tactic and asked Voisin about his movements on the morning the remains had been discovered, 2 November. It was known that there had been a heavy shower of rain early that morning but the parcels were not wet when they were found. It was simple to deduce that they must have been dropped after the rain, which placed the time between 6.15 a.m. and 8.30 a.m., when they were found by Thomas Henry.

Voisin claimed that he had been at Smithfield market until just before 7.45 a.m. but when other butchers there were interviewed, they swore that Voisin had left the market at 6.30 a.m. He had had more than enough time to dump the parcels in Regent Square.

It was time to search Voisin's basement flat at Charlotte Street. Spilsbury noted that there were bloodstains near a doorway which led out into the yard. A search of the cellar revealed a sawdust-filled barrel and when this was tipped out, Emilienne's head and hands were found. Finally, asked to write out the words 'Bloody Belgium', Voisin made the same spelling mistake seen on the paper in one of the gruesome parcels. On 6 November, both Voisin and Roche were charged with murder.

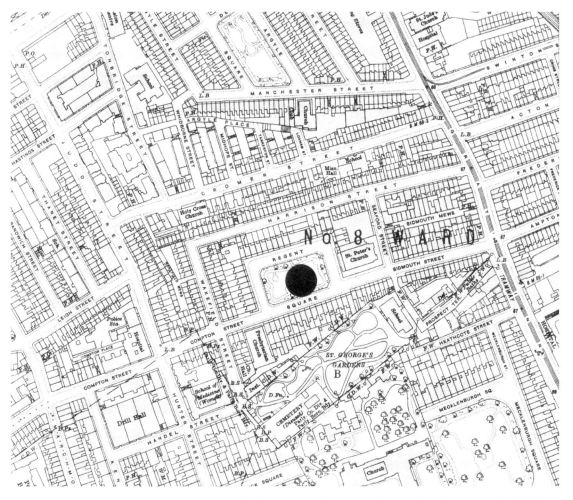

Regent Square, where Louis Voisin dumped the dismembered body of Emilienne Gerard in November 1917.
(Reproduced with the permission of Alan Godfrey Maps)

The two defendants appeared before Mr Justice Darling at the Old Bailey on 16 January 1918, in a trial lasting three days. Voisin claimed that on the morning of 1 November he had gone to Emilienne's home to find that she had been murdered and her body cut into pieces. It seemed that someone was trying to frame him and in a panic, he had hidden the body parts in his cellar, later disposing of some in Regent Square. This did not fit in with the scientific evidence and so the story was given little credence.

In the event, the judge decided that there was not enough evidence to convict Berthe Roche of murder and directed the jury to find her not guilty. A lesser charge of being an accessory after the fact would be held over until the next session of the court. Voisin was not so lucky; the jury took just fifteen minutes to find him guilty.

Louis Voisin was originally due to be hanged on 26 February, but this was postponed by the Home Secretary pending the outcome of Berthe's trial as an accessory. She was duly convicted and sentenced to seven years in prison.

Fifty-year-old Voisin was finally executed at Pentonville on Saturday, 2 March 1918 by John Ellis and Edward Taylor. Berthe Roche died in prison on 22 March 1919.

Henry Perry (Beckett), 1919

Henry Beckett, who also like to use the name Henry Perry, was about to be demobbed from the army and needed somewhere to stay. So it was that his sister introduced him to the Cornish family who lived at 13 Stukeley Road, Forest Gate. In fact, the lady of the house there, 43-year-old Alice Cornish, was Beckett's step-aunt, and 36-year-old Beckett was warmly received by the entire family.

Life seemed to be looking up for the newly demobbed soldier for he had not been with the family very long when he developed an emotional attachment with a local widow, Mrs Sparks, and there was even talk of an engagement. Things were, however, about to change.

After living at Stukeley Road for some five weeks, Beckett argued with Mrs Cornish and, as a result, was asked to find new lodgings. For a few nights he stayed with Mrs Sparks but then, on Monday, 28 April 1919, something inside him snapped.

At 10 a.m. on that day, he left Mrs Sparks's house, visited a local pub and then went for a walk. He had no destination in mind but then, at 1.30 p.m., he found himself outside the Cornish house. He walked up to the front door and knocked.

The only person home at the time was Mrs Alice Cornish. Despite what had passed between them, she invited Beckett in but soon yet another disagreement flared up. At the height of the argument, Beckett picked up a heavy poker and battered Alice over the head.

Alice was badly injured but still alive. Beckett now picked up her unconscious body and carried her into the garden at the back. He took her into a shed there, placed her on the floor, returned to the kitchen and collected a large carving fork. He then returned to the shed and stabbed Alice in the throat. He then cut off one of her fingers in order to steal the ring it carried.

Six-year-old Marie Cornish returned home from school soon afterwards to find Beckett waiting for her. At one stage she turned her back on Beckett who then hit her on the head with a hammer. Satisfied that she was dead, he opened the door to the cellar and threw her body down the steps.

Not long after this, 15-year-old Alice Cornish Junior arrived home. She too was battered to death with the hammer that had claimed her sister's life. Then, to make sure the young girl was dead, Beckett struck her in the throat with an axe. Her body too was thrown down into the cellar.

Only 48-year-old Walter Cornish had yet to come home. When he did, he was not too pleased to see Beckett there and demanded to know where his wife was. Beckett replied that she had gone to the station to meet him and must have missed him somewhere along the way. Satisfied with this explanation, Walter decided to cook himself some bacon and it was while he was attending to the pan that Beckett hit him over the head with the axe he had used on Alice Junior.

Walter Cornish was not to be taken easily and he fought back. Repeated blows from the axe were needed to subdue him, and at one stage a finger was cut off as he tried to ward off a blow. Walter tried to escape and managed to get outside where his screams for help were heard by a neighbour, Charles Henry Amey. As Amey rushed next door, Beckett ran off up the street, his clothing covered in blood.

Three people were already dead and Walter himself passed away two days later, on Wednesday, 30 April. Before he did, though, he was able to give police a meticulous detail of the attack upon him. The killer had been identified. All the police had to do now was find him.

On 2 May, four days after the attacks, an off-duty special constable named William James Green was serving in his shop on Barking Road, East Ham, when a strangely dressed man walked slowly past the premises. The man looked very nervous and wore trousers that were much too long for him. Green popped outside to get a closer look and became sure that this was Beckett, whose description had been widely circulated. Green followed until they passed a police station where he summoned help. The man was apprehended and taken into the station where he was positively identified as Beckett. He even had the ring he had cut from Alice Cornish's finger in his pocket.

On 27 May 1919, Beckett's trial opened at the Old Bailey before Mr Justice Darling. The only possible defence could be one of insanity.

Beckett's defence outlined how he had been captured by the Turks during the Great War. He had been wounded and hit in the head by shrapnel and ever since, he had had terrible dreams and heard voices telling him to do things.

Medical testimony was given by Sir Robert Armstrong-Jones, the superintendent of the Claybury Asylum, who testified that he believed Beckett to be insane. Two other doctors agreed that he was not responsible for his actions. Yet despite three eminent medical opinions, the jury still took just ten minutes to decide that Beckett was sane and guilty of murder.

An appeal against the sentence was dismissed and on Thursday, 10 July, Beckett was hanged at Pentonville by John Ellis and William Willis.

Thomas Foster, 1919

Thomas Foster and his wife, Minnie, had been married for fifteen years and had six children. Thomas, though, was a heavy drinker and had been known to use violence on his wife on occasion.

On the evening of Tuesday, 10 June 1919, the couple were seen walking together. They appeared to be friendly enough, possibly because for once, Thomas was sober. The same could not be said for the following morning.

At 6.45 a.m. on the Wednesday, terrible screams were heard coming from the family home in Shaftesbury Street, Bethnal Green. The commotion was concluded by one very loud scream and soon afterwards Foster was seen trying to run away from his house. The neighbours, however, knew that he must have done something terrible to Minnie so held him until the police arrived.

Something terrible had indeed happened to Minnie. She lay on her bed, with her youngest child still clutched tightly in her arms. Minnie's throat had been cut and a bloodstained razor lay on the mantelpiece.

Put on trial before Mr Justice Avory at the Old Bailey on 25 June, Foster tried to blame his wife, claiming that she had led an immoral life. Her behaviour had driven him insane and he had not known what he was doing when he had attacked her. The prosecution showed that Minnie had actually led a blameless life and the jury found it impossible to believe that Foster had not known what he was doing.

Found guilty and sentenced to death, Foster was hanged at Pentonville on Thursday, 31 July 1919 by John Ellis and Edward Taylor.

Frank George Warren, 1919

At 2 a.m. on the morning of Tuesday, 29 July 1919, Henry Hall walked into his local police station and announced that he had just found a woman's body at his home, 13 Prah Road, Finsbury Park. Naturally he was then detained, pending further enquiries.

Hall had certainly been telling the truth about the body. Twenty-six-year-old Lucy Nightingale had been lodging at the house for just two weeks. Although officially she was described as a housekeeper, it soon became clear that Lucy had been working as a prostitute from that address, with the full knowledge of her landlord.

Hall told police that he was a married man and his wife was in a mental institution. On Monday the 28th, he had been to visit her. Before that he had enjoyed a quiet drink in the Blackstock public house where he had been in the company of two men, Harold Horatio Morgan and Frank George Warren, who also used the surname Burke. The previous night, Morgan had been one of Lucy's clients and he and Warren were both about to visit her again.

Hall returned home from visiting his wife at 9.30 p.m. The house appeared to be empty and he fell asleep in an armchair downstairs. He woke very early on the Tuesday and called out for Lucy but received no reply. Going upstairs, he found her in her in room, tied up and strangled, and had immediately gone to the police station to report the matter.

The two men Hall had mentioned, Morgan and Warren, were soon picked up. They told very different stories.

According to Warren, Morgan had visited him at his home in Harringay and told him that a prostitute had stolen £1 from him and he had determined to have his revenge. At Morgan's request, Warren had accompanied him to the house in Prah Road and it had been Morgan who had killed the woman.

Morgan's story was that he and Warren had gone to the house together and Lucy had suggested that they stay the night. She then asked Warren to sleep with her that night while Morgan shared a room with the landlord, Henry Hall, which he did. During the night he heard a scream and then Warren came downstairs. The two men left soon afterwards.

It was plain that perhaps no one was telling the entire truth, so the police charged all three men. Morgan and Warren were charged with murder and Hall with being an accessory. In fact, the charges against Hall were soon dropped, leaving the other two to face their trial together.

Mr Justice Darling, who sentenced to death Frank Warren, as well as with thirteen others mentioned in this book.

This trial took place before Mr Justice Darling at the Old Bailey on 17 and 18 September. Here it soon became clear that Warren had not told the entire truth. When he had returned to his home in Harringay he had given his landlady, Olive Parton, three rings which were shown to have belonged to Lucy. How could he have taken those if he was not also responsible for Lucy's death? On the final day of the trial, Warren was found guilty and Morgan was acquitted.

There was no appeal and just over three weeks later, on Tuesday, 7 October, Frank Warren was hanged at Pentonville by John Ellis and George Brown.

Arthur Andrew Clement Goslett, 1920

Arthur Goslett never denied that he was responsible for the death of his wife Evelyn, but the reason he gave for killing her was never believed.

On Sunday, 2 May 1920, the body of a woman was found floating in the river Brent close to Brentmead Place, Golders Green. A police search of the area revealed signs of a struggle having taken place at the bottom of Weston Avenue. There were smears of blood on the grass and signs that something, probably a body, had been dragged to the edge of the river and dropped in. A subsequent post-mortem would show that the woman must have been alive when she was thrown into the river for the cause of death was drowning.

It didn't take long to identify the woman as 43-year-old Evelyn Goslett who lived in Golders Green Road. She had four children: three by her first husband and one by her second, 44-year-old Arthur Goslett.

The next step was to visit Evelyn's home and determine her movements on Saturday, 1 May, the day she had been killed. At 8 p.m. she had eaten some supper with two lodgers who lived with the family, Marjorie Orell and Daisy Holt. Soon afterwards Evelyn had left the house, never to be seen alive again.

At some time after 10.30 p.m., Arthur Goslett returned home, having also been out that evening. The next morning the housemaid, Constance Hanrahan, entered the kitchen at 7.50 a.m. to see Arthur making himself a cup of tea. They chatted for a few moments and Arthur said that his wife had not come home the previous night. This fact was soon common knowledge in the busy household and at one stage Arthur asked his stepson, Jules, to go around to his grandmother's house to see if she was there. Jules did as he was asked but found the request puzzling. After all, he knew that his mother had arranged to meet up with his stepfather, close to Brent Bridge, on the night she had vanished.

Naturally, when police told the family that Evelyn's body had been found in the river, Jules told them about the meeting his mother had arranged. When Arthur Goslett was asked about it, he immediately admitted that he had killed his wife.

Goslett said that he had asked his wife to meet him near the Prince Albert pub to look at a house he wanted to buy. She agreed and they arranged to meet at 9.15 p.m. They met and walked down to the river where he took a tyre lever out of his pocket and hit her on the back of the head. After giving her three or four blows, Goslett gently placed her into the river and walked home.

The reason he gave for committing this crime was, to say the least, astounding. He claimed that one of the lodgers, Daisy Holt, had forced him into doing it. When asked about this, Daisy denied all knowledge.

Goslett was placed on trial before Mr Justice Shearman at the Old Bailey on 21 June. The proceedings would last for two days.

In court, two marriage certificates were produced by the defence. One showed that Arthur Goslett had married Evelyn Mear on 12 June 1914. The other showed that Arthur, using the surname Godfrey, had married Daisy Ellen Holt on 7 February 1919.

It appeared that Goslett had started a relationship with Daisy and as a result, she had found herself to be pregnant. Her lover did the decent thing and married her, the child being born in July of that same year and placed into care. Soon afterwards, the man Daisy had married as Arthur Godfrey admitted that his real name was Goslett and that he was already married. He did have a solution to this problem though. Daisy could move into the house as a lodger, claim to be his sister-in-law – her husband having been killed in the Great War – and they could carry on their relationship. Somewhat reluctantly, Daisy had agreed.

For a time the situation was fine, but after a few weeks, Daisy had put pressure on Goslett, demanding that he do away with his wife and threatening to expose him as a bigamist if he didn't. Finally, he felt he had to give in to her and killed Evelyn.

Daisy's story was rather different. Yes, she had married Goslett and yes, she had given birth to his child. However, soon after moving into the house, a neighbour who had known her previously exposed her real identity to Evelyn Goslett who was quite nice about things and offered to find her a new home where she might live with her child. Goslett had then told Evelyn that if Daisy were forced to leave, he would be forced to take drastic action. This was why he had killed his wife, not because Daisy had asked him to.

It was obvious that Goslett would be found guilty, but if the jury accepted his story then Daisy would be arrested and also charged with murder. In the event, they believed her story and Goslett was sentenced to death.

Goslett was hanged at Pentonville on Tuesday, 27 July 1920 by John Ellis and Edward Taylor. Daisy Holt was never charged with any offence.

Frederick Alexander Keeling, 1922

Although he was a married man, Frederick Keeling had lived apart from his wife for some time and had known a succession of lovers since. By November 1921 he was living with a woman named Mrs Haines, but in the same lodging house in St Georges Road, Tottenham, lived 46-year-old Emily Agnes Dewberry.

Keeling was never very fond of honest work and by way of a little fraud had managed to obtain a £4 pension he was not legally entitled to. Somehow Emily found out about this and reported the matter to the pension's officer. As a result, a warrant was issued for Keeling to appear in court. Naturally, as she was a witness, Agnes would have to appear too. The date set was 24 November 1921.

On that date, neither Emily nor Keeling appeared in court and officers were sent to the house in St Georges Road to find out why. They received no reply to their knocking and, having suspicions that something might have happened, forced the door to Emily's room. She lay on the floor, battered to death. Near her head lay a bloodstained hammer and on that weapon were the initials F.K. A warrant was then issued for the arrest of F.K. – Frederick Keeling.

No sign of Keeling could be found so a watch was placed on his latest paramour, Mrs Haines. Finally, on 9 December, she was seen meeting Keeling in a public house. He was arrested but denied all knowledge of the murder, claiming that a stranger must have killed her. The story was backed up by Mrs Haines, who said that on the day of the murder he had only been out of her sight for a couple of minutes so he wouldn't have had time to do it. Nevertheless, he was charged with wilful murder and appeared before Mr Justice Darling at the Old Bailey on 6 March. The case lasted two days.

The hammer with Keeling's initials, found at the scene, was a damning piece of evidence. So too were the bloodstains found on Keeling's clothes. The jury felt they had more than enough to convict.

On Tuesday, 11 April 1922, Keeling was hanged at Pentonville by John Ellis and Seth Mills.

Edmund Hugh Tonbridge, 1922

Twenty-five-year-old Margaret Evans had known 38-year-old Edmund Tonbridge for quite a few years. A relationship had developed and even though they had never married, she had borne him a child and was now pregnant again. Would he now do the decent thing and marry her?

After the first child had been born, Tonbridge had paid maintenance of 15s a week and this had continued from the birth, in November 1920, until the child was adopted in August 1921. Now it seemed as if he might well have to pay Margaret money all over again.

Marriage was discussed a number of times and finally, on Saturday, 14 January 1922, the couple arranged to meet to sort out the arrangements. The pair met at Clapton station and then went for a walk along the banks of the River Lea. It didn't really matter what was discussed though, for in his pocket Tonbridge knew he had the solution to all of his problems: a bottle of potassium cyanide.

The couple walked down Spring Hill, Clapton, onto the banks of the river. A policeman standing in the middle of a bridge nearby saw the young lovers walking slowly towards him. They were still some way off when the officer saw them embrace and, not wishing to stare at what was obviously a private moment, turned his head away.

Almost instantly there was a loud splash. There was something in the water now and though the policeman couldn't make out what it was, he did see that the man was now alone. As he came up level with the bridge, the officer stopped the man and demanded to know what had happened to the woman he was with.

The man, Tonbridge, denied that he had been with a woman and this lie led the officer to take him back to where he had been seen with the woman. There, in the water, was the body of Margaret Evans. Tonbridge was then taken into custody and charged with murder.

The spot on the River Lea, at the bottom of Spring Gardens, where Edmund Tonbridge poisoned Margaret Evans.

Tonbridge faced his trial before Mr Justice Darling at the Old Bailey on 5 March. His defence was that he and Margaret had gone for a walk to iron out their marriage plans. At that point he had produced a letter from a gentleman named George Andrews which proved that he was the father of the child she was carrying. Faced with this, Margaret reached into Tonbridge's pocket and took out a bottle of prussic acid that he claimed to have been carrying for photographic purposes. She drank down the liquid and then fell dead into the river.

It was a simple matter for the prosecution to show that the letter from Andrews was a forgery and that in addition to the effects of the poison, the post-mortem on Margaret's body had also shown bruising on her face which was probably caused by a blow from a fist.

The jury decided that Tonbridge had first struck Margaret and then forced the poison down her throat while she was stunned. This was nothing more than a cold-blooded murder and, as a result, Tonbridge was hanged at Pentonville on Tuesday, 18 April by John Ellis and Robert Baxter.

Henry Julius Jacoby, 1922

Lady Alice White had lived in room 14 at the Spencer Hotel in Portman Street for some time. She had a routine, part of which was that the chambermaid would clean her room at about the same time each day. However, on the morning of Tuesday, 14 March 1922, the maid received no answer to her gentle knocking.

Perhaps the old lady was still asleep? The chambermaid slowly entered the room and saw immediately why Lady White had not replied. She still lay in bed but her pillow was saturated in blood. Someone had given her a very severe beating indeed and part of her brain protruded through her skull.

Surprisingly, Alice White was still alive, though too seriously injured to be moved, and had to receive medical treatment in her hotel bed. However, despite the ministrations of the doctor, Alice died from her injuries the following morning. This was now a case of murder.

The most obvious conclusion was that Lady White had been the victim of an attempted burglary, had disturbed an intruder and been struck by some heavy object as a result. An inventory showed that nothing had been taken so the suggestion that the assailant had been disturbed did seem to ring true. It was time to interview all the staff to see if anyone had seen or heard anything.

One of those whom the police spoke to was a pantry boy, 18-year-old Henry Jacoby. He reported that he had heard whispering in the small hours of 14 March and had mentioned this to Mr Platt, the night porter. They had searched the premises but found nothing.

It was natural for the police to look into the backgrounds of all the staff and it was this that led to some very interesting information on the helpful pantry boy. Jacoby had lived in lodgings before coming to work at the hotel just three weeks before, and some money had been reported missing from these lodgings. Jacoby was then arrested and charged with that theft but then closely questioned about the murder of Lady White.

It wasn't long before Jacoby admitted that after he and Platt had searched the hotel, he had gone back to his bedroom where he picked up a hammer and then gone to see if he could find any cash. The first door he tried was locked but the second one, to room 14, was unlocked.

Jacoby went inside, but no sooner had he switched on his torch than Lady White woke and cried out. In order to silence her, Jacoby struck her with the hammer before going downstairs, washing the bloody weapon and then retiring to his room.

Placed on trial before Mr Justice McCardie at the Old Bailey on 28 April, Jacoby pleaded not guilty to murder. His story had now changed. He now claimed that after parting from Platt he, as he had said before, went to collect the hammer and had gone upstairs to see if he could find out who was whispering. He saw the door to room 14 slightly open and going inside, saw a shadowy figure. He lashed out with the hammer and only then did he realise that he had hit Lady White.

The jury retired to consider their verdict but after a short time returned to court to ask for guidance. They asked if they could return a verdict of manslaughter if they were convinced that Jacoby had not intended to kill. The judge pointed out that even if the intention was just to inflict grievous harm then manslaughter was not an option. After further deliberation, the guilty verdict was returned but with a strong recommendation to mercy.

That recommendation did nothing to save Jacoby, who was executed at Pentonville on Wednesday, 7 June by John Ellis and Thomas Phillips. He was one of the youngest men to be hanged in the twentieth century.

Reginald Dunne & Joseph O'Sullivan, 1922

Thursday, 22 June 1922 was a glorious summer's day, and as Field Marshal Sir Henry Wilson put his key into the front door of his home at 36 Eaton Place, he did not notice the two men approaching him. Without warning, both men drew revolvers and fired at close range. Six bullets hit Sir Henry, the two fatal wounds being chest wounds fired from opposite sides, proving that both men were responsible for his death.

There was no shortage of witnesses to the murder. A group of workmen were busy in the street and there were two policemen in the streets nearby. Bravely, some of these men chased the assailants as they tried to hail a taxi cab in order to make good their escape. The driver had thrown open his door but upon hearing the cry of 'Stop them!' he concluded that there might have been a robbery. He slammed the door of his cab shut and began to follow the two running men.

The escape attempt was a desperate one. The two fugitives fired their guns at anyone who came close to them and three more men were wounded: Constable Marsh, Constable Sayer and Alexander Clarke. Even seeing so many men shot, others continued the chase and eventually both the killers were apprehended. Taken into custody, they readily identified themselves as James Connelly and John O'Brien.

It didn't take the police long to determine that Connelly was actually Joseph O'Sullivan and O'Brien was Reginald Dunne. At first, both appeared to be highly respectable men. Both had been in the army in the Great War, serving with distinction. Both had been wounded in France and O'Sullivan had actually lost his right leg below the knee. Now Dunne was training to be a teacher while O'Sullivan

Eaton Place where Reginald Dunne and Joseph O'Sullivan shot dead Field Marshall Sir Henry Wilson. The murder spot is close to where the middle carriage is parked.

worked at the Ministry of Labour. Both men, though, had sympathies with the Irish Republican movement and Sir Henry was a military advisor to the Ulster government. This was why he had been made a target.

The trial of both men opened before Mr Justice Shearman at the Old Bailey on 18 July. Both refused to enter a plea but admitted the shooting, claiming that it was a political act. They then refused to enter a defence and so the entire proceedings lasted just three hours.

The men who had killed together were hanged side by side at Wandsworth on Thursday, 10 August. John Ellis officiated alongside two assistants: Edward Taylor and Seth Mills.

William James Yeldham, 1922

On 20 May 1922, William Yeldman married Elsie Florence. Within days of that ceremony, both would be facing a murder charge.

Yeldman was not the most pleasant of men. He had poor personal habits and lived in squalor in some outbuildings on a farm near Ilford, but he was still fond of the ladies and, somewhat surprisingly, Elsie was attracted to him. Unfortunately, there was another man who was also fond of Elsie, even though he was almost three times her age, and that was 54-year-old George Stanley Grimshaw.

On Wednesday, 17 May, three days before his marriage, Yeldman saw Elsie walking into some woods in the company of George Grimshaw. He decided to follow them and as he watched from a distance, he saw, to his dismay, that George had his arm around Elsie. It was more than Yeldman could stand. He walked up to the couple, pulled out a spanner, and battered George to death.

On 22 May, Yeldman sold Grimshaw's watch and in due course, the couple were picked up and questioned about the murder. They told rather different stories.

According to Yeldman, Elsie had lured Grimshaw to the woods deliberately so that he could rob him. After Grimshaw was dead, Elsie had stolen £15 from his body. He explained that when he had first met Elsie she was a prostitute and he objected to her earning her living in this manner. He had stolen a bicycle to get some money but had been caught and received a six-month prison sentence. When he came out, he discovered that Grimshaw was paying attention to Elsie. That was when he had asked Elsie to lure him to the woods and he ended by denying that there had been any intention to kill.

Elsie's story was that she much preferred Yeldham to Grimshaw but on 17 May they had argued and she had gone with Grimshaw to make Yeldham jealous. They went for a walk in the woods and suddenly Yeldham appeared from nowhere and attacked Grimshaw. Having said that, Elsie did admit that she had taken money from the body.

It was for the court to decide the truth and the pair appeared before Mr Justice Shearman at the Old Bailey on 17 July, the proceedings lasting three days. At the end of that time the jury decided that they had acted together and both were found guilty and sentenced to death.

A few days before she was due to be executed, Elsie Yeldham's sentence was commuted to life imprisonment. William Yeldham found no such escape and on Tuesday, 5 September, he was hanged at Pentonville by John Ellis and William Willis.

Frederick Edward Bywaters & Edith Jessie Thompson, 1923

In July 1920, Percy Thompson and his wife, Edith, moved into 41 Kensington Gardens, Ilford. The Thompsons did not have what could be described as a happy marriage. He was a rather dull, serious man with little sense of humour while she was a vivacious, younger woman with a romantic attitude to life. It could be said that she was in love with love. Still, the couple muddled along until a catalyst arrived in their lives in June 1921.

That catalyst was Frederick Bywaters, a friend of Edith's younger brothers and sisters. He was employed as a steward on board a ship and in that summer returned home from a four-month long voyage to Australia. Upon his return, he was invited to join Edith's sister, Avis Graydon, on a holiday in the Isle of Wight. There were others from the family on that holiday, including Percy and Edith Thompson.

There was an instant attraction between Edith and Frederick. Even so, the relationship was innocent enough but it is likely that sometime during that stay on the island they kissed for the first time. In fact, according to letters that Edith wrote, it is probable that this momentous event took place on 14 June 1921.

The friendship was, however, more complex than a simple attraction between a young man and a married woman. Frederick Bywaters was a most pleasant man and even Edith's husband Percy found him personable. In fact, Percy liked Frederick so much that he even invited him to lodge with them at Kensington Gardens. Naturally this idea appealed to both Frederick and Edith and he accepted. Again, judging by her letters, it is likely that at some time over the next month, Frederick and Edith became lovers.

For a month or so all was well. Then, on 1 August, Percy and his wife argued and this developed into violence. Frederick was not prepared to stand by and watch the object of his affections treated in this way, so he intervened. Later that same day, Percy and Edith discussed the possibility of a separation but then Frederick interfered again and asked Percy if he would grant Edith a divorce.

We cannot know if, up to this point, Percy had had any suspicions about the relationship that existed between his wife and Frederick Bywaters. It is likely, however, that Frederick's interference and his request for a divorce for Edith did intimate that something might have been going on. What is definite is that Percy asked Frederick to leave the house.

Over the next few months Frederick went back to sea a number of times and letters were exchanged between him and Edith. The letters that she sent to him were long, rambling and filled with that romantic love that so attracted her. She spoke of her unhappiness with her marriage and discussed the possibility of suicide. She even enclosed clippings from newspapers, some of which related to murder cases of the time. In one she even suggested that she had tried to poison her husband by means of broken glass in his food. It is almost certain that there was no truth in these ramblings and that they were nothing more than the outpourings of a sad, frustrated and desperate woman. The letters must also have had an effect on Frederick, who by now must have been extremely worried about the woman he had fallen in love with.

On Saturday, 23 September 1922, Frederick returned home from his latest sea voyage. He and Edith met a number of times over the next few weeks. They had lunches together, met for tea and went for walks. They met for lunch on 3 October in Cheapside and parted at around 5.30 p.m. It was perhaps during that lunch that Edith mentioned that she and Percy were going to the Criterion Theatre that evening with friends.

Edith spent a pleasant enough evening at the Criterion and after the show she and Percy made their way home by tube and train, arriving at Ilford station at around midnight. They then began the short walk back to Kensington Gardens.

It was as they strolled down Belgrave Road, just as they were about to turn into Kensington Gardens itself, that a man wearing an overcoat came up behind them. The man pushed past Edith and began to grapple with Percy. A knife was brandished and Percy Thompson fell to the pavement and lay against a low brick wall. He had been stabbed a number of times. Most of those wounds were defence wounds, or very superficial ones but the one in his neck had cut his carotid artery. The assailant ran off down Seymour Gardens as Edith called for help. It was too late. Percy Thompson was already dead.

Although she said nothing at the time, Edith knew who the man with the knife had been. She recognised his overcoat and his voice from the few words he had spoken. She knew that Frederick Bywaters had just stabbed her husband to death.

It didn't take long for the police to discover the relationship between Edith and Frederick. He was arrested on 4 October, the same day that the murder had taken place. Later that same night, Edith was also arrested.

To begin with, both made statements denying all knowledge of the murder. It was only when Edith was being transferred from one room to another, on 5 October, that she finally gave away Frederick's part in the crime. She caught a glimpse of her lover and suddenly cried, 'Oh God! Why did he do it? I didn't want him to do it. I must tell the truth.'

Edith went on to make a statement in which she confirmed that she had recognised Frederick as her husband's killer. Both were then charged with murder and one week later, in a routine search of his cabin on his ship, the letters Edith had written to him were discovered.

Edith and Frederick appeared before Mr Justice Shearman at the Old Bailey on 6 December. The trial would last until 11 December.

There could be no doubt that Frederick would be found guilty of murder but it was suggested by the prosecution that he had murdered Percy at Edith's instigation. If the jury accepted this then she would be equally guilty and would receive the same sentence: death by hanging. Frederick denied vehemently that he had acted on Edith's instructions or that she had had anything whatsoever to do with the crime, but passages from her letters were read out in court and these damned her in the eyes of the jury. Guilty verdicts were returned on both defendants.

On Tuesday, 9 January 1923, Frederick Bywaters was hanged at Pentonville by William Willis and Thomas Phillips. At the same time, an hysterical Edith Thompson was hanged at Holloway by John Ellis and two assistants, Robert Baxter and Seth Mills.

Bernard Pomroy, 1923

Herbert Richard Golding was not a happy man. The cab driver had picked up a young couple at Leicester Square at 11 p.m. on Tuesday, 6 February, and was asked to drive to Watford. Once there, however, he had been asked to drive on to Templewood Avenue, Hampstead, where they arrived at around 1.30 a.m. on 7 February. Still the couple were apparently not satisfied because all the houses there were in darkness, so Golding was asked to drive them back to Leicester Square. If only they could make their minds up!

In due course the taxi approached Swiss Cottage and as it did, Golding thought he might have heard a low scream. He assumed he was simply mistaken and drove on to Leicester Square. Here, to his utter dismay, Golding was asked to drive on yet again, this time to the nearest police station. Muttering under his breath, Golding then headed for Vine Street.

Upon arrival at the police station, the young man in the back of the cab rushed out, insisting that he had to talk to the officer on duty. As he did so, Golding noticed two things: the man's hands were heavily bloodstained and the woman in the back did not move.

Inside the police station the young man identified himself as 25-year-old Bernard Pomroy and confessed that he had just murdered his girlfriend, 21-year-old Alice May Cheshire. He calmly added that the body, along with the knife he had used, were on the back seat of a taxi cab waiting outside.

Pomroy appeared before Mr Justice Horridge at the Old Bailey on 1 March 1923 to answer the charge of murder. He refused any defence and insisted on pleading guilty. Nevertheless, some of the history of the couple was now revealed.

Pomroy and Alice had been together for about three years and had, very recently, become engaged. Not long afterwards, Alice's sister, Mabel announced to her father, Esau that she was pregnant. As if that were not surprise enough, she then said that the father was none other than her sister's fiancé, Pomroy.

After a long talk with Esau Cheshire, Pomroy said that he should be the one to tell Alice and it was arranged that he should do this on the Tuesday. Pomroy was determined to see Alice before then and so invited her to the theatre on Monday, 5 February. There could be little doubt as to his intentions, for as the couple left Alice's home he shouted, 'Why not say goodbye properly in case she does not come back again?'

The death sentence was a formality and, on Thursday, 5 April, Pomroy was hanged at Pentonville by John Ellis and Edward Taylor.

Rowland Duck, 1923

Rowland Duck was not a stable man. He had served in the Great War where he had been blown up by a shell. He survived without much in the way of physical injury, but afterwards his mental health appeared to be rather suspect. He became nervous and emotional and easily upset.

Rowland lived with his wife and three children in Cambria Street, Fulham, and in order to eke out the family finances, it was agreed that they should take in a lodger. So it was that 18-year-old Nellie Pearce moved in.

Nellie, an attractive girl, earned her living as a prostitute and one of her clients happened to be none other than Rowland himself. Unfortunately, she gave him venereal disease and this did not rest well on the shoulders of the already unstable Rowland.

On Wednesday, 2 May 1923, Rowland announced to his wife that Nellie would have to leave the house. Whether his wife agreed to that course of action or not is unimportant, for the very next morning, Rowland walked into Nellie's bedroom and cut her throat while she slept. He then wrapped her body in a blanket, shoved it underneath the bed and walked to the nearest police station where he admitted what he had done.

Rowland's trial took place before Mr Justice Swift at the Old Bailey on 31 May, where it was suggested that he was not responsible for his actions. Rowland's mother, Charlotte, told of his injury during the war and how he had been 'funny' ever since: sometimes he would even have to be held down until one of his episodes had passed.

Dr Eric Coplans stated that the prisoner was a very nervous individual and showed clear signs of epilepsy, something he had not had before he had been blown up in the trenches. Other medical evidence showed that while suffering an attack, Rowland could commit acts and have no memory of them afterwards. Despite all this testimony, the jury still took just thirty minutes to decide that he was guilty as charged.

An appeal was heard but the judges ruled that since Rowland had confessed at the police station, he must have known what he had done and that it was wrong. Indeed, his statement had described in precise detail exactly what he had done. This was not consistent with a man who had no memory of events.

On Wednesday, 4 July, 25-year-old Rowland Duck was hanged at Pentonville by John Ellis and Robert Wilson.

George William Barton, 1925

In 1917, Mary May Palfrey's husband died. Soon afterwards she also lost her sister and in time, Mary found herself growing ever closer to her sister's husband, George Barton. Soon an engagement was announced and a day fixed for the wedding: 5 February 1925.

Mary lived at 12 Bartle Avenue, East Ham, and on the night of Wednesday, 21 January her son, 10-year-old Edward Charles, had a friend, 13-year-old Ivy Stevens, over to stay. Ivy's family lived at no. 23 but they were quite close to Mary and the children often stayed at each other's houses. The children went to bed at 10.30 p.m. The next morning both children had breakfast together and then went off to school. At that time, Mary Palfrey was alive and well.

It was 12.10 p.m. by the time Edward returned home for lunch. All thoughts of food were soon forgotten though, for there, on the kitchen floor, lay his mother's body. She had been battered with an iron pipe that lay nearby and her throat had been cut.

Police spoke to the neighbours and from them, the time of the attack could be pinned down. Elizabeth Carroll had seen Mary in the garden between 9 a.m. and 9.45 a.m. and Alice Batford had seen George Barton leaving the house soon afterwards, at around 10 a.m. Of George himself, no trace could be found.

The next day, 23 January, Barton's son, Albert received a postcard. Written by George, it apologised for what he had done and expressed his intention to flee abroad. In the event, George must have changed his mind, for the day after that, 24 January, he gave himself up to the police. He claimed that he had no involvement in the crime and had only come forward because he had seen reports in the newspaper and realised that he was being sought.

Questioned at length, George Barton finally admitted that he had killed Mary, but said that he had done so out of jealousy. Apparently, Mary had told him that a sailor she knew was going to visit her once he had left for work so he lashed out with the iron pipe. Then, while she lay on the floor he had used his razor to cut her throat.

Placed on trial before Mr Justice Avory at the Old Bailey on 28 February, it did not take long for the jury to find Barton guilty. Asked if he had anything to say, he replied that it was a pity he wasn't Ronald True, a killer who had been found guilty but subsequently reprieved on the grounds that he was insane. Sentenced to death, Barton then turned to the judge and exclaimed, 'May you be hung tomorrow.'

An appeal was dismissed and on Thursday, 2 April, Barton was hanged at Pentonville by Robert Baxter and Robert Wilson.

Arthur Henry Bishop, 1925

There is a hierarchy among servants in a gentleman's household. Francis Edward Rix was the butler to Sir George Lloyd, the High Commissioner to Egypt, who lived at 24 Charles Street, Mayfair. Each morning there was a routine whereby the maidservant, Rix's junior, would bring the butler a cup of tea at 7.30 a.m.

That routine was unchanged on the morning of Sunday, 7 June 1925. The maidservant made the tea and took it to Rix's room. She knocked politely and entered, only to find that Rix would not be drinking this particular cup. He was still in bed, covered in blood and a hatchet lay on the floor. It was later discovered that some money, a ring, a watch and a pair of boots were missing from the room.

It is perhaps routine to enquire of any other members of staff who might have left recently or had some sort of grudge against the butler. This led to the name of Arthur Bishop who had been employed as a hall-boy until recently. Bishop had been there for about six months and it had been Rix who had dismissed him, in February.

The police did not have to work hard to find Bishop, for on 8 June, the day after the murder, he walked into the police station at Sittingbourne and gave himself up. In his hand he had a newspaper, which carried a detailed account of the murder, and Bishop showed this to the officer on duty and admitted that he was responsible. Bishop was then searched and some of the stolen property was found in his pockets.

Eighteen-year-old Bishop appeared before Mr Justice Swift at the Old Bailey on 16 July. Here he admitted that the motive for the crime had been robbery. He had already committed one robbery in Cranbrook and decided that his next port of call would be the home of his ex-employer in Mayfair.

At around 1.30 a.m. on 7 June he had gained entry through a basement window. That was where he had found the hatchet and took it with him in case anyone should try to apprehend him. He crept silently into the butler's room but, thinking that Rix might wake, pre-empted that possibility by hitting him with the axe.

The guilty verdict was a formality and on Friday, 14 August, Bishop was hanged at Pentonville by Robert Baxter. Since this was a double execution, with the subject of the next entry, there were three assistants: Henry Pollard, Edward Taylor and Robert Wilson.

William John Cronin, 1925

Lightning can sometimes strike twice in the same place. That was certainly true for William Cronin who went on trial for his life twice.

On 23 July 1897, an argument broke out between a group of men in Limehouse. One of the men, Henry Cuthbert, had been accused of breaking a strike and it was during the altercation that Cronin, one of the protagonists, rushed into Cuthbert's house at 16 Carr Street and battered his 10-month-old daughter, Eliza to death with a spade. He was charged with murder and appeared in court on 14 September.

It soon became clear that there was some doubt in this case. Cronin claimed that at the time of the attack upon Eliza, he was with a woman named Mary Farrow, and she backed this story. Another witness, Henry Corcorna, claimed that it had been Cuthbert himself who had first wielded the spade and there was the possibility that the child had been struck accidentally in the fracas. In the event, the jury decided that Cronin was guilty of manslaughter, not murder, and he received seven years' imprisonment. That would have been the last history ever heard of William John Cronin but for events that took place twenty-eight years later.

In 1924, Alice Garrett's husband had died, but soon afterwards she became involved with Cronin and eventually moved in with him at 126 Old Street, Stepney. The relationship was not a happy one however, and their neighbours at no. 128, Rose and William Blanks, often heard the sounds of heated arguments.

Yet another argument broke out just before midnight on Friday, 12 June 1925, but this time Alice was heard to cry, 'Murder!' William Blanks went to investigate and found, to his horror, that not only had Alice's throat been cut, but her head had almost been severed from her body.

William went back to his wife to tell her what he had discovered. Perhaps showing more curiosity than sense, Rose went next door to take a look for herself. As she entered the house, Cronin pushed past her. He did not get very far. Rose shouted, 'Stop him!' and a gentleman named Charles James Edmead, who was passing at the time, leapt upon Cronin and held him until the police arrived. Edmead did not escape unscathed, though. Cronin struggled, pulled out his razor and managed to slash one of Edmead's fingers.

Cronin appeared before Mr Justice Swift at the Old Bailey on 17 July. His defence was that he was not responsible and someone else must have committed the crime.

Cronin explained that he had first met Alice about six months before she was killed. They had been introduced by Cronin's married sister, Emma Jane Sartain, who lived on the floor above Alice. It was Emma who later told Cronin that Alice had been seeing other men while he had been at sea. It must have been one of those men who had killed her.

Unfortunately for Cronin, while his sister did agree that she had introduced him to Alice, she denied that she had ever said anything about Alice being unfaithful to him. The jury did not even bother to leave the box before deciding that he was guilty as charged.

On Friday, 14 August 1925, Cronin was executed at Pentonville alongside Arthur Bishop, the subject of the last entry.

Ewen Anderson Stitchell, 1926

At 7.50 a.m. on Friday, 1 January 1926, Mrs Walker left her home at 58 Arlington Road, Camden Town. The only person left in the house at that time was her 16-year-old daughter, Polly Edith Walker.

At some time within the next thirty minutes, Kathleen Lukey, who lived in rooms below the Walkers, heard a scream. Shortly after this she also heard someone leaving the house, but did not report any of this to the police.

It was 1 p.m. when Mrs Walker returned home. Going into her daughter's room, she found Polly lying on the floor, partly underneath her bed. The young girl had been battered and a bloodstained poker lay by her head. There was also a broken pair of fire tongs. Finally, for good measure, Polly's assailant had also strangled her and a stocking was still tied tightly around her throat.

When police interviewed Mrs Walker, she gave them the name of a man who lived nearby: Eugene de Vere. He had been paying attention to Polly but she had not encouraged him in any way. This had only served to make him very jealous indeed if Polly showed the slightest sign of affection for any else. An example of this feeling was given at a Christmas party held at no. 58 just a week or so before.

Alfred Leonard Miall had been at the Walkers' house and had offered to take Polly for a ride on his motorcycle. De Vere had made such a scene that Polly had been forced to turn down the offer. Things were no better when Miall then offered to take Polly to a dance and de Vere even threatened to punch Miall if he persisted. The police decided that it was time to interview de Vere, but he was no longer at home.

De Vere's description was circulated and he was eventually picked up on 3 January at a temperance hotel in Hitchin. He readily admitted responsibility for Polly's death.

Charged under his real name of Ewen Stitchell, de Vere appeared before Mr Justice Salter at the Old Bailey on 11 February. The proceedings would last for two days.

De Vere said that on the evening of 31 December he had lain awake in his room at 32 Delaney Street. The next morning, at around 7.30 a.m., he had risen and left the house, walking directly to Polly's home. He had a key to the house, let himself in and put the kettle on. Polly must have heard him for she came down almost immediately, wearing her nightdress and a dressing gown. They argued and he ran after her into her bedroom, where he killed her.

De Vere claimed, however, that he had been provoked, and when arrested, had shown officers a small bite wound on one of his fingers. It was pointed out by the prosecution that even if Polly had bitten him, it hardly justified the level of retaliation that de Vere must have used. The jury agreed and de Vere was sentenced to death.

On Wednesday, 24 March 1926, Ewen Stitchell was hanged at Pentonville by Robert Baxter and Thomas Phillips.

James Frederick Stratton, 1927

Madge Dorothy Maggs hated her first name and insisted that everyone call her Daisy. She was an attractive, vivacious 25-year-old and lived with her brother and sister at 5 Grinstead Road, Deptford.

It was natural that such an attractive young lady should have a paramour and for some years, Daisy had been seeing James Stratton who lived with his grandmother at 7 Homerton Terrace, Morning Lane, Hackney. Things were wonderful between the two until 25 December 1926, when Daisy suddenly announced to Stratton that the relationship was over.

Stratton didn't want things to end and for a time at least they remained on friendly enough terms, even meeting occasionally. One such meeting was arranged for Sunday, 20 February 1927, but Daisy did not turn up. A concerned Stratton travelled over to Deptford to see what the problem was, only to find Daisy with another man.

The next day, Monday the 21st, Daisy was working at the International Exhibition at White City. Frederick knew her routine, of course, and paid Edmund Hean, an errand boy, a few coppers to take a message to her. There was no reply from Daisy. A second message was sent with John Welch and this time Daisy did reply. She agreed to meet Stratton at Liverpool Street station at 7.30 p.m.

Stratton returned home and got ready for his meeting. He dressed neatly, made sure he looked his best, and took with him a sharp knife and an iron last wrapped in an old rag. The couple met, and at one stage he had a drink in the Mermaid public house while she waited outside. Stratton, fortified by a pint of beer, then asked Daisy why she had stood him up the previous evening. An argument developed but eventually things calmed down a little and the couple walked to Broad Street station together.

Stratton bought two return tickets to Hackney and the couple were seen getting into a third-class carriage together. Nothing else was heard of them until the train stopped at signals near Graham Street, Hackney. Stratton was then seen leaping down from the train and walking along the track towards the engine. When he had drawn level, Stratton shouted up to the fireman, Walter Edward Tidd, that he had just murdered his girlfriend.

A check was made inside the carriage and it was seen that Daisy was indeed dead. She had been battered with the last and then stabbed a number of times. The police were called as the train moved on to Dalston Junction station, the same one mentioned in the very first case in this book.

Stratton appeared before Mr Justice Branson at the Old Bailey on 8 March. He insisted on pleading guilty and admitted that he had been looking for a chance to 'do her in' since Christmas. Sentenced to death, Stratton was hanged at Pentonville by Robert Baxter and Lionel Mann on Tuesday, 29 March. It was just thirty-six days since Daisy's death.

John Robinson, 1927

The wicker trunk had been in the left-luggage department at Charing Cross station for just a few days but now it was beginning to give off a rather unpleasant smell. Perhaps something inside had gone off or spilled. It couldn't simply be ignored so, on 9 May 1927, it was forced open.

The trunk contained five brown paper parcels, all neatly wrapped. Further investigation revealed that each parcel contained a separate portion of a female body.

The remains were sent on to Sir Bernard Spilsbury for examination and he was able to determine that the cause of death had been strangulation. Further, he was able to add that the woman had been dead for a week or less and that there were also signs that she had been struck with something.

The parcels contained one other clue. One contained a pair of knickers and upon these were sewn the name P. Holt. Excellent police work led to Mrs Holt being traced and she identified the underwear as hers. Of even more help was the fact that, given a description of the dead woman, Mrs Holt was able to give her a name. The body in the trunk was that of 36-year-old Minnie Alice Bonati.

Minnie was a known prostitute and checks showed that she had last been seen alive on Wednesday, 4 May. More dogged police work brought forward two more valuable witnesses. The first, a Mr Ward, identified the trunk as one he had sold, while the second, a taxi-driver, recalled delivering the trunk to Charing Cross. He gave the police the address he had collected the trunk from: 86 Rochester Row. The next port of call was Rochester Row. All the tenants there were accounted for but one, John Robinson, who hadn't been seen for some days.

The premises were searched and police found a telegram which had been sent to 'Robinson' at the Greyhound Hotel in Hammersmith. Upon checking there, the police discovered that this Robinson was John's wife. She agreed to assist the police in any way she could.

Charing Cross station, where Minnie Bonati's body was found inside a trunk.

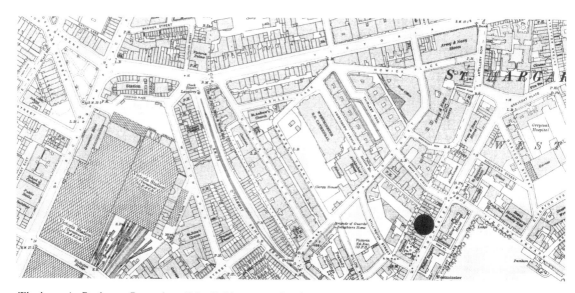

The house in Rochester Row where John Robinson murdered Minnie Bonati. It is notably close to the police station. (Reproduced with the permission of Alan Godfrey Maps)

John Robinson was in regular contact with his wife and they occasionally agreed to meet up. At the next meeting, Mrs Robinson brought along a friend to meet her husband. That 'friend' was Chief Inspector George Cornish. Taken into custody, Robinson denied having anything to do with Minnie's death.

Robinson appeared before Mr Justice Swift at the Old Bailey on 11 July. The hearing would last for three days during which Robinson claimed that it had all been an accident.

He said that he had been at Victoria station when Minnie had propositioned him. He had agreed and took her back to Rochester Row. An argument broke out and they struggled but she fell back and banged her head on a coal scuttle. In a panic, he had fled the building.

The next day he returned and found that Minnie hadn't moved. She was dead and he knew he would be blamed so he bought the trunk and a large knife to dismember her with. Unfortunately for Robinson, scientific evidence showed that Minnie could not have died in this way and as a result, Robinson was found guilty and sentenced to death.

A subsequent appeal was dismissed and on Friday, 12 August, Robinson was hanged at Pentonville by Robert Baxter and Robert Wilson.

Frederick Stewart, 1928

Every day Clifford Webb called at his father's office and drove him home after work. Things were little different on Thursday, 9 February 1928, except for the fact that Clifford had another passenger, Frank Sweeney, in addition to Alfred Charles Bertram Webb.

It was around 6.30 p.m. when the three men arrived at 20 Pembridge Square, Notting Hill. Going up to his home, Flat 3, Alfred was surprised to find that he could not gain access. Someone had put a chair against the door, which in turn meant that someone must have broken into the flat. Indeed, a figure could be seen moving about through the glass panelling.

Alfred asked his son and Frank Sweeney to go for the police while he stayed where he was in case the burglar tried to escape. Even as Clifford and Frank turned to go, a deep voice from inside the flat shouted, 'Put 'em up!' and a shot rang out.

Clifford turned in time to see a man making good his escape and his father lying on the floor, a bullet wound over his left eye. Alfred Webb would die in hospital the following day.

A police search of the area soon turned up the murder weapon, a Browning automatic, in a nearby garden. A bullet had jammed in the breech, which was probably why it had been discarded. The serial number was checked and the gun traced to a Corporal James O'Brien of the RAF. He reported that the weapon had been stolen from him while he was in Tadcaster, some years before. This information led to the deduction that the most probable thief was Frederick Stewart who lived in Southend. He was picked up there on 23 February.

At first Stewart denied any knowledge of the murder but then changed his story and admitted that he was the burglar. He claimed, however, that the shooting was an accident. He had been trying to make his escape when he was hit in the face by Mr Webb. The shock of the blow caused his hand to close, the trigger to be pulled and the gun to go off. In fact, he had not even known that Mr Webb had been hit until he had read about it in the newspapers.

Stewart appeared before Mr Justice Avory at the Old Bailey on 18 April, when it was shown that his story of an accidental shooting was most unlikely. Medical testimony stated that the most likely result of a blow was in fact a loosening of the grip. More telling perhaps was the absence of any burning around the wound. This in turn showed that the gun had been held at some distance when it was fired.

Convicted and sentenced to death, Stewart was hanged at Pentonville by Robert Baxter and Thomas Phillips on Wednesday, 6 June 1928.

Frank Hollington, 1929

Nathan Markovitch ran a butcher's shop from 17 Loddiges Road, Hackney. He lived above the shop with his wife, two young children, and a servant, 18-year-old Annie Elizabeth Hatton, who had worked for the Markovitch family since February 1928.

On Saturday, 17 November, Nathan and his wife went to the theatre, leaving the children in the care of Annie. By the time they returned home, it was 11 p.m. and they immediately knew that something was wrong. The children were both crying.

Going into the kitchen, Nathan saw immediately why Annie had not seen to her duties. She was lying on the floor, bound and gagged, and had been battered to death.

The police soon discovered that Annie had had a male friend named John Dennis. It seemed that Dennis had already exhibited violent tendencies where Annie was concerned. Once she had returned home with a bloody nose and had told Nathan that Dennis had done it.

In due course, officers discovered that John Dennis was a name used by Frank Hollington and he was interviewed at his home at 65 Warner Place, Bethnal Green, on 29 November. He freely admitted that he had killed Annie, but claimed that it had been an accident.

According to Hollington, he had arranged to meet Annie at the Empress Picture Palace on Wednesday, 14 November. She had not turned up and he had telephoned her to find out why. That much was certainly true, for the end of the call had been overheard by Mrs Markovitch.

On the night Annie died, Hollington had gone to visit her. She was ironing in the kitchen as he arrived and he sat down nearby and started reading a newspaper. He happened to ask her again why she had stood him up on the previous Wednesday and she lied to him. He lost control and hit her a couple of times before tying her up. He then stole a few items to make it look as if there had been a robbery.

At his trial before Mr Justice Humphreys at the Old Bailey on 14 January 1929, Hollington tried to say that he had not even known that Annie was dead until he read it in the newspapers. Unfortunately, that story did not ring true. If he had really thought that Annie was alive and well when he left her, why had he gone to the trouble of faking a robbery? Surely the only reason for that was to hide the fact that she had been killed by someone she knew.

The jury had little trouble in deciding that Hollington was guilty and he was hanged at Pentonville on 20 February by Robert Baxter and Robert Wilson.

William John Holmyard, 1929

William Holmyard, now in his seventies, still ran a successful furniture business from premises at 37 Tachbrook Street, Pimlico. Next door, at no. 39, lived his son and his grandson, 24-year-old William John Holmyard.

On Friday, 7 December 1928 old Mr Holmyard was found battered in the office at the back of his shop. Various witnesses came forward and reported that at about the time he had been attacked, his grandson had been seen leaving the premises. Young William was then taken in for questioning.

William John admitted that he had attacked his grandfather. He explained that until fairly recently he had been in the army and serving in India, having been discharged on 18 November. Somewhat short of cash, he had borrowed £7 from his grandfather. Some had been repaid but he had then borrowed more so that the debt now stood at £17.

On the day in question, William John had walked into the office, only to be greeted by demands that the money be repaid. An argument developed and William John picked up some copper fire irons and struck his grandfather twice. As a result of that statement, William John Holmyard was charged with wounding.

Unfortunately, the old man died from his injuries just over a month later, on Monday, 10 December, and the charge was now amended to one of murder. Holmyard appeared to answer that charge before Mr Justice Humphreys at the Old Bailey on 15 January 1929. The case lasted for two days.

Once his grandfather died, Holmyard changed his story. He claimed that the statement he originally made was not voluntary and he had actually been in Kennington at the time of the attack. Later still he had gave a third story, again admitting his part but claiming that it had all been an accident.

The prisoner was a slightly built man while his grandfather had been well built and nearly 6ft tall. Now the story was that as the argument developed, his grandfather had lifted a heavy chair above his head and was about to batter Holmyard with it. He had then struck out in self-defence. The jury were not convinced and Holmyard was sentenced to death.

An appeal was entered and here a most interesting point was raised. It was claimed by the defence that at the Old Bailey a court bailiff had supplied the jury with newspapers and they carried reports of the trial. This invalidated the entire proceedings and a retrial should be ordered.

The appeal court judges did not agree and as a result, on Wednesday, 27 February, William John Holmyard was hanged at Pentonville by Robert Baxter and Lionel Mann.

Alexander Anastassiou, 1931

Twenty-two-year-old Evelyn Victoria Holt was a happy girl who enjoyed life. She lived with her aunt in McFarlane Road, Shepherd's Bush, and loved her job at a Lyons Corner House in the West End. Her love life too was going well for, just before Christmas 1930, she had met a new man, a Cypriot named Alexander Anastassiou, and now they were engaged to be married.

On Thursday, 26 February 1931, Evelyn left for work at 7.50 a.m. That same afternoon she saw Alexander talking to some girls and objected strongly. This book is filled with men who suffered from insane jealousy but in this case it was Evelyn who suffered from that green-eyed monster. Despite her outburst, the couple arranged to meet for a meal that evening.

In fact, Evelyn and Anastassiou went to see a film, had supper and then returned to his room on the top floor of 65 Warren Street, off Tottenham Court Road. They arrived there at a few minutes after 11 p.m.

It was around 11.30 p.m. when Anastassiou's landlady, Lena Ballerini heard a loud crash from upstairs, followed by a scream. Running up to investigate, Lena found that Anastassiou's door was locked. She demanded to be admitted and when the door opened slightly, she saw a bundle lying in a pool of blood. Without waiting to see more, Lena ran to fetch the police.

Constable James Murphy was the first officer to arrive and he took Anastassiou to the station. Here the prisoner said that after arriving at his room, Evelyn had asked if she could borrow a comb. He opened a drawer and she must have noticed that he also kept his razor there.

They had a conversation about her jealousy and the way she had reacted that afternoon, and finally Anastassiou told her that he didn't see how he could go ahead with the wedding as long as she was like this. He added that he was even thinking of emigrating to America.

Hearing that, Evelyn had gone to the drawer, taken out his razor and threatened him with it. She had then lunged forward and attacked him. They struggled and he managed to overpower her. Fearful for his life, he had then cut her throat without really knowing what he was doing.

At Anastassiou's trial, which took place before Mr Justice Swift at the Old Bailey on 27 April, the jury had to decide between murder and manslaughter. Scientific evidence showed that in addition to the wound that claimed her life, Evelyn also had numerous other wounds on her hands and arms, which were almost certainly defence wounds. Anastassiou had wounds of his own but these had only been inflicted by fingernails. The most likely scenario is that he had attacked her with the razor and she had tried to fight him off.

The verdict was one of murder and on Wednesday, 3 June Anastassiou was hanged at Pentonville by Robert Baxter and Henry Pollard.

Oliver Newman & William Shelley, 1931

In 1931 there existed, in the Scratchwood Sidings area between Mill Hill and Elstree, a shanty town of small huts where homeless and unemployed men lived. They cooked on open fires, slept under ragged blankets and generally tried to eke out an existence.

On Monday, 1 June, Mr McGlade was cutting through the sidings on his way home from work. As he passed a small, smouldering bonfire, he noticed something sticking out at the bottom. Closer inspection revealed that it was a human arm. The police were called and when the fire had been doused they discovered a charred and unrecognisable male body.

It was Sir Bernard Spilsbury who examined the remains and he deduced that the man had been dead for about three days, putting the date of his demise at Friday, 29 May.

The cause of death had been repeated blows to the head by some implement rectangular in shape. Then only form of identification on the body was a tattoo on one hand of a heart pierced by a sword.

The various occupants of the huts were questioned and this led to the identification of the dead man as 45-year-old Herbert William Ayers, who had been known by the rather unattractive nickname of Pigsticker. It was then that a most valuable witness was discovered.

John Armstrong had now found himself a job and lodgings, but at the time that Ayers had last been seen, he had been an occupant of one of the huts, which he shared with two men whom he knew only as Tiggy and Moosh.

One night Armstrong had been woken by some noise outside the hut and, looking out, he saw Tiggy and Moosh attacking Pigsticker. Later still he saw what he thought was the unconscious form of Pigsticker being carried to the rubbish dump where his body would eventually be found. He had said nothing at the time in case Tiggy and Moosh turned on him.

It was a simple matter now to identify the two attackers. Tiggy was 61-year-old Oliver Newman and Moosh was his close friend, 57-year-old William Shelley. They were arrested and seemed to be surprised to be told that they had done anything wrong. Shelley admitted killing Ayers because he had been found stealing tea and sugar from their hut. For that he had been given a beating but when, a few days later, some bacon had also vanished, he and Newman battered Ayers to death using the back of an axe. The police now went back to the hut where, underneath the floorboards, they found the bloodstained axe. The flat back fitted exactly the depressions seen on Ayers's skull.

Despite their admissions, both men pleaded not guilty at their trial before Mr Justice Swift at the Old Bailey on 24 June. At the end of the second day, largely due to the testimony of John Armstrong, both men were judged to be guilty and sentenced to death.

Just over four weeks later, on Wednesday, 5 August, Shelley and Newman were hanged together at Pentonville by Robert Baxter and three assistants: Lionel Mann, Thomas Phillips and Robert Wilson.

Maurice Freedman, 1932

Annette Friedson had started walking out with Maurice Freedman in August 1930. They were happy enough for a time but then, in October 1931, she discovered that he was a married man. From that moment on her family tried actively to discourage her from having anything more to do with him. The couple did go on seeing each other but there was a distinct cooling in the relationship after that time.

The fact that Freedman was married caused many arguments between him and Annette and these came to a head on Saturday, 23 January 1932. Things had to be sorted out once and for all and Annette agreed to meet Freedman the next day, 24 January, to settle things. During that evening she thought better of it and failed to turn up. She knew that this would incense Freedman and Annette was concerned for her safety.

So scared was she that on Tuesday, 26 January, she asked her brother, Samuel, to escort her to her train as she headed off to work at 103 Fore Street. Samuel did as he was asked and waved to his sister as the train pulled out. Later that same morning, Annette was found on the staircase at her office, her throat cut from ear to ear. A trial of blood led down the stairs to the point where she had been attacked.

There was only one suspect and Freedman was arrested at his lodgings in Oakfield Road, Clapton, that same evening. He admitted that he had killed Annette but claimed that it was not murder. He had gone to her offices to wait for her; this was backed up by two witnesses, Ernest Carr and Arthur Samuel Barnaby, who had seen him.

Continuing his story, Freedman admitted that he and Annette had argued. Annette had said that the relationship must end, whereupon he had taken a razor from his pocket and held it to his own throat. She reached out to try to stop him from cutting his throat and in the ensuing struggle, he must have accidentally cut her.

At his trial before Mr Justice Hawke at the Old Bailey on 8 and 9 March, the prosecution pointed out that if this had been a tragic accident as Freedman described, why had he not gone for help? That was a most telling point and the jury only took thirty minutes to decide that the accused was guilty as charged.

An appeal was entered and dismissed and on Wednesday, 4 May, 36-year-old Freedman was hanged at Pentonville by Robert Baxter and Robert Wilson.

Jack Samuel Puttnam, 1933

There were four people living on the top floor of 13 Blackstock Road, Finsbury Park. In addition to 44-year-old Elizabeth Mary Standley, there was her husband and two lodgers.

At around 8 a.m. on Saturday, 4 March 1933, Elizabeth was alone in the house. At noon, one of the lodgers, Mr Cox, returned to the house for lunch only to find that his landlady was dead, her body stuffed underneath her bed and a length of flex knotted tightly around her throat.

The police began by talking to Elizabeth's neighbours to determine if any of them had seen anything. Elizabeth Kerswell, who lived on the ground floor of no. 13, said that at 9 a.m. she had heard someone ring the bell to the top floor. She hadn't seen who the caller was but she did hear Mrs Standley shout, 'Are you coming up for a few minutes, Jack?'

It didn't take long to discover that 'Jack' was almost certainly Jack Puttnam, Elizabeth's nephew. After speaking to Mr Standley, officers found that Puttnam owed his aunt money. He had borrowed various amounts so that now his debt stood at £35 and Elizabeth had been pressing him for payment.

When Puttnam was spoken to, he claimed not to have seen his aunt for some weeks. The investigating officers knew that this was a lie for Elizabeth had visited Puttnam at his home the day before she was killed, again to discuss the money he owed her. Puttnam was spoken to a number of times and finally was arrested and charged on 24 March.

Puttnam appeared before Mr Justice Hawke at the Old Bailey on 1 May, the trial lasting three days. One of the witnesses was a bus conductor, Louis Zachis, who had seen a man rushing from the murder house. He had climbed on the bus almost opposite to Elizabth's house and the conductor had subsequently picked out Puttnam at an identity parade.

Puttnam had then agreed that he had gone to his aunt's house and they had argued about money. Personal accusations had been made, including that Puttnam might be involved in a relationship with his brother's wife. Finally, Elizabeth had pushed him backwards and he had lashed out with his fist. Not content with that however, he had gone on to stab her with a meat cleaver and strangle her with the flex from a radio.

Now, at his trial, Puttnam withdrew the above statement, claiming that he had only made it to protect his sister-in-law. Once again, he had not called at his aunt's house that day and someone else must have killed her.

The jury found Puttnam guilty and he was hanged at Pentonville on Thursday, 8 June by Robert Baxter and Stanley Cross.

Varnavas Antorka, 1933

Varnavas Antorka had worked very hard. A Cypriot, he had come to England in 1928 knowing hardly a word of the language of his new country. He had taught himself English and even found work for himself, as a silver washer at Bellometti's Restaurant which was situated at 27 Soho Square. There were, however, two flaws in the make-up of Varnavas Antorka; he had a short temper and he had no respect for authority.

Thirty-five-year-old Boleslar Pankorski was head chef at the restaurant and as such, his word was law. He was responsible for all the staff and often barked out orders to them. Antorka did not appreciate this treatment from his superior.

On Friday, 12 May 1933, one of the cooks, Zacharias Panagi, was in the larder with Antorka. Pankorski came in and told Antorka to put some plates into an oven so that they could be warmed. Unfortunately, Antorka did not, as expected, jump to obey. Pankorski then escalated matters somewhat by saying that if Antorka did not obey immediately, he would be dismissed. Antorka was not intimidated and threatened Pankorski, who promptly sacked him on the spot. It was then around 12.45 p.m.

Fifteen minutes later, at 1 p.m., one of the waiters, William Richard Summers, saw Antorka at the bottom of a flight of stairs at the back of the restaurant. Almost immediately, Pankorski appeared at the top and started to walk down. He was met at the bottom by Antorka who shouted, 'You gave me the sack you bastard! You take me back or else I'll shoot you!'

Pankorski moved forward and the two men grappled together. Suddenly a shot rang out, followed swiftly by two more, one of which hit another employee, Michael Kikilaron in the leg. As Pankorski fell to the ground, two other waiters, Guiseppe Negrori and Antonio Antoniades grabbed Antorka and held him until the police arrived.

Placed on trial before Mr Justice Humphreys at the Old Bailey, from 27 June to 30 June, Antorka tried to claim that he had not known what he was doing at the time of the shooting. This was not supported by the evidence of Louisa Nutti, Antorka's landlady who lived at 19 Arthur Street. She testified that just after noon, Antorka had rushed into the house, gone to his room and after a few

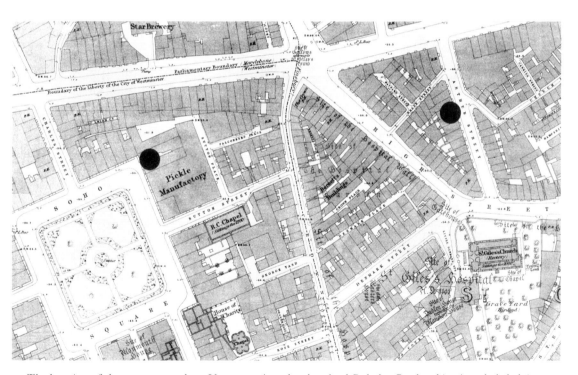

The location of the restaurant where Varnavas Antorka shot dead Boleslar Pankorski. Antorka's lodgings,
where he returned to get his gun, are also marked on the right of the map.
(Reproduced with the permission of Alan Godfrey Maps)

minutes, had dashed out again. The suggestion was that Antorka had gone to collect his gun from his lodgings. He had therefore known exactly what he was doing.

The guilty verdict was almost a formality and on Thursday, 10 August, Antorka was hanged at Pentonville by Robert Baxter and Henry Pollard.

Harry Tuffney, 1934

It was, to say the least, a most unusual complaint. At 8.30 a.m. on Saturday, 30 June 1934, 36-year-old Harry Tuffney walked into Marylebone Lane police station and complained that he had been unable to kill himself. He then went on to add that he wished to end his life as he had just killed his girlfriend, Edith Kate Longshaw.

Tuffney was taken into custody and officers then went around to his home on the second floor of 75 Star Street, Paddington. Tuffney had lived at that address for some seven weeks, having been introduced to the landlady, Elizabeth Warren, by Edith who also lived on the second floor. Soon after moving in, Tuffney and Edith had started going out together.

One day, Edith's handbag broke and Tuffney kindly said he would mend it for her. It was while effecting the repair that he found a letter, signed Sidney, which suggested that he had been Edith's lover. The couple did have a mutual friend, Sidney Briggs, who had just split from his wife. Tuffney convinced himself that not only was Briggs the letter writer and Edith's lover, but that she was about to go off with him.

On Friday, 29 June, Tuffney paid 1s 3d for a nice shiny new axe. That night he took the axe with him when he called on Edith. Tuffney did ask her about Sidney and she reassured him that nothing was going on. Apparently satisfied, Tuffney watched as Edith drifted off to sleep. Then he took the axe and brought it down on her head, with all his strength behind the blow. Edith died instantly, the blade embedded deep in her head.

Tuffney now tried to kill himself by placing a couple of cushions on the floor, turning on the gas ring and making himself comfortable. Some four hours later he was, to his deep regret, still alive, so he walked to the police station and gave himself up.

The trial took place before Mr Justice Atkinson at the Old Bailey on 20 September. Tuffney tried to claim that he was insane and evidence was called to show that there was a good degree of madness within his family background. His mother had died in a mental hospital in 1928, a brother had been diagnosed as a congenital idiot and another had died in a home.

None of this helped and Tuffney was found guilty and hanged at Pentonville on Tuesday, 9 October by Robert Baxter and Alfred Allen.

John Frederick Stockwell, 1934

Monday, 6 August 1934 was a Bank Holiday. As a result, Dudley Henry Hoard, the manager of the Eastern Palace Cinema on Bow Road, East Ham, had been unable to bank the takings and now held around £100 in cash on the premises.

On Tuesday, the cleaners arrived for work at 8 a.m. and were surprised to find that the doors were still locked. They all had to stand around on the pavement until a keyholder arrived. They soon found out why Mr Hoard had failed to open up.

Dudley Hoard lay at the front of the balcony. His wife, Maisie, lay a short distance away – both had been brutally battered. In time, Maisie would make a full recovery but Dudley Hoard died from his injuries later that same day.

The motive for the crime was obviously robbery, but there was no sign of a forced entry. This suggested that the killer had been admitted to the premises, which in turn meant that he was probably known to the manager. This was later confirmed when Maisie Hoard regained consciousness. She said that they had been woken by someone ringing the doorbell. Her husband had gone to see who it was and he must have let his killer in.

The next development occurred on Wednesday, 8 August. One of the employees had been entitled to a day off on the Tuesday but he now failed to turn up for work on the Wednesday. His name was John Stockwell and it was soon discovered that he had left his lodgings. A full description was circulated.

Mrs Tripp ran a boarding house in Lowestoft and she was surprised when one of her new guests threw down a newspaper he was reading and announced that he was moving on to Yarmouth. Curious to see what might have upset him, she picked up the paper and read the story of the cinema murder in London. The description given matched her guest so she contacted the police. By the time they arrived, the guest, none other than Stockwell, had moved on.

To their surprise, the next day police received a letter from Stockwell himself. In this he admitted attacking Hoard but said that he had not meant to kill him. The letter went on to say that he saw no way out now but suicide. Later than same day a pile of clothes, which were shown to belong to Stockwell, were found on Lowestoft beach.

Meanwhile, a Mr Smith was checking into the Metropolitan Hotel in Yarmouth. Asked to sign in, the manager noticed that his new guest gave a home address at Luton, Hertfordshire, instead of Bedfordshire. Surely a man should know which county his hometown is in? The manager contacted the police who called around to find that Mr Smith was none other than John Stockwell.

Placed on trial before Mr Justice Goddard at the Old Bailey on 22 October, Stockwell entered a plea of not guilty. The trial was only a few minutes old when the prisoner passed a note to his counsel, Mr Frederick Levy. The note stated that he wished to change his plea to guilty. That plea was accepted and as a result, Stockwell was hanged at Pentonville on Wednesday, 14 November by Robert Baxter and Robert Wilson.

Charles Malcolm Lake, 1935

George Hamblin was an inmate of the Westminster Poor Law Institute on Fulham Road, Chelsea, and liked to act as an unofficial bookie for the other occupants. One of his most regular customers was 37-year-old George Frank Harvey.

On the evening of Thursday, 25 October 1934, Harvey went out with a lady friend of his, Mrs Barnes, and told her he had lost a great deal of money on a horse race. The next evening, Friday the 26th, George Hamblin was found in a storeroom, battered to death. The murder weapon, a hammer, lay nearby.

On the night that the body had been found, Harvey had asked for a pass so he could stay out all that night. At the same time, he handed in some clothing for cleaning and it was noticed that a shirt was missing. Before he could be asked about it, he had already left the home.

For the next two days, Harvey stayed with Mrs Barnes. At one stage he took her to the cinema and sometime later, a bloodstained shirt was found left in the toilet at that same cinema. There was also a cash wallet, which had belonged to George Hamblin.

When Harvey finally returned to the home he was arrested and charged with murder. A total of £3 5s was found in his possession, but of more significance was a postal order which had been sent to Hamblin.

Harvey claimed to know nothing of the murder and had only read about it in the newspapers. He then tried to throw suspicion on a mysterious blackmailer and said that Hamblin had confided in him and shown him a scribbled note that read, 'Yes, 13, yes,' but he would not say what it meant.

Harvey was tried before Mr Justice Atkinson at the Old Bailey on 21 January 1935, the proceedings lasting until the 24th.

Witnesses were called to show that Harvey had been seen in the storeroom where Hamblin's body had been found at 4.30 p.m., the time of the attack. That, plus the money and the postal order were more than enough to convict Harvey, who was then sentenced to death.

Harvey was hanged at Pentonville on Wednesday, 13 March 1935 by Robert Baxter and Henry Pollard. At his trial he had admitted that Harvey was not his real name but asked that the real one not be revealed as his mother was rather ill. Once the death sentence had been carried out, his real name was revealed and Harvey was shown to be Charles Malcolm Lake.

Allan James Grierson, 1935

Dorothy Maud Helen Riley had arranged a nice holiday for herself in Scotland but was a little concerned about her house, 19 Gloucester Road, Regent's Park, being properly looked after. Luckily, there was a solution. She would ask her best friend, Louise Gann, to live in it while she was away. On 1 June 1935, Louise Gann moved into the flat on the top floor. The next day Louise's daughter, Maxine, moved in with her.

On 3 June, Maxine received a telephone call from the young man she had been seeing, 27-year-old Allan Grierson. He was down on his luck and had nowhere to stay. Grierson was kindly invited to the flat at Gloucester Road and allowed to stay. On 7 June, he showed his gratitude by stealing some of Dorothy Riley's jewellery and pawning it at a shop in Oxford Street.

When the postman arrived on the morning of 8 June, Maxine received a note from Grierson admitting what he had done and begging for forgiveness. The letter also contained the pawn tickets he had obtained for the jewellery. Apparently, if the Ganns wanted the jewellery back, they would have to get it out of pawn themselves.

On 10 June, Grierson telephoned the flat and apologised yet again for what he had done. Surprisingly, he was allowed to return to Gloucester Road, after he had promised that he would get the jewellery back.

Three days later, on 13 June, Grierson announced that he had found work at last. He would be starting the following Monday, 17 June, and would soon be able to get back the goods he had pawned.

On the day he was supposedly due to start work, Grierson stole more jewellery, though the Ganns did not notice at that time. Four days later he explained that his new job would require him to drive down to Torquay. He asked both Ganns if they would like to come with him. Maxine agreed but her mother declined. They would journey down on Saturday, 22 June.

On the Saturday, Maxine went to work as usual, having arranged to meet Grierson near Oxford Circus at 1.20 p.m. She turned up at the appointed hour but Grierson did not show. Thinking that he might have let her mother know of any change of plan, Maxine rang the flat but there was no reply.

It was 2 p.m. by the time Maxine got back to Gloucester Road. The door was locked and, concerned that her mother might have fallen ill, Maxine went to a nearby electrician's where she told the proprietor, Frederick Summers, of her worries. Summers returned to no. 19 with Maxine and forced the door. The flat had been ransacked and there, in the bedroom, lay the battered body of Louise Gann. She was still alive but died in hospital the next day.

Grierson's description was circulated and he was arrested on 1 July. He appeared before Mr Justice Porter at the Old Bailey on 10 September, the case lasting until 18 September.

With all the evidence against him, the guilty verdict was easy to come by and Grierson paid the penalty on Wednesday, 30 October when he was hanged at Pentonville by Robert Baxter and Henry Pollard.

Frederick George Murphy, 1937

The entire country was celebrating. Wednesday, 12 May 1937 was Coronation Day for King George VI. That day and the next were both public holidays and people were not due back to work until Friday the 14th.

It was early on the Friday that Stanley Herbert Wilton received a visitor in the form of Ethel Marshall. She gave him a note which read, 'Don't be frightened. There is a dead woman in no. 22 and you can believe me Stan. It is nothing to do with me, but you know what the police will say.' The note was signed 'Fred'.

Stanley was a salesman at a furniture warehouse at 22 Islington Green, the address referred to in the letter, and Fred was Frederick Murphy, an odd-job man at that warehouse. As for Ethel Marshall, she was Murphy's girlfriend.

The first thing for Stanley to do was check out the warehouse. Sure enough, there was a woman's body in the basement. She had been strangled and her body hidden behind an old tin trunk. She would later be identified as 49-year-old Rosina Field.

A widespread search was launched for Murphy but on Saturday, 15 May he walked into the police station at Poplar and said he wished to make a statement about the body in the warehouse.

According to Murphy's statement, he had gone to the warehouse on 13 May to do some cleaning. It was then that he found the body. He admitted that he had moved the body behind the trunk but denied any involvement in the murder itself. Unfortunately for Murphy, two witnesses had already come forward who showed that this story was a lie.

Morris Felberg knew Murphy well and said he had seen him going into the furniture store on Coronation Day and that Murphy was with a woman who was not Ethel Marshall. Morris could not positively identify the woman but could describe a rather distinctive coat she was wearing. Rosina Field's body was dressed in an identical coat.

Herbert Robert Fleming had seen Rosina, whom he knew as Rosie, on Coronation Day and she had borrowed 2d from him for a cup of tea. Later that day he saw her again, with Murphy. It was then around 8 p.m.

Charged with murder, Murphy appeared before the Lord Chief Justice, Lord Hewart, at the Old Bailey on 30 June. The case lasted until 2 July and after a forty-five minute deliberation, the jury agreed that he was guilty as charged.

On Tuesday, 17 August, Murphy was hanged at Pentonville by Alfred Allen and Thomas Phillips. This was the second time that Murphy had faced the hangman's noose. In 1929 he had been accused of murdering Katherine Peck but had been found not guilty. Katherine had also had a nickname and, by coincidence, that name too was Rosie.

Leonard George Hucker, 1939

Mary Alice Maud Moncrieff and her daughter, Beatrice Maud Fullick, lived together at 13 Victoria Villas, Willesden, and were happy enough together. There had been a few problems a year or two back, when Beatrice's boyfriend, Leonard Hucker, had also lived with them for he had something of a temper. This had led to a number of arguments between him and Mary and eventually they had all agreed that he should find fresh lodgings.

The relationship between Hucker and Beatrice had never been a very serious one so it was no real surprise when it cooled even further. This culminated in a letter Beatrice sent to him on 13 August 1939 in which she wrote, 'Dear Len, I shall not be seeing you again, as I have made further arrangements. Trix.' Though Beatrice had not gone into any further detail, these 'further arrangements' were a new boyfriend named Reg.

Four days after that letter had been penned, on 15 August, Hucker bought himself a new knife from a shop run by Walter Cecil Silver. Not satisfied that the knife was sharp enough for his purpose, Hucker then proceeded to hone the blade even further.

Beatrice left for work at 8.50 a.m. on Wednesday, 16 August, leaving her mother alone in the house. Almost seven hours later, at 3.45 p.m., Hucker walked into the police station on Harrow Road where he told the officer on duty, Constable John Reginald Bass, that he had murdered a woman. He then threw a key onto the counter adding that this would open the door back at Victoria Villas.

Mary Moncrieff was indeed dead. She had been stabbed and the new knife Hucker had purchased the day before was embedded up to the hilt in her chest. Hucker was charged with murder.

The trial took place before Mr Justice Oliver at the Old Bailey on 22 September. Hucker's defence was that he had acted on the spur of the moment, had not intended to kill and so was only guilty of manslaughter. He told the court that he had simply called at the house to talk to Beatrice's mother. An argument developed because Mary thought that Beatrice might be pregnant and Hucker was the father. During the course of the argument, he lost his temper and stabbed Mary without really knowing what he was doing.

The story did not hold water. To begin with, Beatrice testified that there had been no discussion of any pregnancy whatsoever. Allied to this, Hucker had bought the murder weapon the day before and sharpened it to make it even more deadly.

There was more than enough evidence to show that the crime was premeditated and Hucker was sentenced to death. This sentence was carried out at Wandsworth on Tuesday, 10 October by Thomas Pierrepoint and Herbert Morris.

Udham Singh, 1940

History is said to repeat itself. Perhaps no clearer illustration of this could be found than the case of Udham Singh, which was similar to that of Madar Lal Dhingra from 1909.

The East India Association and the Royal Central Asian Society had joined forces to arrange a discussion on affairs in Afghanistan. It was to take place in the Tudor Room at Caxton Hall, in Westminster. Proceedings would begin with a lecture by Brigadier General Sir Percy Sykes. Other distinguished speakers would then have their say and the meeting then thrown open to a general discussion. All this was set for Wednesday, 13 March 1940.

The meeting finally ended at 4.30 p.m. and people began to gather in small groups to talk. No one noticed the stocky, well-built Asian gentleman walk down the central gangway towards one small knot of people. Equally, no one saw him draw out a revolver.

In all, six shots were fired into the group standing near the platform. Sir Louis Dane was hit in the arm and Lord Lanington was wounded in the wrist. Lord Zetland was hit twice in the chest but luckily would make a full recovery from those wounds. The other two bullets struck 75-year-old Sir Michael O'Dwyer. One bullet hit him in the heart, the other penetrated a kidney and Sir Michael died immediately. The crowd, galvanised into action, grabbed the assassin, wrested the gun from him and held him until the police arrived. He would later be identified as 37-year-old Udham Singh.

Placed on trial for murder, Singh appeared before Mr Justice Atkinson at the Old Bailey on 4 June. The case was heard over two days.

Singh's defence was that the killing had been accidental. It had not been his intention to kill or wound anyone. He had wished to fire at the ceiling just to frighten everyone in the room but, as the prosecution pointed out; six shots fired and six wounds seemed to destroy this line of defence. Singh was found guilty and sentenced to death.

On Wednesday, 31 July, Singh was hanged at Pentonville by Stanley Cross and Albert Pierrepoint. It was the same scaffold that had claimed the life of Madar Lal Dhingra in 1909.

Antonio Mancini, 1941

In 1941, the Palm Beach Club in Wardour Street, Soho, was run by Tony Mancini, known to all as 'Babe'. The club was on the ground floor and above it was a second establishment, a billiards club. Mancini was also a member there and spent a good deal of time in both premises.

Most clubs have elements of their clientele who occasionally get out of hand and one such occasion was 20 April when a fight broke out at the Palm Beach. Mancini was more than able to handle most troublemakers, and in this case he simply banned the ringleader. In return, Mancini was threatened with violence and he must have taken that threat seriously for he henceforth took to carrying a knife.

On Thursday, 1 May there was another fracas, this time in the billiards club at 3 a.m. Mancini felt it was his duty to go and see if he could help but as he was walking up the stairs, he heard a familiar voice behind him saying, 'Here's Babe, let's knife him.'

Mancini was not one to run from a fight but there was a group threatening him so he thought it a good idea to run up to the billiards room. Two of the men, Edward Fletcher and Henry Distleman, decided to follow and a fight broke out inside the club.

Snooker cues, billiard balls, chairs and knives were used in the fight that followed. Fletcher received a stab wound to the wrist and Distleman received a 5in deep wound under his left armpit. That particular wound proved fatal and Mancini found himself facing a charge of murder.

The trial opened before Mr Justice Macnaghten at the Old Bailey on 4 July and, naturally, Mancini claimed that he had acted in self-defence. There had been over forty witnesses to the fight and they described the fury with which Mancini had defended himself. The prosecution argued that he had used too great a level of violence. The jury accepted that and Mancini was found guilty and sentenced to death.

An appeal was entered and here, for the first time, it was revealed that the dead man, Distleman, had had six previous convictions for assault. Despite this, the appeal was dismissed and the sentence confirmed.

On Friday, 31 October, 39-year-old Mancini was hanged at Pentonville by Albert Pierrepoint and Stephen Wade. It was the first ever execution at which Pierrepoint was the 'number one'.

Lionel Rupert Nathan Watson, 1941

Mrs Brown was most concerned. For some reason, the flats around Goring Way, Greenford, seemed to be permeated by an awful smell.

Mrs Brown and other tenants had first noticed the smell around the end of May 1941, but as the days and weeks passed, it grew stronger and stronger. Attempts were made to pin down the source and finally it was decided that it was coming from the garden of the flat below. Mrs Brown determined that she should speak to the occupant, Lionel Watson.

In fact, technically, Mr Watson had already moved out. The woman he lived with, Phyllis Elizabeth Crocker and their 18-month-old daughter, Eileen Alice, had gone to stay with friends in Scotland on 21 May and soon afterwards, Watson himself had moved out. He did call back from time to time and it was on one of these visits that Mrs Brown waylaid him and spoke to him about the foul aroma.

Watson was most conciliatory and said he would look into the matter without delay. He said that it might well be the drains and, true to his word, he was seen pouring disinfectant over the drains and the garden, on 27 June.

It didn't have any effect. In fact, the smell got worse and so three days later, on 30 June, Mrs Brown and another neighbour decided to do some investigating themselves. If the problem was the drains then it might be beneath the paving stones so a few of these were lifted. Beneath them was some sort of white powder and something that looked like flesh. The source of the smell had finally been discovered. It came from two decomposing bodies.

When he was interviewed, Watson made no attempt to deny that he had buried the bodies of Phyllis and Eileen. It would have been no use to do so anyway for the ubiquitous Mrs Brown had seen him digging at the exact same spot on 26 May. Watson denied, however, that this was a case of murder.

A medical examination showed that both bodies contained cyanide and it was true that Watson had access to that poison as a moulder at the Bakelite factory where he worked. His story was that he had gone to work as usual on 20 May and when he had returned that night, had found two dead bodies. Obviously Phyllis had killed her daughter and then taken her own life. He admitted that he had then panicked and buried the bodies.

Watson appeared before Mr Justice Cassels at the Old Bailey on 15 September. The trial lasted until 18 September and here the history of Lionel Watson came out in full. A married man with four children, he had left his wife for Phyllis Crocker. When his wife wouldn't give him a divorce, he married Phyllis anyway, even though it was bigamous, in January 1941.

The defence claimed that surely he had no motive for killing his lover and their daughter, but the prosecution showed that Watson had been making advances to a young girl who worked at his factory. Were Phyllis and the child simply in the way? The jury thought so and Watson was found guilty.

On Wednesday, 12 November, 30-year-old Watson was hanged at Pentonville by Thomas Pierrepoint and Harry Critchley.

Harold Dorian Trevor, 1942

By the autumn of 1941, London was suffering quite badly from the effects of the German bombing. Sixty-five-year-old Theodora Jessie Greenhill was scared and came to the conclusion that she would be safer out of the capital. She spoke to a local estate agent and decided to rent out her home in Elsham Road, Kensington.

On Tuesday, 14 October, Theodora received a visit from a very nice elderly gentleman who showed a great deal of interest in the property. He had a look around and said that he would take the house and wished to pay the deposit immediately. Cash was handed over and then, as Theodora wrote out the receipt, the 'gentleman' smashed a beer bottle over her head. Theodora fell to the floor unconscious and the new tenant then strangled her.

He ransacked the flat, stole money from a cash box and made good his escape. Theodora's body would be found later by her daughter.

Solving the crime was the easiest thing possible for the police. The unfinished receipt that Theodora had been writing still lay on the table. It read: 'Received from Dr H.D. Trevor the sum of...'

The name H.D. Trevor was already well known to the police. Harold Dorian Trevor had spent thirty-nine of the last forty years in prison for dozens of offences, including theft and fraud. To make absolutely sure they had the right man, the beer bottle used to bludgeon the victim, which had been left behind, was examined. One set of fingerprints were found and these matched those of Trevor held on file.

Details of the stolen items were published and soon two rings turned up at a pawnshop in Birmingham. Further sales showed that Trevor was moving north and eventually, on 18 October, he was picked up in Rhyl. He admitted killing Theodora but claimed that it wasn't a case of murder.

Trevor confessed to striking his victim with the beer bottle but his intention had been just to knock her out and steal what he could before she recovered. His mind had gone blank then and he had no recollection of the strangulation.

The two-day trial opened before Mr Justice Asquith at the Old Bailey on 28 January 1942. Not surprisingly, Trevor was found guilty and on Wednesday, 11 March he was hanged at Wandsworth by Albert Pierrepoint and Herbert Morris.

Gordon Frederick Cummins, 1942

On the morning of Sunday, 8 February 1942, the body of Evelyn Margaret Hamilton was found in an air-raid shelter in Montagu Place. She had been strangled with her own scarf and her handbag was missing. Investigations showed that the bag had contained about £80, so it was assumed that the motive for the crime had been robbery.

Two days later, on Tuesday, 10 February, a second body was discovered. Evelyn Oatley, a prostitute who used the name Nita Ward, was found in her flat in Wardour Street. She too had been strangled but her killer had also mutilated her body by using a can-opener on her. He had also cut her throat after she was dead.

A further two days passed and on Thursday, 12 February, two more bodies were added to the total. One was another prostitute, Margaret Florence Lowe, who was killed in Gosfield Street. She had been strangled and mutilated with a razor. Finally, Doris Jouannet, also known as Doris Robson, had been strangled and mutilated in her flat at 187 Sussex Gardens, Paddington. Four women had died in less than a week.

The police assumed that one man had carried out all four murders. Even more worrying was that they saw no reason why the killer would stop. Surely more bodies would follow.

On Friday, 13 February, a man in uniform picked up Margaret Heywood, who was known as Greta. At first he was the epitome of charm, taking her for a drink and later going for a walk with her. It was while they were strolling down the Haymarket that his attitude changed and she tried to leave but he caught up with her, forced her into a doorway and began strangling her. Margaret slipped into unconsciousness but, luckily for her, a curious delivery boy went to see what was going on. The assailant fled, leaving behind an RAF gas mask. This bore a name, rank and serial number: 525987. The police now knew that they were looking for Gordon Cummings.

Of course, at this stage, it might well have been that Cummins was only guilty of the one attack, that on Margaret Heywood. The fact that he was more than a one-off attacker was proved by the experience of Kathleen Long, another prostitute. She had picked up an airman and took him back to her flat at 29 Southwick Street where she was given a £5 note for her favours. As she began to undress, the airman leapt upon her and started to strangle her. She screamed and kicked out at his shins. The assailant gave her another £5 and left, leaving behind his service belt. That too was traced to Cummins.

Cummins was interviewed at his billet in St John's Wood, but unfortunately for the police, he had an excellent alibi for three of the murders. His passbook showed that he had been in his billet before midnight all week. Since those murders were committed after that time, Cummins could not be the killer. However, further enquiries showed that the men were in the habit of signing each other's passbooks so they could sneak out, and a witness was found who swore that one night he and Cummins had left the billet after midnight, using a fire escape. Cummins was arrested on 16 February.

A search of his belongings revealed a cigarette case that had belonged to Margaret Lowe, a fountain pen belonging to Doris Jouannet and other items which had belonged to Evelyn Oatley. Further, Cummins's fingerprints matched some found at Margaret Lowe's flat and on the tin opener used on Evelyn Oatley. Cummins was then charged with four murders.

Gordon Cummins appeared before Mr Justice Asquith at the Old Bailey on 27 April. The trial lasted for two days and at the end, the jury took just thirty minutes to reach a guilty verdict on the one charge that had been proceeded with; the murder of Evelyn Oatley.

Hanged at Wandsworth during an air raid, on Thursday, 25 June by Albert Pierrepoint and Harry Kirk, it is possible that Cummins was responsible for two more murders; that of Mabel Church in Camden, and that of Mrs Humphries in Gloucester Crescent, both in October 1941.

Arthur Anderson, 1942

Pauline Barker had been married twice but both these relationships had ended and she was now living with a Greek man, Arthur Apergis, who preferred to use the surname Anderson.

The couple lived in rooms at 184 Belsize Road and their relationship was not all it should have been. Anderson was rather lazy and did little to help Pauline around the house. As a result, there were many arguments between them and on one occasion, he had even threatened to shoot her. These arguments and threats had been overheard by Katherine Patricia Maher, who lived at the same address.

On 27 May 1942, another argument led to Anderson packing his bags and moving back in with his parents. He confided in his brother, Hector Demetrius Apergis, that the real cause of his troubles was Pauline's mother, Lydia Barker. Apparently, she interfered too much.

It was around 1 p.m. on Sunday, 31 May when Anderson returned to Belsize Road to visit Pauline. He called out to her and this was overheard, again, by Katherine Maher. She also heard Pauline reply that she was too busy. Nevertheless, Pauline did go down to talk to Anderson for a few minutes before returning to her house. Anderson stood around the house for a few more minutes and then walked to the Price of Wales public house for a drink.

Later that same day, at around 7 p.m., Anderson was back at the Price of Wales where he fell into conversation with the landlord, Alfred Herbert Rice. In the course of their chat, Anderson casually announced that he was going to commit a murder. Alfred naturally thought that Anderson was joking, even if the joke was in rather poor taste.

Anderson left the pub but twenty minutes later he was back again. He walked up to Rice, showed him a revolver and even removed a spent cartridge from the chamber. He then handed the gun to Rice and asked him to hide it.

Apparently, Anderson had walked back to Belsize Road and shouted up for Pauline. When there was no reply, he asked another occupant, Alan Philip Sedgewick, where she was. Told that she was downstairs in the kitchen, Anderson then walked into that room and after a brief argument, shot Pauline dead. It was 7.45 p.m. by the time Anderson was arrested. He claimed that he had no memory of the crime, nor of telling Arthur Rice that he was going to kill someone.

Anderson appeared at the Old Bailey on 23 June 1942. The jury had no problem in finding him guilty of murder and he was hanged at Wandsworth on Tuesday, 21 July by Albert Pierrepoint and Herbert Morris.

Samuel Sydney Dashwood & George William Silverosa, 1942

On Thursday, 30 April 1942, two men met at a café in Bethnal Green. One of them, Samuel Dashwood, produced a gun and told his friend, George Silverosa, that he was going to use it to 'do a job'. Silverosa thought it a good idea and said he would tag along.

In due course, the two men found themselves walking down Hackney Road, Shoreditch, looking for a suitable place to rob. Dashwood noticed a pawnbrokers and said that it might make a good target. Silverosa agreed and pointed out that it was early closing day in the area and added that it might be better to wait until the owner was shutting up shop for the day. The two men then waited until 1 p.m., when 71-year-old Leonard Moules came out to put up the metal shutters.

Moules was followed back into the shop and battered into unconsciousness. The safe was then ransacked and valuables stolen. What was a vicious robbery soon became something more though, for Moules died of his injuries in hospital nine days later on Saturday, 9 May.

The police had two excellent clues. A palm print had been left on the inside of the opened safe. Since that print did not belong to Moules, it was reasonable to assume that it must have belonged to one of his attackers. In addition, a soldier came forward after the robbery. He had been in that same café in Bethnal Green when Dashwood had shown Silverosa the gun. He gave excellent descriptions of both men and said that they had referred to each other as George and Sam.

Dashwood was arrested first and immediately put all the blame for the murder onto Silverosa. As expected, when Silverosa was picked up, he blamed it all on Dashwood. In fact, both men were implicated in the attack. The palm print in the safe belonged to Silverosa but Moules's injuries were consistent with Dashwood's gun being used to batter him.

The trial of both men opened before Mr Justice Wrottesley at the Old Bailey on 17 July. The case would last until 21 July.

On 20 July, Dashwood created a sensation by dismissing his counsel and defending himself. Both men were found guilty and sentenced to death. An appeal was entered and now Dashwood created even more commotion by claiming that because he had dismissed his counsel, he must have been insane and the verdict should be quashed!

The appeal court judges pointed out that this would set a precedent. If the appeal was granted then any defendant in future could just sit back, watch how things were going and if it looked like he might be convicted, dismiss his counsel and claim that he was insane. The appeal was rejected.

On Thursday, 10 September Dashwood and Silverosa were hanged together at Pentonville by Albert Pierrepoint and three assistants: Herbert Morris, Stephen Wade and Harry Kirk.

Gerald Elphistone Roe, 1943

On the morning of Monday, 17 May 1943, Elizabeth Canfield was on her round, delivering milk, along Greenhill Park, Barnet Vale.

As she approached no. 9, Elizabeth detected a strong smell of gas. She knocked on the front door but received no reply. Bending down and looking through the letterbox, she realised that the smell was stronger now. There seemed to be a leak inside no. 9 and the occupants were not answering her calls. At that point, Constable William Warner strolled down the street and Elizabeth told him of her concerns.

Constable Warner went around the back of the house to see if he could rouse anyone there. Looking through the kitchen window, he saw the body of a woman, dressed in blue pyjamas, lying on the floor. Thinking that she might have been overcome by the gas, Warner dashed to no. 4 Greenhill Park where the owner, Nigel Stephen Arnold, had a telephone. He then rang his station for assistance and also for an ambulance. Then, knowing that time was of the essence, he and Mr Arnold returned to no. 9 and smashed their way in through the French windows.

The grill on the gas stove had been left on: obviously the cause of the apparent leak. Warner turned this off and then, with Mr Arnold's assistance, took the woman, Elsie Roe, out into the garden. It was too late. She was already dead.

It was then that Nigel Arnold volunteered the information that he had heard screams at 6.50 a.m. Looking through his window he saw a woman, dressed in blue pyjamas, being dragged about her kitchen by a man. The screaming had stopped and later that moring, Arnold had seen Gerald Roe leaving the house, carrying two suitcases.

A later post-mortem, carried out by Keith Simpson, showed that Elsie had been struck once, from the front, and knocked unconscious. Then, while she was probably lying on the floor, five more heavy blows had been rained down upon her head. The actual cause of death, however, was carbon monoxide poisoning from the gas and the time of death was put at around 8 a.m.

Roe, who was in the forces, had returned to his billet in Hampshire. He was interviewed there later that day and bloodstains were found on some of his clothing. He was then arrested and charged with murder.

Roe's trial took place before Mr Justice Humphreys at the Old Bailey on 18 June. Initially, Roe claimed that he had had nothing to do with Elsie's murder but when it became clear that this line of defence would not work, he tried to say that there was insanity in his family. This too failed and Roe was sentenced to death.

At his subsequent appeal, a third tack was attempted. Now it was suggested that the gas tap, the direct cause of death, might have been left on accidentally. The judges, quite rightly, pointed out that Elsie's other physical injuries had played their own part in Elsie's death and Roe was responsible.

The appeal having been dismissed, Roe was hanged at Pentonville on Tuesday, 3 August by Albert Pierrepoint and Stephen Wade.

Charles William Koopman, 1943

The neighbours were concerned. Although it was late morning, the blackout curtains at 1 Grove Flats, Grove Place, Ealing, had not been drawn back. Perhaps 22-year-old Gladys Lavinia Brewer had fallen ill. Further, there was no answer when people knocked on the door.

By 3 p.m., there was still no sign of Gladys or her 2-year-old daughter Shirley, so the police were called in. They forced an entry in the early evening of Wednesday, 8 September 1943 and found out immediately why there had been no reply to the neighbours. Gladys and her daughter had both been battered to death with a hammer. On the arm of a chair lay a note, addressed to Gladys's husband, who was in the forces. It read, 'Dear Ernie, I am sorry to do this to you and please God forgive me, but I am afraid your wife is very immoral. We don't know you personally but we know your heart.' The letter was not signed.

The letter had been written in the plural so the police believed they were now looking for two possible killers. A further clue was a tunic, which had been placed beneath Gladys's head. It was an RAF tunic and since Ernie Brewer was in the navy, it obviously didn't belong to him.

The police soon determined that the tunic belonged to Charles Koopman, an aircraftman. He had married in 1941 and been given a weekend leave before being posted to Bridlington. He had not, however, reported for duty but had run off with his new wife, Gladys Patricia. He was also known to be a friend of Mrs Brewer. Officers were now looking for Koopman and his wife.

The couple were eventually arrested in Slough and both were charged with murder. After a number of interviews, Koopman maintained that his wife had not been involved in the killings and, at the magistrates' court, the charges against her were dropped, leaving Charles Koopman to face his trial alone.

This trial took place before Mr Justice Asquith at the Old Bailey on 26 October. Here, Koopman admitted that he and his wife had arrived at Grove Place on 5 September. Three days later, on the 8th, he had been teasing Gladys Brewer by turning down the gas when she was trying to read. She argued with him and he picked up a hammer to scare her. Before he knew what was happening, he had battered her to death.

Koopman said that it had been his wife who stopped him attacking Gladys Brewer but the next part of his statement made it something of a puzzle as to why charges against her had been dropped, for she had made no attempt to interfere when Koopman went on to kill the child. Koopman had heard the child crying, took her through to the bedroom and battered her to death with the same hanner. The reason he gave for this appalling act was that he didn't think Shirely should be without her mother.

Found guilty and sentenced to death, Koopman was hanged at Pentonville on Wednesday, 15 December by Thomas Pierrepoint and Stephen Wade.

Christos Georghiou, 1944

For some time in the early 1940s, Christos Georghiou and Savvas Demetriades had been close friends and business partners, running a café together in Cardiff. In early 1943, the two argued over the relatively piffling sum of 30s and as a result, the partnership was dissolved. Soon after that, in April, Georghiou left Cardiff and moved to London.

On Sunday, 24 October, Savvas also travelled down to London on business. He needed somewhere to stay while he sorted out his affairs so contacted an old friend, Nicola Costas. He owned a café at 4 Goodge Place and told Savvas that he was welcome to use his spare room there.

That same day, Savvas and Nicola went to a café at 42 Dean Street, another establishment that Nicola owned. By coincidence, Georghiou was also there. Wishing to avoid any sort of scene, Savvas and his friend moved on to yet another café, at 91 Charlotte Street, but Georghiou followed them there. No words were exchanged but there was a very tense atmosphere.

The next day, Monday, 25 October, Savvas walked around to Nicola's establishment in Dean Street. The two friends had a nice chat and then left the premises together. It was just on 3 p.m. as the two men turned from Dean Street into Old Compton Street. Suddenly, a hand appeared on Savvas's shoulder and he began to turn.

A number of witnesses saw what happened next. Alwyn Childs saw two men exchange blows. He then saw Savvas fall to the ground and the other man then stepped forward and plunged a knife into his chest. Another witness, Martha Zurrer, a Swiss tourist, was in Old Compton Street and saw a grey-suited man, a knife in his hand, running away from the prone figure of Savvas. Other witnesses, including Nicola Costas, identified that grey-suited man as Christos Georghiou.

Savvas was badly injured and died at Charing Cross Hospital half an hour later, at 3.30 p.m. He had actually been stabbed three times, with the fatal wound being one that had passed through a lung.

Georghiou lived in Conway Street but when police called there, he was nowhere to be seen. Eventually, on the Tuesday, Georghiou was traced to 26 Marlborough Hill, Harrow, where he was staying with a friend of his, Christina Douglas.

Placed on trial at the Old Bailey on 10 December 1943, Georghiou claimed to have no memory of the actual crime. He claimed that he had been very drunk at the time and all he could recall was some sort of argument and someone being pushed. Nevertheless, he was found guilty and executed at Pentonville on Wednesday, 2 February 1944 by Albert Pierrepoint and Herbert Morris.

Karl Gustav Hulten, 1945

In mid-August 1944, an American soldier named Karl Hulten went absent without leave from his unit. On 3 October, the fugitive was in a café in London with a friend of his, Len Bexley, and he introduced Hulten to an attractive 18-year-old, Elizabeth Maud Jones, who liked to call herself Georgina. Even though Elizabeth already had a steady boyfriend, she readily agreed to meet Hulten the next night.

On 4 October, Elizabeth waited outside the cinema as arranged but Hulten did not appear. After waiting for a short time, Elizabeth Jones marched off towards her home at 311 King Street, Hammersmith. Suddenly, a ten-wheeled American truck pulled up beside her and there, in the driving seat, was Hulten.

The two went for a drive, heading towards Reading and on the journey, Hulten told Elizabeth that he had been a gangster back in Chicago and that he had stolen the truck he was now driving. This didn't seem to bother Elizabeth. If anything, it seemed to excite her. Towards the end of the trip, the couple robbed a girl near Reading.

They met again on 5 October and Hulten, using a gun, tried to rob a taxi driver. He failed in that attempt but later did succeed in robbing a young girl near Windsor. The next meeting took place on the evening of 6 October and they again discussed the idea of robbing a cab driver. So it was that in the early hours of Saturday, 7 October, Hulten flagged down a cab driven by George Edward Heath and asked him to drive him and Elizabeth to Chiswick.

Once at Chiswick, Heath told his two passengers what the cost of the ride was and turned around to collect his money. Hulten drew out his gun and shot Heath once. Heath was badly injured and when told to move across to the front passenger seat, did as he had been asked. Hulten then took over the driving and headed off towards Staines. Somewhere along that journey, George Heath died from his injuries. His body was dumped in a ditch as Hulten and his companion drove back to London.

Once George Heath's body had been found, details of his stolen cab were circulated to all police officers. The cab was spotted by Constable Walters, parked in Hammersmith at 8 p.m. on 9 October. Walters contacted his superiors and soon he was joined by two colleagues. All three officers now kept a keen watch on the cab.

At 9 p.m., Hulten climbed into the cab and started the engine. He was stopped, and gave his name as Second Lieutenant Richard Allen of the US Army. He claimed he had found the cab near Newbury and had taken it. Second Lieutenant Allen was taken into custody and was later positively identified as Hulten.

Two days later, on 11 October, Hulten told officers about his partner, Elizabeth Jones, and she was picked up later that same day. She was questioned and released but later talked about the murder to a friend of hers, Henry Kimberley, a War Reserve policeman. As a result, she was arrested and charged with murder.

Each blamed the other for what had happened to George Heath. Elizabeth claimed that she had only acted out of fear of Hulten, while he in turn said that she had encouraged him in all that he had done. It was for a jury to decide the truth and the two appeared at the Old Bailey before Mr Justice Charles on 16 January 1945.

The jury decided that both were guilty and both were then sentenced to death. Elizabeth Jones was reprieved on 6 March but two days later, on Thursday, 8 March, Hulten was hanged at Pentonville by Albert Pierrepoint and Henry Critchell. Elizabeth Jones remained in prison until January 1954.

Ronald Bertram Mauri, 1945

At 5.30 p.m. on Wednesday, 11 July 1945, screams were heard emanating from a house in Denecroft Crescent, Hillingdon. Neighbours determined which house they came from and then saw a man, dressed in some kind of uniform, leaving that house. Going to see if they could offer any help, these same neighbours got no answer to their knocking so forced an entry. They found the strangled body of 18-year-old Vera Guest inside.

Having checked into Vera's background, the police wished to interview her boyfriend, a lorry driver named Ronald Mauri, but he was missing from his usual haunts. No sooner had the search been launched than an astonishing letter arrived at Mauri's employer's office in Nottingham.

The letter, written by the fugitive, was a confession. Mauri admitted that he had strangled Vera and added that he intended to kill six more people before he took his own life. Two of the intended victims were neighbours in Denecroft Crescent, three more lived elsewhere in London and the last one lived in Nottingham. The letter ended with the information that the writer had a gun and would not hesitate to use it if any policeman tried to apprehend him.

In due course another letter was received by Vera's parents, Frank and Nora Guest. Now Mauri was claiming that Vera had asked him to kill her. Threats against the six people were repeated and there was the added message that he blamed the police, whom he said had framed him for a robbery in Nottingham.

On 15 July, four days after Vera's death, Mauri's car was spotted in Monmouthshire, Wales. The threats he had made had to be taken seriously so armed officers were called in to make the arrest. The car was later found to be abandoned but Mauri was seen running into some woods. The police followed and called out for him to stop. When he didn't, shots were fired and Mauri was wounded in the head. That wound was not life threatening and the prisoner was taken to Monmouth Hospital for treatment.

Once he recovered, Mauri made a full statement. Apparently, the police had framed him for a cigarette robbery in Nottingham and he knew he would be sent to jail. He had told Vera about this and said that he wanted to kill himself. Vera had then said that she did not want to live without him and asked him to kill her. Eventually he had done as she asked.

Put on trial at the Old Bailey on 20 September, before Mr Justice Tucker, the defence found that Mauri's letters and his own statement to the police after his arrest were more than enough to convict their client. Just over a month later, on Wednesday, 31 October, Mauri was hanged at Wandsworth by Albert Pierrepoint and Harry Kirk.

Reginald Douglas Johnson, 1945

Captain John Alexander Ritchie of the Canadian Army travelled to London on Thursday, 13 September 1945. He booked into the YMCA Officer's Club and the following evening, Friday the 14th, he dined with some friends at the Criterion Restaurant. At 10 p.m. Ritchie left the restaurant with another Canadian soldier, Lieutenant James Alexander Findlay.

Less that two hours later, at 11.45 p.m., Police Sergeant John Dimsey and Constable Charles Pearce were strolling down Bouchier Street, Soho, when they passed two British soldiers in uniform, walking in the opposite direction. Moments later, the two police officers found the body of John Ritchie, his head lying in a pool of blood. Turning around, the police officers saw the two soldiers break into a run. They gave chase.

The two soldiers split up but Sergeant Dimsey was able to capture one of them. He gave his name as Robert Blaine, but whose real name was Reginald Johnson. He was taken back to where Ritchie lay and asked to explain what had taken place. Blaine replied that the other soldier, the one who had escaped, had hit the Canadian.

Taken in for further questioning, Blaine gave the name of the soldier he had been with as Jack Connolly. They had first met up three or four weeks ago and since then had gone drinking in Soho quite regularly. Sometimes they would use the Duke of York and at other times the Alfred's Head.

On the night in question, he and Connolly had left the pub and as they walked, they passed a pile of house bricks. Connolly picked one up, handed it to him and asked him to keep it for him, adding that he might need it later. Then, as they passed down Bouchier Street, Connolly had asked for it back and used it to batter Ritchie to death.

When searched, police found the dead man's bankbook and wallet on Blaine, together with £5 in cash. Blaine admitted that he had rifled Ritchie's pockets but still insisted that it had been Connolly who killed him.

Johnson, alias Blaine, appeared before Mr Justice Humphreys at the Old Bailey on 13 November, the trial lasting until 16 November. There could be little doubt that another soldier had taken part in the attack upon Ritchie and may well have struck the fatal blow, but no trace of him had been found and Johnson had taken a full part in the crime. Consequently, he was found guilty and sentenced to death. Only then was it revealed that he had a long record of theft dating back to 1938.

An appeal was heard on 13 December, but once this had been dismissed, Johnson's fate was sealed. He was hanged at Wandsworth on Saturday, 29 December by Albert Pierrepoint and Harry Kirk.

Marion Grondowski & Henryk Malinowski, 1946

The body of 39-year-old Reuben Martirosoff, known as Russian Robert, lay in the back of his car in Chepstow Place, Notting Hill. There was a bullet wound to the back of his head and a bullet fired from a Walther automatic was found on the front seat. There were also fingerprints inside the car which did not belong to the dead man.

The date was Thursday, 1 November 1945, and over the next few days, investigations led police to two Polish soldiers, Grondowski and Malinowski, who lived together in a flat in Ilford. When that flat was raided, the murder weapon was discovered and both men were taken into custody.

A third man also lived in the flat. Josef Novakhalcz stated that he had been with the two Poles on the evening of 31 October and they had spoken of their intention to lure the dead man into going out for a drink with them, rob him and, if he gave any resistance, shoot him.

Faced with this evidence, Grondowski and Malinowski began to blame each other. Grondowski claimed that he didn't own a gun. His story was that all three men had been in a club close to Marble Arch where they had been drinking whisky. Not long after midnight they all got into Reuben's car. He was in the front passenger seat while Malinowski got into the back. Suddenly, there was a loud bang. Reuben fell forward and he, Grondowski, made a run for it but Malinowski called for him to come back, adding that he had shot one and would quite happily shoot another.

Grondowski's story was that he had been a close friend of Reuben's and knew where he had hidden his money. If he had wanted to rob him he could have done so without having killed him. Having said that, he did admit that he and Malinowski had taken £160 from Reuben's body.

Both men were charged with murder and appeared before Mr Justice Croom-Johnson at the Old Bailey on 11 February 1946, the hearing lasting until 13 February.

At the outset of the proceedings an attempt was made to have the men tried separately, but this was refused. Further drama followed when one juror said he objected to capital punishment and was then excused and replaced.

Found guilty, Grondowski was hanged at Wandsworth at 9 a.m. on Tuesday, 2 April by Albert Pierrepoint and two assistants, Harry Kirk and Alex Riley. One hour later, at 10 a.m., Malinowski was hanged on the same scaffold.

Neville George Clevelly Heath, 1946

Neville Heath was not the most honest of men. By the time the Second World War was over he had been court-martialled three times, served a three-year sentence in Borstal for theft, and been fined for wearing medals and a uniform that he was not entitled to wear.

In early 1946, Heath met 32-year-old Margery Aimee Brownell Gardner. What might, under normal circumstances, be described as a pleasant relationship developed into something more sinister once they discovered each other's sexual proclivities. Heath was a sadist who liked to inflict pain on his partners; Margery was a masochist who liked bondage and flagellation. The couple seemed to be made for each other.

On 1 May, the couple booked into the Pembridge Court Hotel in Notting Hill. This was their first attempt at satisfying each other's tastes and so successful was it that her screams attracted the attention of the hotel detective. The couple were politely asked to keep it quiet.

Heath was nothing if not a ladies' man. On 15 June he went to a dance, and there met 19-year-old Yvonne Symonds. He swept her off her feet, took her to the Panama Club in South Kensington and finally got her to agree to spend the following day with him. The charm continued and Heath ended up proposing marriage, which Yvonne accepted. She even agreed to spend that night with him, back in the Pembridge Court Hotel. The next day, 17 June, she returned to her parents' house in Worthing to tell them all about her new fiancé.

Three days after this, on 20 June, Heath met Margery Gardner again. She too was dined at the Panama Club and then taken back to the Pembridge Court Hotel where she and Heath took room 4. It was now about midnight and none of the guests heard any noise during the night.

The next morning, Alice Wyatt was taking care of her duties, cleaning the rooms in the hotel. She knocked on the door to room 4 and when she got no reply, assumed that the occupants must have checked out. She used her key and went into the room.

Both beds appeared to have been slept in and there was some sort of bundle in one of them. Upon closer inspection, Alice found the body of Margery Gardner, covered over with bedclothes. She lay on her back, naked, with her right arm underneath her. Her ankles were tied together and marks on her wrists showed that they too had been bound at some stage. Her face was bruised and there were seventeen scourge marks on her body, inflicted with some sort of whip. Both breasts had been bitten and one nipple had almost been removed. Finally, something rough had been inserted into her vagina and then removed, causing massive bleeding. Worse still would come after the post-mortem, when it would be revealed that many of these injuries were inflicted while Margery was still alive. Death was actually due to suffocation, a gag or a pillow being forced into her mouth, probably to stifle her screams.

Heath was nowhere to be found. What the police could not know was that early that morning he had telephoned Yvonne Symonds in Worthing and arranged to go down to see her. He arrived in Worthing that afternoon and booked into the Ocean Hotel.

The next day, details of the London murder appeared in the papers. Heath knew that Yvonne would almost certainly read those reports and she would take an especial interest since she had stayed in the same hotel. In order to diffuse this possible problem, Heath mentioned the murder to her first. All he would say is that he knew something about it and would tell her later. He was then taken to meet her parents, whom he charmed. That evening he bought dinner for Yvonne at the Blue Peter Club in Angmering.

It was while they were eating that Yvonne reminded Heath of his promise to tell her something about the murder in London. To her horror he told her that it had taken place in the very room that they had shared and even that he had viewed the body. He explained that he had met the dead woman and a male companion of hers the day before. They had had nowhere to stay so he let them use his room. It must have been this companion who had brutally murdered Miss Gardner.

The next day, 23 June, Yvonne's parents read about the murder and were even more dismayed to read reports that the police were looking for Neville Heath. At their request, Yvonne rang Heath at his hotel and asked him to explain. He said that the police probably wanted to talk to him because he had information on the crime. He ended by saying that he was going back to London immediately to offer what help he could.

Heath did indeed leave Worthing on the 23rd, but he did not go back to London. He went on to Bournemouth instead where he booked into the Tollard Royal Hotel using the name Group Captain Rupert Brook.

In one respect, Heath had not lied to Yvonne because he did actually contact Scotland Yard. He wrote a letter to Chief Inspector Barrett, whom the newspapers had said was investigating the case, and repeated the story he had told Yvonne about Margery and her companion using his room. He added the one detail that he had returned to his room at 2 a.m. and found the body.

Oblivious to the massive police hunt for him, Heath continued to enjoy himself. On 27 June he went to a dance at the Pavilion where he met and charmed a girl named Peggy. A few days later, on 3 July, Heath took a walk along the promenade and sat on a bench to take the air. By coincidence, Peggy walked past with a friend of hers, 21-year-old Doreen Marshall. The three fell into conversation, Heath turned on the charm again and when Peggy carried on with her walk, Doreen stayed behind to chat to the handsome Group Captain.

Doreen Marshall lived in Pinner but was in Bournemouth recuperating after a short illness. She was staying at the Norfolk Hotel but readily accepted an invitation to take tea at the Tollard. Later, she accepted an invitation to dinner and they met again at 8.15 p.m. After eating, they chatted in one of the hotel lounges and were seen leaving the hotel together at 11.30 p.m.

On Friday, 5 July, the manager of the Norfolk Hotel, concerned that he had not seen Miss Marshall for almost two days, telephoned his opposite number at the Tollard. He knew that Doreen had arranged to have dinner on the evening of the 3rd with a Group Captain who was staying there. The manager was asked to see if his guest had any news about the missing lady.

It was Saturday before Mr Bell, the manager of the Tollard, had a chance to speak to Group Captain Brook. The dashing Group Captain admitted the dinner date, expressed his own concerns for Miss Marshall and readily agreed to talk to the police about her.

Eventually, Heath, still posing at the Group Captain, went to the police station where he was seen by Detective Constable Souter, who showed him a picture of the missing girl. Heath agreed that this was the young lady he had taken to dinner and even consoled Doreen's parents who had travelled down to Bournemouth from Pinner.

As a matter of routine, Heath was asked to give an account of his movements. As he spoke, Constable Souter couldn't help but notice how much Brook resembled the description of a man wanted by Scotland Yard. Souter passed his suspicions on to his superiors and Brook was asked outright if he was really Neville Heath. He denied it, but did agree to wait in the station and speak to Detective Inspector George Gates.

It was during the talk with Gates that Heath asked if he might pop back to his hotel to fetch his jacket. Gates refused Heath permission, and instead went to the Tollard himself to search Heath's room. Inside the jacket that Heath had been so keen to get his hands on was a cloakroom ticket for Bournemouth station. Once this was redeemed, a suitcase was found and upon opening this, the police found items of clothing with the word 'Heath' stitched into them. There was also a bloodstained scarf and a diamond weave whip that matched patterns found on the flesh of Margery Gardner.

On 7 July, Heath was escorted back to London and the following day was charged with the murder of Margery Gardner. That same evening, Doreen Marshall's body was found in bushes in Branksome Chine in Bournemouth.

Doreen's body was naked except for one shoe, the rest of her clothing having been thrown over her body to conceal it. She had been battered about the head and her throat had been cut. One nipple had been completely bitten off and there were jagged cuts all along her body. Finally, something rough, possibly a tree branch, had been pushed into her vagina and her anus.

Neville Heath appeared before Mr Justice Cassels at the Old Bailey on 22 July. The case lasted until 25 July and Heath's defence was one of insanity. Medical evidence was called and although this showed that the prisoner was a sexual degenerate, a sadist and a pervert, it did not show that he was insane.

On Wednesday, 16 October Heath was hanged at Pentonville by Albert Pierrepoint and Harry Kirk. The condemned man's last request had been for a double whisky.

Arthur Robert Boyce, 1946

In late May 1946, 41-year-old Elizabeth McLindon obtained employment as housekeeper at 45 Chester Square, Belgravia, at a house owned by the King of Greece. He seldom used the house so most of the time Elizabeth was alone there.

Before she had taken the job in London, Elizabeth had lived in Brighton and it was there that she had met the man in her life, 45-year-old Arthur Boyce. He worked on the Palace Pier and the couple were soon lovers, despite the fact that Boyce was a married man. Indeed, so close did they become that on 1 June, Elizabeth took advantage of having the house in Chester Square to herself and moved Boyce in.

Exactly one week later, on 8 June, a neighbour saw Elizabeth slam the door of no. 45 and walk off purposefully. Very soon after this, Boyce entered the square, walked past no. 45 and headed off in the same direction Elizabeth had gone. He looked very angry. The neighbour found it easy to remember the exact date because it was the first anniversary of VE-Day and there were many celebrations.

The next day, 9 June, the King of Greece paid one of his rare visits to the house. The place was tidy enough, even though there was no sign of his new housekeeper, and one of the downstairs rooms was locked. The King couldn't be bothered with such mundane matters and left the house later the same day.

The next visitor to the house was the King's private secretary, Sophocles Papanikoladu. He called on 12 June and again there was no sign of Elizabeth McLindon but there was a letter for her on the mat behind the front door. Then the telephone rang. The caller gave his name as Boyce and asked to speak to the housekeeper. Told that she didn't appear to be in the house, Boyce said that he was very concerned about her.

The letter on the mat was also from Boyce and again expressed concern that he had not heard from Elizabeth. A second letter followed the next day. The housekeeper had now been missing for some days and of course, there was the mystery of the locked room downstairs. The police were called in and they forced the door open. Inside the room they found the body of Elizabeth McLindon. She was sitting in a chair and had been shot through the back of the head.

Boyce was interviewed in Brighton. He said that he had last seen Elizabeth on 8 June. They had gone out together to watch a parade, then returned to Chester Square where they made love. They were still in bed when the doorbell rang. Elizabeth told him to stay where he was and keep quiet but he did overhear a male caller say that the King would be calling and the place must be made ready for him.

Asked if he possessed a gun, Boyce admitted that he had owned a Colt .45. He had shown it to Elizabeth and she had objected to him having it so he had thrown it into the sea off Brighton Pier.

Number 45 Chester Square, where Arthur Robert Boyce killed Elizabeth McLindon.

Elizabeth had been shot with a .32 and, questioned further, Boyce admitted that he had once had one of those too. A man named Rowland had given him this in Brighton and asked £5 for it. He thought this was too high a price and intended returning it to him but Elizabeth said she was scared of being at the house in London by herself so he had bought it for her as protection. This made the police rather suspicious. Why had Elizabeth apparently objected to one gun and yet wanted to keep another?

A search of Elizabeth's belongings in London revealed some letters from Boyce. The gist of these was that marriage had been discussed between them. Yet Boyce was a married man. Had she been pressing him for marriage without knowing his true circumstances? Here was a possible motive for murder.

The evidence against Boyce was circumstantial. He had lived with Elizabeth and been with her on the day she died. He had supplied the murder weapon and he did have a motive if she was pressing him for marriage. He was duly arrested and charged with murder.

Boyce appeared before Mr Justice Morris at the Old Bailey on 16 September, the proceedings lasting until 19 September. He was found guilty and sentenced to death, but the case did not end there.

On 3 July, a man named Arthur Clegg was arrested. When he was searched, police found a piece of paper on him which bore Elizabeth's name and her London address. This same Clegg was being held at Maidstone Court for a hearing when a note, written in block capitals, was found beneath the cell windows. It read: 'The man Clegg is mixed up in a case of murder. He say's [sic] they can't touch him now as they have a man called Boyce in Brixton Prison.'

Clegg was never rated as a serious suspect and the note and its implications did not save Boyce from the gallows. He was hanged at Pentonville on Friday, 1 November by Albert Pierrepoint and Henry Critchell.

John Mathieson, 1946

Mona Victoria Vanderstay had led a most colourful life. She had been a weightlifter, a jujitsu expert and even a variety artiste. As if that were not enough, she was also the mother of five children. Now, at the age of 46, she lived with her husband, Robert in Camden Road, Holloway.

On the evening of Saturday, 20 July 1946, Mona went to the cinema alone. She caught a bus home at some time between 10 p.m. and 11 p.m. but she never arrived back at Camden Road. The following morning her strangled body was found in St Luke's churchyard, close by her home. Whoever had killed her had also rifled through her handbag and taken what he wanted. He had, however, missed a purse containing £12 in cash.

This would have been a very difficult case to solve for the police, but for the arrest of a sailor who was serving on HMS *Victory* at Portsmouth. He had been caught stealing clothing but when he was searched, a chequebook in the name of Robert Vanderstay was found, along with other items taken from Mona's handbag. His clothing was then examined and bloodstains found. Tests showed that these were of Group B, the same as Mona's. The sailor, who gave his name as John Mathieson, was now questioned about Mona's murder.

Mathieson said he had no memory of any murder. He did recall drinking heavily on that Saturday night and had seen Mona on a bus. He also had a very hazy recollection of being in some sort of garden and having an argument and striking someone after she had hit him first.

Arrested and charged, Mathieson appeared at the Old Bailey on 19 October. The presiding judge was Mr Justice Stable and the case lasted until 23 October.

Mathieson persisted in having no knowledge of the attack but what counted heavily against him was that he had then sorted through the dead woman's handbag and taken the items he wanted. It was then suggested that he had acted during some form of sleepwalking trance and so could only be guilty of manslaughter. Finally, a psychiatrist, Dr Paterson, suggested that the prisoner should be found guilty but insane.

None of this moved the jury who decided that Mathieson was sane and had known exactly what he was doing. Found guilty of murder, he was hanged at Pentonville on Tuesday, 10 December by Albert Pierrepoint and Harry Allen.

Frederick William Reynolds, 1947

Frederick Reynolds, a bookmaker, and Beatrice Greenberg had been having an affair for eighteen years, even though they were both married to other partners. In that time, they had developed a routine. He would approach her home whistling a Bing Crosby tune and if Beatrice's husband, Sidney was out of the way, she would rush to the front door and let Reynolds in.

On Tuesday, 17 December 1946, the ritual was acted out as usual. Reynolds had gone out for a drink and once the pubs had closed, approached Beatrice's house in Avenell Road, Highbury, whistling his chosen tune.

At first there was no sign of Beatrice so Reynolds took a walk around the block and returned some minutes later. This time Beatrice opened the door and Reynolds went up to her flat.

What happened next was a puzzle. According to Reynolds's later statement to the police, he spent some time with Beatrice and then she told him to leave as her husband would be home at any time. Almost immediately she gave a loud scream and there was a blinding flash. Reynolds had taken a gun from his pocket and shot Beatrice dead. He claimed, however, that he had no recollection of actually taking the gun from his pocket and using it. In his statement he wrote: 'Now I know it was my hand that took her life. I am ready to die to be with her.'

Reynolds appeared at the Old Bailey on 7 February 1947. At one stage there was some drama when Reynolds claimed that both his wife and Beatrice's husband had known of the long-standing affair. At that, Sidney Greenberg shouted, 'That is a damned lie sir!'

There could be no doubt that Reynolds had killed Beatrice, and the fact that he was probably very drunk at the time was no defence. Found guilty, he was hanged at Pentonville on Wednesday, 26 March by Albert Pierrepoint and Harry Kirk.

Christopher James Geraghty & Charles Henry Jenkins, 1947

For most of the day it was business as usual at Jay's Jewellers at 73–75 Charlotte Streeet. Then, at 2 p.m., all hell broke loose. Three men ran into the shop carrying guns and announced that they were going to rob the place. Bravely, the staff resisted.

Ernest Stock, the director, slammed the safe shut and was clubbed over the head for his trouble. Bertram Keates, the assistant manager, set off the alarm and was shot at. Fortunately for him, the bullet missed and embedded itself in a wall behind him. The three would-be robbers then panicked and fled empty handed. Outside, their car waited, but there was no way they could use it. A lorry making a delivery had blocked them in. They had no choice but to make a run for it.

The alarm sounding loudly meant that everyone knew there had been a robbery. One of the people who heard it was 35-year-old Alec de Antiquis who was travelling down Charlotte Street on his motorcycle. Bravely, he positioned himself directly in front of one of the gunmen, blocking his path. Immediately another shot rang out and a bullet hit Alec in the head. The three men made good their escape, just as another gentleman, Albert Pierrepoint, passed the scene on his way to an appointment.

Alec de Antiquis died from his injuries later that day. The police now made an appeal for witnesses and two days later, on 30 April, this appeal bore fruit. A taxi driver came forward to say that he had seen two men, in an obvious hurry, dash into an office block at 191 Tottenham Court Road, not long after the shooting had taken place. It may be that the robbers had split up after the attack so the premises were checked out and there, in an empty office, police found a discarded raincoat.

Whoever had left the coat had carefully cut out all the identifying labels but had not known that there was another label inside the lining. This enabled the police to trace the coat to a manufacturer in Leeds and they in turn gave a list of outlets in the capital. Further diligent work led to one such establishment in Deptford High Street.

During this time, many items were still rationed and in order to avoid fraud or black marketing, purchasers of clothing had to leave a name and address with the shopkeeper.

The shop was able to say that the coat had been sold on 30 December 1946 to a gentleman in Bermondsey. When he was interviewed in turn, he told the police that the coat was his, but that his wife had lent it to her brother, Charles Jenkins.

It was a simple matter to trace Jenkins. Although witnesses failed to pick him out as one of the robbers, he was held in custody pending a charge of murder. Soon afterwards, the other two were identified as Christopher Geraghty and Terence John Peter Holt. They too were arrested and all three then charged with murder. Soon after this, two guns were found in the mudflats of the River Thames. Tests showed that one had fired the bullet that killed Alec de Antiquis and the other had fired the bullet that had just missed Bertram Keates.

The trial of all three men opened before Mr Justice Hallett at the Old Bailey on 21 July. It would last for a full week and end on 28 July. All three men were found guilty. Holt was only 17, and so was sentenced to be detained during His Majesty's pleasure. The other two men were sentenced to death.

Tottenham Court Road. It was into an office here that Geraghty and Jenkins dashed after shooting Alec de Antiquis.

On Friday, 19 September Geraghty and Jenkins were hanged together at Pentonville by Albert Pierrepoint, the man who had passed the scene of their crime on 28 April. As it was a double execution, Pierrepoint had two assistants: Henry Critchell and Harry Allen.

Walter John Cross, 1948

At 9.30 p.m. on the night of Friday, 14 November 1947, Florence Wright heard screams coming from 11 King Edward's Road, Barking, the house next door. Knowing that the premises were occupied by 55-year-old Percy Bushby, a crippled watchmaker who lived alone with his cat, Toby, Florence went to investigate.

Just as she reached her own front door, Florence saw a young man coming out of Percy's house, leaving the door open. Florence went inside to find Percy lying dead on the floor. He had been strangled and the motive appeared to be robbery as his empty wallet lay nearby on a table.

Police investigations led to them picking up 21-year-old Walter Cross. He admitted that he and another man, Walter Leslie Bull, had been to Percy's shop three weeks before in order to sell some items to him. They had returned on 12 November when Bull had sold some more items for which he received 12*s* 6*d*, but Cross went on to deny that he had been anywhere near the shop since that date.

Questioned further, Cross finally admitted that he and Bull had discussed robbing the old man but, in the end, he had acted alone. During their last visit, Bull had noticed that Percy had a wallet stuffed with money and he suggested that they should go back and steal it. In the event, Bull had failed to turn up at the appointed time so Cross had gone in alone.

As he entered the shop, Percy Bushby had come towards him, shouted out suddenly and then collapsed onto the floor. Cross denied even touching him, apart from taking his wallet out of his pocket and stealing the money. Someone else must have strangled Percy after he had left.

When Walter Bull was interviewed, he said that he had only known Cross for a few weeks. He agreed that they had been to the shop together but claimed it was Cross who had spotted the wallet full of money, and Cross who had suggested the robbery. Bull had told him that he didn't want anything to do with it and knew nothing more about it.

Cross was charged and appeared before Mr Justice Cassels at the Old Bailey on 14 January 1948, the case lasting three days. Cross persisted in his claim that someone else must have gone into the shop after him but this suggestion was, of course, not believed as Florence Wright had gone into the premises as Cross had left.

Found guilty and sentenced to death, Cross was hanged at Pentonville on Thursday, 19 February by Albert Pierrepoint and Harry Allen.

Harry Lewis, 1949

Harry Saul Michaelson was badly hurt but he had no idea how he had been injured. He was found by the night porter, staggering around outside his flat at 75 Furzecroft, George Street, Marylebone on the evening of Sunday, 26 December 1948. He had a deep wound on his forehead and the injury was so severe that he had to undergo brain surgery to repair the damage. It did no good, for Michaelson died on 27 December.

A search of the dead man's flat showed that there was no sign of a forced entry. The murder weapon had, however, been determined. A tubular metal chair bore bloodstains and it appeared that the assailant had used this to batter Michaelson about the head. That chair bore other marks among the blood; a clear set of fingerprints which led officers to their owner, 21-year-old Harry Lewis. He was arrested on 18 January and charged with murder. He freely admitted that he had been responsible for Michaelson's death.

Lewis's story was that he had been wandering the streets, short of money and looking for something to steal. As he passed down George Street, he saw a basement window open and crept into the premises. There was a man asleep in bed and Lewis then sneaked quietly around the flat until he found a wallet. He helped himself and was just making good his escape when he heard a voice demand to know who was there. Picking up the nearest weapon, the tubular chair, Lewis then struck the man twice before leaving through the basement window.

Lewis faced his trial at the Old Bailey, before the Lord Chief Justice, Lord Goddard, on 7 March. Since he could not deny that he had attacked Michaelson, Lewis's defence tried to suggest that the attack was not responsible for the man's demise.

The suggestion now was that Michaelson had died not as a result of being battered with a chair, but from the surgery upon his brain. Even had this been accepted as fact, it would still not have helped Lewis as it would have been argued that the surgery was only necessary because of his initial attack. However, this line of defence was ruled useless when Dr Donald Teare testified that Michaelson would have died with or without the surgery.

Lewis was found guilty but with a recommendation to mercy on account of his youth. It did nothing to save him and he was hanged at Pentonville on Thursday, 21 April by Albert Pierrepoint and Harry Allen.

Bernard Alfred Peter Cooper, 1949

On the afternoon of Friday, 1 April 1949, Bernard Cooper was arrested by police in Islington for being drunk and disorderly. Once he had sobered up, he was released and told to report back to the station the following day. Cooper never did turn up on the Saturday and had an excellent reason for wanting to avoid contact with the police, for he had just strangled his wife, Mary Elizabeth, and stuffed her body underneath their bed at Davisville Road, Shepherd's Bush.

On the Saturday evening, Mary's body was found by her 14-year-old daughter, Sheila, and a full-scale police search was then organised for Bernard, the missing husband. For some days, no sign of him could be found and then, on 6 April, the caretaker at the Girl's County School in Maidstone Road, in Ashford, Kent, reported a prowler on the premises at 7.30 a.m. The police took the prowler into custody and found that they had captured Bernard Cooper. The story that Cooper now outlined to the police was a most sordid one.

Some time before, Sheila Cooper had had a legal abortion. At the time, the story was that a stranger had raped her but now Cooper confessed that he was the father of his own daughter's child. He had told his wife the truth about the 'relationship' and Mary had forgiven him. For a time things were allowed to rest but then, on the morning of 1 April, Mary had broached the subject of his incest once again.

The discussion became more heated and developed into a full-scale argument. Mary became hysterical and Cooper had slapped her face to quieten her. When this did not work, he had taken one of her stockings, which lay over the edge of the bed, and strangled her.

Cooper appeared at the Old Bailey on 18 May and, after listening to the story, the jury took just eleven minutes to decide that he was guilty as charged. He was hanged at Pentonville on Tuesday, 21 June by Albert Pierrepoint and Harry Kirk.

John George Haigh, 1949

Constance Lane was at a loss to understand it. One of her closest friends, a lady with the rather grand name of Olive Henrietta Helen Olivia Robarts Durand-Deacon had apparently vanished off the face of the earth.

The two ladies had lived for some time at the Onslow Court Hotel in South Kensington and Constance had last seen Olive on Friday, 18 February 1949. Olive had failed to appear for dinner that evening and the next morning, even a charming gentleman, Mr Haigh had expressed concern about her disappearance. It was surely time to involve the police in this matter.

It was 20 February by the time Constance Lane and John Haigh walked into Chelsea police station. Haigh explained that he was an entrepreneur with a small factory at Crawley. He was a guest at the same hotel, and had stayed in room 404 for some time. In due course, he had chatted with Mrs Durand-Deacon and she had expressed interest in an idea he had for making false fingernails for cosmetic purposes. They had agreed a time when he would take her down to Crawley and show her the process. Mrs Durand-Deacon had indeed been waiting in the hotel foyer at the appointed time but said she needed to go to the Army and Navy Stores in Victoria Street first. He waited, but she had never returned and he was at a loss to know what had happened to her.

On Monday, 21 February, Divisional Detective Inspector Shelley-Symes called at the Onslow Court to speak to Haigh again. Asked for further details, Haigh was happy to assist and said that he had last seen Mrs Durand-Deacon at 1.50 p.m. on the 18th. When she did not return, he had travelled down to Crawley alone. After attending to his business, he had a meal in a local pub and returned to the hotel at about 7 p.m.

The entire affair just did not make sense. On a hunch, Inspector Shelley-Symes ran a police check on Haigh and discovered that he had been in prison three times, the last occasion being during the war when he was caught looting from bombed houses. It was time to look a little deeper into the affairs of John Haigh.

Hilda Kirkwood, the bookkeeper at the hotel, confirmed that until recently, Haigh had had financial problems. He had been pressed for payment of his outstanding room account and at one stage, a cheque had been returned unpaid. Fortunately, he had settled his bill in full on 16 February, two days before Mrs Durand-Deacon had vanished.

Further checks revealed that the 'factory' in Crawley was little more than a storeroom. It was actually owned by a company called Hurstlea Products. The managing director, Edward Charles Jones, confirmed that he had known Haigh for some years and allowed him to use the premises to conduct experiments. Further, Jones confirmed that Haigh had visited him on 15 February and borrowed £50. For the police, this explained how Haigh had been able to pay his hotel bill the next day.

On 19 February, the day after Mrs Durand-Deacon vanished, Haigh had repaid £36 of the money Jones had lent to him. Where had he obtained that cash? The police decided to take a much closer look at the storeroom in Leopold Road, Crawley.

On 26 February, Detective Sergeant Patrick Heslin entered the storeroom at Crawley and began a thorough search of the premises. He found, among other things, three carboys containing acid, a rubber apron, a pair of long rubber gloves and an army respirator. There was also a stirrup-pump and on the bench was a locked hat box. Some papers were also found, including a receipt for a fur coat from a cleaner's in Reigate. Why would Haigh have had a fur coat?

Checks at the cleaner's shop revealed that the coat had been brought in by a well-dressed and well-spoken gentleman. The coat, which was still there, was a Persian and was identical to one Mrs

Durand-Deacon was known to possess and which she had been wearing when she disappeared. As a result, Haigh was asked to report back to the police station at Chelsea, which he did on 28 February.

At first, Haigh continued to deny any knowledge of the disappearance of Mrs Durand-Deacon, but when faced with the evidence of the fur coat, he sat in silence for a few moments and then asked, 'Tell me frankly, what are the chances of anybody being released from Broadmoor?'

The story that Haigh now told was incredible. He claimed that he had shot the missing woman inside the storeroom at Crawley and then dissolved her body in acid. He was cocky and arrogant, claiming that the police would be unable to prove murder without a body. That was not all, for Haigh went on to admit to other murders and claimed that in each case he had then dissolved the bodies in acid.

The trial of John George Haigh opened at Lewes in Sussex on 18 July before Mr Justice Humphreys and lasted for two days.

Haigh had been wrong in thinking that the prosecution needed a body in order to pursue a case of murder. In the case of Mrs Durand-Deacon, scientists had taken the top layer of soil from the yard at Crawley and carefully sifted it. Among the items found were a set of dentures, which were confirmed as belonging to the missing woman. Also found were fragments of bone and three gallstones, and it was shown that these were from a female in late adult life who suffered from arthritis. Olive Durand-Deacon would have been 69 on 28 February and did suffer from that complaint.

Although evidence was only heard on the one charge of murder, that of Mrs Durand-Deacon, Haigh had actually confessed to a total of nine. He was now claiming that he had killed three members of the McSwann family; Archibald Henderson and his wife, Rosalie; a woman he had met in Hammersmith; a young man he had met the same year; and a woman named Mary. The last three 'murders' were given little credence but details of the others were read out in court when Haigh's confession was heard.

Haigh had once worked as a repairman for William Donald McSwann who ran amusement arcades in London. In the summer of 1944, McSwann had told Haigh that he was concerned about being called up into the armed forces. Haigh had solved his problem by inviting him to a basement he had rented at 79 Gloucester Road, London SW7 where he shot him in the head, dissolved his body in acid and then washed the resulting sludge down the drain.

Soon after this, in July 1945, McSwann's parents, William and Amy were both lured to Gloucester Road and received the same treatment. It was a profitable move for Haigh who then helped himself to property they owned, in all making around £4,000.

In 1947, Dr Archibald Henderson wished to sell some flats he owned in Fulham. Haigh replied to his advertisement and even though the sale fell through, the two men kept in touch. So, when Henderson and his wife said they were taking a short break in Brighton, Haigh booked into the same hotel, the Metropole on the seafront.

On 16 February, Henderson and his wife vanished. Haigh admitted that he had taken them both to the storeroom at Crawley, shot them and dissolved their bodies in acid. In short, Haigh was confessing to six murders that the police accepted he was involved in; three murders in London and three in Crawley.

The reason for this was obvious. Surely a man who had killed six people and destroyed their bodies in acid was insane? To back this idea up, Haigh added the detail that he had made a small cut in the throat of each victim, drawn off a glass of blood, and drunk it down with relish. This habit came from a time

Number 79 Gloucester Road. John Haigh began his killing spree in the basement of this address and killed three people here. (Mirror Syndication)

when he had been involved in a car crash, been injured and blood had run into his mouth. Ever since, he had enjoyed the taste of blood and had had dreams involving bleeding crucifixes and chalices of blood.

The jury retired on the second day and took just seventeen minutes to decide that Haigh was sane and guilty of murder. The defence announced that there would be no appeal and they would rely on medical reports to show that he wasn't sane and should be committed to a mental hospital instead.

The reports did not save Haigh and on Wednesday, 10 August he was hanged at Wandsworth by Albert Pierrepoint and Harry Kirk.

Daniel Raven, 1950

October 6, 1949 saw the Raven family celebrating. It was on this day that Marie and Daniel Raven had their first child, a son. The child was born in a nursing home at Muswell Hill and four days later, on Monday, 10 October, Daniel visited the home along with Marie's parents, Leopold and Esther Goodman.

At 9 p.m. Leopold and Esther left Muswell Hill to return to their home at Ashcombe Gardens, Edgware. Daniel Raven left soon afterwards, but at about 10.30 p.m. the telephone rang at Raven's home. It was the police, asking him to come over to his parents'-in-laws' house in Edgware.

It had been 9.50 p.m. when Frederick Fraiman, Marie's brother-in-law, had called at Ashcombe Gardens to enquire after the new mother and baby. He was surprised to receive no reply to his knocking but, finding a window open, climbed into the house, fearful that something was wrong. There was indeed something wrong for inside he discovered the battered bodies of Esther and Leopold Goodman. The police soon determined that the motive for the crime had not been robbery, for a good deal of cash was found in various places around the house.

When Raven arrived at the house, he appeared to be genuinely upset. The police, however, had not failed to notice that his clothing appeared to be extremely pristine. He was taken into the police station for further questioning and asked to hand over the keys to his own house.

It was close to midnight when officers entered Raven's house in Edgwarebury Lane. The first thing they noticed was a strong smell of burning and they soon found the remains of a man's suit, smouldering inside a stove. The remnants were retrieved and sent for examination. Bloodstains were detected and these proved to be the same group as the Goodmans.

The police believed that, after leaving the nursing home, Raven had gone to his in-laws' house and battered them to death with a heavy television aerial. He had tried to wash the blood off his suit but when that failed, he had tried to burn it. No motive for the double murder could be determined, but a motive is not necessary to bring a charge of murder.

Raven appeared before Mr Justice Cassels at the Old Bailey on 22 November. His defence during the three-day hearing was that he had indeed called on the Goodmans at their home but had left them alive and well. He had then visited a cousin to tell her about the baby before returning to Ashcombe Gardens. This time he had received no reply and so climbed in through the same window Frederick Fraiman later used to gain entrance. He had found the bodies and in examining them, must have got some blood on his suit. As for burning that suit, he had panicked when the police had telephoned him.

The defence did not convince the jury and Raven was found guilty. An appeal was entered and here a different defence was put forward. Raven now claimed that he was suffering from insanity. He had served in the RAF and had been in a plane crash. Ever since, he had suffered from blackouts and a form of epilepsy.

The new defence failed and the appeal was dismissed. As a result, Raven was hanged at Pentonville on Friday, 6 January 1950 by Albert Pierrepoint and Harry Kirk. Raven's new son was exactly three months old.

Timothy John Evans, 1950

At 3.10 p.m. on Wednesday, 30 November 1949, a young man walked into the police station at Merthyr Tydfil and asked if he might speak to an inspector or if one wasn't available, a sergeant.

The officer on duty, Detective Constable Gwynfryn Howell Evans said that there was no senior officer available and asked if he might be able to assist. After a few moments pause, the frightened looking young man announced, 'I want to give myself up. I have disposed of my wife. I put her down the drain.'

The man identified himself as 25-year-old Timothy John Evans and, after being cautioned, said he wished to make a full statement. He asked Constable Evans if he could write it down as he was unable to read and write properly. He was then handed over to Detective Sergeant Gough, who took down Evans's words, read the statement back to him and then had him sign it.

According to this statement, Evans and his family lived in London. At the beginning of October, Evans's wife, Beryl had told him that she was expecting their second child and, because they couldn't really afford another baby, wanted to get rid of it. By Sunday, 6 November, Beryl was so desperate that she told Evans she was thinking of doing away with herself.

The next day, 7 November, Evans had gone to work and at one stage pulled up at a transport café between Ipswich and Colchester. It was while he was enjoying a cup of tea that he got into conversation with a stranger and told him about his problem. The man said he could help and gave him a bottle which he said would do the trick and abort Beryl's pregnancy.

On the morning of the 8th, Evans went to work as normal. That night when he returned home he found his daughter, Geraldine crying in her cot and Beryl lying dead on the bed. She had obviously taken the liquid in the bottle and died as a result. In the early hours of the morning, Evans had taken his wife's body to a drain in the street outside, lifted the manhole cover and deposited Beryl inside. After a couple of days, he had then got someone to look after the baby, sold some furniture and travelled up to Merthyr, where he originated from. The matter had played on his conscience ever since and now he wanted to get it off his chest. Finally, Evans gave the officer his London address: 10 Rillington Place, Notting Hill.

The Welsh police contacted their colleagues in London and asked them to check out Evans's story. It was late afternoon by the time officers arrived at Rillington Place. They found the drain, exactly where Evans said it was. It took three officers to lift it, a task which Evans said he had accomplished alone. The drain was empty and a message to that effect was then sent back to Merthyr.

At 9 p.m., Evans was interviewed again and told that nothing had been found in the drain. He was asked if he wished to make a second statement and agreed that he did. Once again it was written down by an officer and later signed by Evans as a true copy of what he had said.

This second statement began by saying that there had been no meeting with a man in a transport café. In fact, Evans wasn't responsible for his wife's death at all. The real culprit was the man who lived on the ground floor of 10 Rillington Place, one John Reginald Halliday Christie.

In this statement Evans said that about a week before Beryl died, or around 1 November, he had been approached by Christie who said he knew about Beryl's delicate condition and would be able to help him out of this predicament. Christie said he had trained as a doctor before the war and could perform an abortion for Beryl, adding that the 'stuff' he used would kill one in ten, but was the only way to sort things out. Evans then discussed this with his wife and though he was against the idea, Beryl was adamant that she wanted to go through with it.

The arrangements were made and Christie said he would perform the process on 8 November. Evans had gone to work as normal that day and when he returned home he was met by Christie who said he had some bad news: Beryl had died during the operation.

Working with Christie, they had hidden the body in the middle flat at Rillington Place. The occupant was in hospital at the time so they knew they wouldn't be disturbed. They then discussed what to do with the body and Christie said he would put it down the drain outside. As for the baby, Geraldine, Christie knew a couple in Acton who would take her. It would be best all round if Evans got away for a time and that was why he had travelled up to Merthyr where his aunt lived.

Once again the London police were contacted and officers returned to Rillington Place. A search of the premises was organised but an error led to nothing of interest being found. One officer noticed a wash-house in the yard at the back and asked if it had been checked out. He was informed that it had been. In fact, no one had looked inside so it was left unchecked.

On Friday, 2 December, Detective Inspector James Neil Black and Detective Sergeant Corfield travelled up to Wales to escort Evans back to London. Later that same day, other officers went back to Rillington Place to search the premises again, and this time the wash-house was properly checked.

Inside the wash-house officers found a large package wrapped in a green tablecloth and blanket and tied very tightly indeed. When the parcel was opened it was found to contain the doubled over body of a woman. Behind the door, hidden under some planks of wood, was the body of a baby girl. Beryl and Geraldine Evans had been found.

Back in London, Evans was faced with this discovery and made another, short statement. In this he admitted to strangling Beryl because she was running up debts. He also admitted to strangling his daughter two days later, on 10 November. Later still he made a fourth statement, his longest yet, in which he again admitted both murders. He was then formally charged.

In British courts, it is usual for a man facing multiple murder charges to only appear in court on one of those charges. So, when Evans appeared before Mr Justice Lewis at the Old Bailey on 11 January 1950, he was indicted only with the murder of his daughter. The trial lasted for three days.

Among the most damaging witnesses were John Christie and his wife, Ethel. Christie told the court that very late at night, on 8 November, he and his wife had been woken by a loud bang, which came from Evans's flat on the top floor. This was followed by the sound of something heavy being moved about. The next morning Evans told him that his wife had gone to Bristol, taking Geraldine with her. Ethel Christie confirmed much of what her husband said.

The jury retired on the third day and had little trouble in returning a guilty verdict. An appeal was dismissed on 20 February and just over two weeks later, on Thursday, 9 March, Evans was hanged at Pentonville by Albert Pierrepoint and Syd Dernley.

Matters would have ended there, but for the later story of John Reginald Halliday Christie, which is also detailed in this book (*see* page 114). Christie, after his arrest, confessed that he had killed Beryl Evans but denied any responsibility for the death of Geraldine, the crime for which Evans had been executed. It was difficult to accept that two killers had lived in Rillington Place and a campaign for a pardon for Timothy Evans was organised. Eventually, Evans was granted a posthumous pardon on 18 October 1966.

This decision has led many people to assume that Evans was an innocent man. In fact, once Christie had been convicted of murder, Beryl Evans's body was exhumed and no trace of Christie's tell-tale method of carbon monoxide poisoning could be found. There is also evidence that Beryl was subject to some violence before she died and this was certainly not Christie's style. He was a coward who could only exert any degree of dominance over a woman who was already unconscious.

It is the author's belief that Evans did kill his wife after or during a heated argument over money. As for Geraldine, although Christie always denied it, he was almost certainly responsible for her death. Evans did indeed deserve to be pardoned for the crime he was hanged for; the murder of his daughter, even though he probably did kill his wife. Even so, he should not have been hanged for he had an IQ of just 65 and on medical grounds alone should have faced no greater charge than that of manslaughter.

John O'Connor, 1951

Early on Saturday, 11 August 1951, John O'Connor handed himself into the police and confessed that he had killed his landlady, Eugenie le Maire at 15 Perham Road, West Kensington.

O'Connor told the police that the previous night, 10 August, he had visited a number of pubs in London and, after closing time, had taken a taxi back to his lodgings, arriving there rather late. His 82-year-old landlady welcomed him home and began making him a cup of tea. Then, without any warning, he had seized her by the throat and attempted to strangle her.

Eugenie lost consciousness and fell to the floor in a heap. O'Connor then raped her before going calmly up to his bedroom. For some time he brooded on what he had done, but far from feeling any degree of remorse, he then went back downstairs, picked up a bread knife and stabbed Eugenie through her heart and her lungs.

Put on trial for murder, O'Connor appeared before Mr Justice Barry at the Old Bailey on 2 October. Here the judge explained that there were three possible verdicts in this case. O'Connor could be guilty, not guilty, or guilty but insane. Given the circumstances of the case, the defence would obviously have sought to go for the third verdict, guilty but insane and counsel did have an array of evidence which they wished to present. It was then that, in effect, O'Connor put his own neck inside the noose for he expressly forbade that evidence to be called.

The jury now had only two possibilities: guilty or not guilty. With the evidence of O'Connor's own statement, it took them just ten minutes to decide that he was guilty and he was then sentenced to death. Twenty-two days later, on Wednesday, 24 October, O'Connor was hanged at Pentonville by Albert Pierrepoint and Harry Allen.

Backary Manneh, 1952

Late on Friday, 4 January 1952, the occupants of Oakley Square were just settling down for the evening when loud shouts and screams shattered the calm. Looking through their windows, the residents saw a coloured man leave no. 10 and move quickly down the street.

Some of the neighbours went across to 10 Oakley Square and, finding the door open, went inside. There they found 28-year-old Joseph Aaku. He had been slashed across the face and stabbed a number of times. He was rushed to hospital but died there at 11.17 p.m.

The police investigation soon showed that the killer, whoever he was, had also been injured in the attack. Aaku had had blood of Group A but there were also bloodstains belonging to Group O at the scene. The motive also appeared to be obvious as a large quantity of hemp was found in the flat. There had probably been some sort of argument over drugs, though Aaku's gold watch had also been stolen.

As a matter of routine, all of Aaku's known associates were spoken to and this included his fellow workers at Euston station. It was here that officers interviewed Backary Manneh on 8 January. While Manneh was answering questions, officers noticed a fresh cut on his right hand, which was badly swollen. Asked about this, Manneh said he had been mugged in Tottenham Court Road on the night of 5 January.

By 9 January, Manneh's hand had grown worse and he had to go back to the doctor's. The next day, 10 January, he was admitted to St George's in the East Hospital and it was there, on 12 January, that he was interviewed again. By then other men had been interviewed, one of which was Denba Jadama, an acquaintance of Manneh's who said that on 9 January, Manneh had specifically asked him not to mention his hand to the police. What was Manneh trying to hide?

Soon after this second interview, the police spoke to Simon Litwin who said he had bought a gold watch from Manneh on 7 January. The watch was now with a jeweller for repair and when the police recovered it, they found that it had belonged to Aaku. On 14 January, Manneh was arrested at the hospital.

Manneh appeared before Mr Justice Gorman at the Old Bailey, the trial lasting three days, from 25–27 March. The evidence was enough to convict Manneh who was hanged at Pentonville by Albert Pierrepoint and Harry Smith on Tuesday, 27 May.

John Howard Godar, 1952

On Friday, 6 June 1952 Mr Gillespie picked a young couple up in his cab at Uxbridge station and was asked to drive to Chalfont Road, Maple Cross near Rickmansworth. They had not gone very far when the woman in the back began to scream.

The scream was accompanied by a frenzied knocking and Gillespie pulled over immediately. Going to the back, Gillespie opened the door and the blood soaked body of the woman almost fell out of the cab. The man, sitting quite calmly, said, 'I think I've hurt her.' He then asked Gillespie to take him to the police station.

The woman in the cab, 20-year-old Maureen Jones Cox was certainly dead. She had been stabbed twenty-three times in the left temple and cheek, twenty-eight times in her chest and eight times in her throat. Her killer, 31-year-old John Godar, was now interviewed by Chief Inspector Richardson and Inspector Gladwell.

Godar said that he and Maureen had been seeing each other for ten months but lately, Maureen had expressed reservations about the relationship. It had only been very recently that she had discovered that Godar had been married and had a child, though he was now divorced. He hadn't told her about this and it had made her think hard about whether she wanted to continue seeing him or not.

In the cab, Maureen had spoken about this and then dropped the bombshell that there was another man she was interested in and had even arranged to go out with him on a date on the following Sunday. This was the final straw and Godar had taken out a knife and began stabbing her.

Godar appeared before Mr Justice Barry at the Old Bailey on 7 July, the trial lasting two days. The defence sought to prove that the defendant had been insane at the time of the attack.

Dr Rossiter Lewis said that in his opinion, Godar had mental problems which meant that he would have outbursts of temporary insanity, often lasting less than a minute. He believed that Godar had killed Maureen when suffering just such an episode. However, this was countered by the testimony of Dr Matheson from Brixton Prison who said that he had found no evidence of insanity.

It took the jury forty minutes to decide that Godar was sane and guilty of murder. He was hanged at Pentonville on Friday, 5 September by Albert Pierrepoint and Robert Leslie Stewart.

Dennis George Muldowney, 1952

Countess Krystyna Skarbek was a true heroine. Known by her friends as Christine Granville, she had been born in Poland. When the Second World War broke out Christine was living in east Africa and immediately offered her services to the Allies. She was sent to Hungary where she helped set up the resistance. She was arrested twice by the Gestapo but managed to escape both times.

After leaving Hungary, Christine fought in Turkey, was parachuted into France and fought there too. Finally, she served in Italy. For her efforts she had been awarded the George Medal, the Croix de Guerre and an OBE. Then, when the war was over, she moved to Britain and lived in London.

On Sunday, 15 June 1952, Christine was standing in the foyer of the Shelbourne Hotel at 1 Lexham Gardens, Kensington, when a man suddenly rushed forward and stabbed her in the chest. The blade penetrated her heart and she died instantly. Her attacker was grappled to the floor and held until the police arrived to take him into custody. He identified himself as 41-year-old Dennis Muldowney.

Muldowney claimed that the motive for his crime was jealousy. He said that he and Christine had been lovers and he had found out that she was seeing another man. That was why he wanted to kill her and then take his own life.

On the day in question he had seen her going into the hotel, had stopped her and asked for the return of some letters he had written to her but she replied that she had burnt them and added that she wanted nothing more to do with him. It was then that he had drawn out his knife and stabbed her.

Muldowney appeared before Mr Justice Donovan at the Old Bailey on 10 September, the proceedings lasting for two days. Here it was shown that there was no truth whatsoever in any of Muldowney's ramblings. He and Christine had not even known each other, let alone been lovers.

Found guilty, Muldowney did not bother to enter an appeal or even petition for a reprieve and so, on Tuesday, 30 September was hanged at Pentonville by Albert Pierrepoint and Harry Smith. This was a double execution, Muldowney being hanged alongside Raymond Cull, the subject of the next story.

Raymond John Cull, 1952

There were constant arguments between Raymond Cull and his 17-year-old wife, Jean Frances. Mostly these were over lack of money or his jealousy, and finally Jean said she had had enough and moved back to her father's house in Shadwell Drive, Northolt.

Raymond tried his best to get Jean to return to him, including writing her love letters, but all to no effect. On Sunday, 29 June 1952 she wrote him a note reading, 'I don't want you anymore. Please understand. I just don't want to see you anymore.' As far as she was concerned, that was the end of the matter.

At close to midnight on that same 29 June, Jean's father was woken by a terrible scream coming from his daughter's bedroom. Running in to see what the problem was, he found Jean lying on the floor with her husband Raymond standing over her, a 17in bayonet in his hand. Cull now turned to his father-in-law and chased him from his own home. Satisfied that he could now make good his escape, Cull ran from the house to his sister's home, where he confessed to her that he had stabbed his wife. The police were called and Cull handed over the bayonet without any resistance.

In his interview Cull said that he had been out drinking that night and had drunk no less than seventeen pints of beer. He had then made his mind up to speak to Jean and sort things out once and for all. As for the bayonet, he had taken this just to scare her father if he tried to interfere.

Arriving at Shadwell Drive, Cull found a window open and climbed inside Jean's house. He took off his shoes so he wouldn't disturb anyone and went into his wife's room. He woke her and she started to struggle. It was during this struggle that she grabbed for the bayonet, fell over and landed on the blade. It was all a tragic accident and he had not meant to kill her.

That was Cull's defence when he appeared before Mr Justice Donovan at the Old Bailey on 11 September, the case taking two days to hear. Unfortunately for Cull, medical evidence from

Dr Donald Teare, who had performed the post-mortem, showed that the only way the fatal wound could have been inflicted was for the bayonet to have been deliberately swung around to strike with some degree of force. As a result, Cull was found guilty but with a recommendation to mercy, as he was only 25 years old.

No appeal was entered and the recommendation of the jury had no effect. Cull was hanged at Pentonville at the same time as Dennis George Muldowney.

Peter Cyril Johnson, 1952

Peter Johnson and Charles Mead were the best of friends. They both worked as street traders in London and had known each other for years. Even the best of friends can have arguments, though, and so it was with Johnson and Mead. On Saturday, 28 June 1952, the two argued in Bethnal Green Gardens. This argument developed into a fist-fight that ended when Johnson knocked Mead down, then picked up a 16lb lump of concrete and used it to batter him to death.

Johnson was arrested and readily admitted that he was responsible for Mead's death. He claimed, however, that this was a case of self-defence. It had been Mead who first picked up the concrete and tried to use it as a weapon. Johnson had merely got the better of him, took the concrete from him and used it to defend himself. This was manslaughter, not murder. Of course, that would be for a jury to decide.

Johnson appeared before Mr Justice Donovan at the Old Bailey over two days, 17–18 September, and pleaded not guilty to murder but guilty to manslaughter.

The evidence was then heard. Johnson claimed that at one stage in the fight he had held the concrete block in one hand and removed his coat at the same time, using his other hand. He was asked to demonstrate this action to the jury but was unable to do so. Johnson became frustrated at this and announced that he wished to change his plea. The jury were then asked to retire to consider their verdict and took thirty minutes to decide that the killing had been deliberate and Johnson was guilty of murder. Only now could it be revealed that Johnson had a long record for crimes of violence.

On Thursday, 9 October, that long record came to an end when Johnson was hanged at Pentonville by Albert Pierrepoint and Harry Allen.

John Reginald Halliday Christie, 1953

John Christie was a weak, ineffectual man. By the outbreak of war in 1939, he had already been sacked from a number of jobs and had served prison sentences for petty theft and assault. Such a man enjoyed his brief moments of power, none more so than when he became a special constable in the War Reserve Police. He would patrol the streets at night, making sure that blackout regulations were observed correctly and throwing his authority about if they weren't.

It was in 1943 that Christie developed from a petty criminal into a murderer. In August of that year he met 21-year-old Ruth Fuerst who worked in a munitions factory in Mayfair. They chatted and she confided that the bombing really frightened her. At the time, Christie's wife, Ethel was away from their home at 10 Rillington Place, Notting Hill, and he took advantage of that situation by inviting the nervous Ruth back to his ground floor flat.

According to statements he would later make, Ruth went back to Rillington Place two or three times and then, on one visit, offered herself to him. They made love and while they were doing so, he strangled her to death and hid her body under the floorboards in his front room. Later, when it was dark, he dug a shallow grave in the back garden and buried her body there.

In fact, this scenario was rather unlikely. Judging from his later behaviour, it is more reasonable to assume that somehow Christie managed to render Ruth unconscious and then strangled her while he was raping her. This was the only way he could obtain any degree of dominance over a sexual partner.

In late 1943, Christie took a job at Ultra Radio in Acton. This is where he met 31-year-old Muriel Eady. She became a regular visitor, along with her boyfriend, to Rillington Place and they became quite friendly with both John and Ethel Christie. Then, one day in October 1944, Muriel made the mistake of visiting the house by herself.

Muriel had had a rather bad cold at the time but Christie said he knew something that would clear it up in no time. He then produced a rather strange contraption of his own making which looked like a large glass jar with two tubes passing through the lid. He explained that he would make a solution of Friar's Balsam which he would place inside the jar. Household gas would be bubbled into this liquid through one tube, and the balsam would take out the poisonous element. The other tube led to a mask, which Muriel was to place over her face. She would breathe deeply the now harmless gas and might feel a little sleepy, but that would cure her cold.

Muriel may have had her doubts but Christie persuaded her of the efficacy of his method. Needless to say, she was rendered unconscious and, like Ruth Fuerst, was then raped and strangled. She too was buried in the back garden at Rillington Place. For a time at least, Christie now seemed to control his homicidal impulses.

In 1948 a young family came to live on the top floor of 10 Rillington Place. This was Timothy Evans, his wife, Beryl and their baby daughter, Geraldine. Their relationship had always been tempestous and violent and when, in late 1948, Beryl fell pregnant and said she wanted an abortion, the arguments only intensified. Whatever the truth of the matter, Beryl and Geraldine were both murdered in November 1949 and Timothy Evans, whose story is told earlier in this section, was hanged for the murder of Geraldine (*see* page 108).

For a couple of years, Christie settled down again, no doubt letting the notoriety that Evans had brought to Rillington Place die down a little. Then, in late 1952, the floodgates burst open.

Ethel Christie was last seen alive on Friday, 12 December 1952. When she died is not known with accuracy but what is certain is that she was strangled and her body hidden beneath the floorboards in the front room of Christie's flat. Perhaps because he was now alone or perhaps because he no longer had Ethel's influence to restrict him, Christie went on a murder spree.

In January 1953, Christie sold most of his furniture. All that remained in the squalid hovel he called home was a mattress, a table and two chairs, one of which as a deckchair. That same month he picked up two women; 26-year-old Kathleen Maloney and 25-year-old Rita Nelson. Both were introduced to Christie's gas contraption and both were strangled during intercourse. The bodies were then stuffed into an alcove in Christie's kitchen. Around Friday, 6 March, the process was repeated with 25-year-old Hectorina MacLennan and her body was added to the others in the alcove. Christie now had four bodies hidden in his flat; Ethel's under the floorboards and three more in the kitchen alcove. It was time to move on.

On 13 March, Christie sublet his flat to a Mr and Mrs Reilly, taking three months' rent in advance. He then boarded and papered over the alcove, hiding the three bodies there, took his dog to the vet and had it put down, and then walked out of Rillington Place, never to return.

In due course the Reillys moved into the flat and noticed a rather unpleasant smell emanating from somewhere in the kitchen. They didn't have time to investigate much because the landlord, Charles Brown, visited the premises the next day. He told the Reillys that Christie had had no authority to sublet and they must move out. Besides, he had his own tenants who wanted to move in. Before that, though, the place had to be spruced up somewhat as Christie had left it in such a mess.

On 24 March, Beresford Brown, who lived upstairs, was cleaning some of the rubbish out of Christie's rooms prior to them being decorated. In the course of his duties he struck part of the kitchen wall and noticed that it sounded hollow. Investigating further, he pulled off a piece of loose wallpaper and peered into the alcove. He was horrified to see the naked back of a woman.

The police turned the house upside down and every day the newspapers carried fresh revelations. Medical examinations soon showed that all three bodies in the alcove had been gassed, but not fatally, and had engaged in sexual intercourse at about the time that they died. Each had been strangled by means of a ligature. Finally, Ethel Christie's body was found. In her case there was no sign of gassing or intercourse but she too had been strangled by means of a ligature.

Christie had been staying at Rowton House and almost certainly saw reports of the discoveries at Rillington Place on 25 March for he moved out of his lodgings that same day. He now began to wander aimlessly around the streets of London as the newspapers carried fresh stories of two more bodies in the back garden. A total of six murdered women had now been discovered and the police were rather anxious to talk to John Christie. His description was circulated to all officers in the capital.

On 31 March, Constable Thomas Ledger was patrolling the southern embankment of the River Thames, close to Putney Bridge, when he noticed a rather shabby, unshaven man looking down into the river. Constable Ledger approached the man, who gave his name as John Waddington and said he lived at Westbourne Grove. The officer was not satisfied and asked 'Waddington' to remove his hat. He did so, revealing a telltale bald dome. It was unmistakeable; Christie had been found.

In his interviews, Christie readily admitted all the murders and included that of Beryl Evans in 1949, though he always denied killing Geraldine, her baby. In Christie's own words, '…the more the merrier.' It seemed that he was seeking to escape death by hanging by claiming that he must be insane.

The trial began at the Old Bailey on 22 June before Mr Justice Finnemore and lasted until 25 June. As expected, the defence was that Christie was insane and so not responsible for his actions. Having listened to the mass of evidence, however, the jury took just eighty-five minutes to decide that Christie was sane and guilty of wilful murder.

There was no appeal, Christie preferring to rely on a respite on those same grounds of insanity. That respite never came and on Wednesday, 15 July, Christie was hanged at Pentonville by Albert Pierrepoint and Harry Smith.

Kenneth Gilbert & Ian Arthur Grant, 1954

There were two porters at the Aban Court Hotel in Harrington Gardens, Kensington and on Monday, 8 March 1954, one of them, 55-year-old George Smart, started a week-long stint on the nightshift.

It had just gone midnight when George opened the main door to one of the female residents. Later still, at 1 a.m. on 9 March, George was seen by another of the hotel's employees. The next time anyone saw the porter was at 7.45 a.m. when the head waiter found George's body, bound and gagged, in the serving quarters.

The motive for the crime seemed to be one of robbery. Just £2 in cash was missing but a large quantity of cigarettes had also been taken. It was determined that the thief had gained entrance through the coal cellar, had presumably been disturbed by George Smart who had been battered before being tied up. The actual cause of death was asphyxiation due to a gag being forced into George's mouth.

On the same day that George Smart's body was found, an employee at Olympia, Ian Grant, bragged to a co-worker named Chapman that he and his friend, Kenneth Gilbert, had robbed a hotel and 'done a man in.' He added that they had stolen cigarettes and that these were now stored at Victoria station. The reason for relating all this was that Grant wanted Chapman to pick the cigarettes up for him. Chapman agreed and took the left-luggage ticket, but instead of going to Victoria, took this information directly to the police.

The police checked the left-luggage office and found the missing cigarettes. Further investigations showed that one of the men named, Gilbert, had actually worked at the Aban Court Hotel for three months in 1953, so he would know his way around the place. Both men were picked up and charged with murder.

The trial of Gilbert and Grant took place before Mr Justice Glyn-Jones at the Old Bailey on 10 May. The defendents both pleaded not guilty to murder although they did admit that they had played a part in George Smart's death. They then began to blame each other.

Grant said he had seen Smart in one of the corridors with his arm raised and thought he was about to lash out at him. To defend himself, he had hit him just once, in the stomach. It was Gilbert who then hit him again, very hard indeed. Gilbert admitted that he had hit Smart but said he had only hit him twice before gagging him and tying him up.

The jury thought that both men were equally guilty and both were then sentenced to death. An appeal was entered, during which the defence tried hard to suggest that as neither man had gone to the hotel with the intention of killing, the verdict should correctly be one of manslaughter and not murder. However, the judges ruled that since both men had gone with the intention of committing a robbery, were quite prepared to use violence and did so, that murder was the correct verdict.

Victoria station, where Kenneth Gilbert and Ian Grant stored the cigarettes they had stolen after murdering George Smart.

On Thursday, 17 June, Gilbert and Grant were hanged together at Pentonville by Albert Pierrepoint and three assistants: Royston Rickard, Harry Smith and J. Grant. Although there would be other double executions for murder, this was the last time that two men were hanged on the same gallows at the same time.

Styllou Pantopiou Christofi, 1954

In 1926, Styllou Christofi was put on trial for murder in her native Cyprus. She had argued with her mother-in-law and, in a fit of temper, had killed the old woman by ramming a burning torch down her throat. Surprisingly, she was found not guilty.

The years passed, children were born and in July 1953, the same Styllou Christofi came to England to live with her married son, Stavros, his attractive wife Hella, and their three children. All of them lived at 11 South Hill Park, Hampstead.

There can be no doubt that Stavros and Hella were happy together. He worked as a waiter at the Café de Paris in the West End and she served in a fashion shop. There was, however, one problem:

Styllou was of the old school, knew precisely how a home should be run and constantly interfered. Hella found herself criticised in everything she did and put up with this for some time. Then, one day, she decided that she had had enough. It was time to give Stavros an ultimatum.

Hella had taken the three children on a brief holiday to Germany to stay with her family and upon her return, took Stavros to one side and told him it was time to send Styllou back to Cyprus. After some thought and discussion, Stavros agreed and told his mother of his decision. For her own part, Styllou decided that if someone had to go, it would be Hella.

On the evening of Thursday, 29 July 1954, Stavros went to work as usual. The children were all put to bed, leaving Styllou and Hella alone together. It was then that Styllou picked up a heavy ash-plate from the fireplace and smashed it down onto Hella's head. Still not satisfied, Styllou then took a scarf and throttled the life out of her unconscious daughter-in-law before dragging her body out into the rear garden.

It was close to midnight when John Young, a neighbour, noticed the glow of flames from the garden next door. Going out to investigate, he saw what he took to be a tailor's dummy, on fire. Even as he watched, Styllou Christofi came out into the garden and tried to stoke up the flames.

About one hour later, Mr Burstoff and his wife were walking down South Hill Park on their way home when Styllou dashed out into the street, alomost running into them, shouting, 'Please come! Fire burning! Children sleeping!'

Going to check what the woman was talking about, Mr Burstoff found that the tailor's dummy seen by John Young was actually the body of Hella Christofi. Styllou had tried to burn the body by covering it in newspaper soaked in paraffin.

The police were called and Styllou explained that she had been asleep when the smell of something burning had woken her. She had found Hella's body in the garden and immediately rushed out for help. Unfortunately, she could not explain how Hella's wedding ring, wrapped in newspaper, had found its way into her bedroom. She was arrested and charged with murder.

Styllou appeared at the Old Bailey on 28 October. The evidence against her was overwhelming and she was found guilty and sentenced to death. An appeal was entered and lost and Styllou then knew that she was going to die.

The condemned woman was a member of the Greek Orthodox Church and as such, asked that a cross from her church should be placed inside the execution room. The request was granted and on Wednesday, 15 December, Styllou Christofi saw that cross as she was hanged at Holloway by Albert Pierrepoint.

Ruth Ellis, 1955

In 1926, a girl was born in Rhyl, north Wales. Her real name was Ruth Hornby but her father, a musician, had changed his name for professional reasons. Consequently, the child was known as Ruth Neilson.

In 1941, Ruth Neilson moved to London and became involved with a Canadian serviceman named Clare. By the end of 1943, Ruth was pregnant and it was only now that she discovered that Clare was married and already had three children. Ruth gave birth to a son on 15 September 1944 and christened him Andria Clare, though he was always known as Andy.

Money was tight and so when Ruth saw an advertisement offering £1 an hour for nude models at a camera club, she took up the offer. It was there she met Morrie Conley who owned a number of nightclubs in London. He liked Ruth and offered her a job as a hostess at the Court Club situated at 58 Duke Street. Since this paid £5 per week plus a commision on sales, Ruth jumped at the chance.

In the spring of 1950, Ruth met the next man in her life. George Ellis was a dentist and he was infatuated with Ruth. They became engaged and married on 8 November 1950.

The relationship was not a happy one and they broke up in 1951, but not before Ruth found herself pregnant again. In October of that year she gave birth to a second child, a daughter, Georgina. Alone again, the newly named Ruth Ellis returned to the world of nightclubs run by Morrie Conley.

In 1953 Ruth was on duty at one of Conley's clubs when a man came in. He was rude, boorish and even insulted some of the other hostesses. Ruth left the arrogant man in no doubt that she didn't like him and was pleased to see the back of him when he left. His name was David Moffat Drummond Blakely.

In October 1953 Ruth was promoted to manageress of another of Conley's clubs, the Little Club at 37 Brompton Road, Knightsbridge. This was a real move up in the world for the job came with a flat over the club. Now she had a better income and a new place to live. One of her first customers was David Blakely.

This time, though, Blakely was a different man. He was charming and witty and made Ruth laugh. They chatted all evening and both felt a strong attraction between them. Within a week, they were lovers. This did not go down too well with another customer at that same club. Desmond Cussen also liked Ruth and developed an instant dislike for Blakely. Still, Ruth was happy and that seemed to be enough for Cussen.

So far David Blakely had shown Ruth two sides to his personality. He had been boorish and then charming, insulting and then witty. For the rest of their relationship it was always going to be that way.

Blakely liked to race fast cars. More than that, he liked to build them. With a friend and business partner, Anthony Findlater, he was working on a new project, a racing car they had named the Emperor. This was a rather expensive hobby, proved to be a great drain on Blakely's finances and led to him being constantly short of money. This in turn put a strain on his relationship with Ruth and she saw more and more of his boorish side.

One weekend, Blakely drove Ruth to Penn in Buckinghamshire where his parents lived. David took her to a local pub and, finding his mother already there, made Ruth stay outside. He did buy her a drink but she had to consume it in the car while he went inside to be with his mother.

In June 1954, Blakely took part in the Le Mans twenty-four hour race. He had promised Ruth that he would be back by a certain date and time. When he failed to show, Ruth got her revenge by taking Desmond Cussen to bed. When he found out about this, Blakely was furious but strangely, if anything, it only brought him and Ruth closer together.

Things got worse again in October 1954. The takings at the Little Club had been falling off and Ruth found herself out of a job. More than that, she also lost the flat that went with it. About the only place she could go was Desmond Cussen's flat in Goodwood Court, Devonshire Street. This did nothing to improve Blakely's temper and the relationship with Ruth cooled again.

Once again Blakely ran hot and cold. On one day he would rant and rage about Ruth living with Cussen, the next he was attentive and considerate. Finally the solution presented itself; they would move in together. So, in February 1955, Ruth and Blakely rented a bedsit at 44 Egerton Gardens as Mr and Mrs Ellis.

At the end of March, Ruth discovered that she was pregnant again. A few days later, on 2 April, Blakely's car, the Emperor, blew up during a race. Somehow, he determined that this was Ruth's fault and he called her a jinx. The argument grew into a violent row during which Blakely returned to being a boor. He struck Ruth hard in the stomach and as a result she lost her baby and was ill until 5 April. Things between Ruth and Blakely were growing ever worse now. They would reach a climax over the coming Easter weekend.

Blakely had always been close to his business partner, Anthony Findlater. He was also close to Findlater's wife, Carole. Indeed, some years before, Blakely had had a brief affair with Carole, and Ruth had never managed to convince herself that the relationship was finally over. It was on Friday, 8 April that this began to trouble Ruth again.

David was out drinking with both of the Findlaters in their favourite hostelry, the Magdala Tavern at the bottom of South Hill Park. As they were chatting together, Blakely mentioned that he had agreed to pick Ruth up that evening but things had been so bad between them of late that he couldn't face it. As a solution, Carole Findlater suggested that Blakely should spend the weekend with them at their flat at 29 Tanza Road. A relieved Blakely readily agreed.

At 8.30 p.m. that same evening, Ruth, concerned about Blakely, rang the Findlaters and asked if he was still with them. Anthony Findlater answered the telephone and said that he wasn't. Ruth did not believe him and asked Desmond Cussen if he would drive her to Tanza Road. Cussen agreed to do so.

When they arrived at Tanza Road, Ruth immediately saw Blakely's station wagon. This meant that he was inside and the Findlaters had lied to her. She rang the doorbell but there was no answer. Ruth then walked to a telephone box and rang the Findlaters again. This time there was an answer but as soon as Ruth spoke, the receiver was put down on her. Furious at this treatment, Ruth returned to Cussen's car, took his torch and smashed the rear window of Blakely's car. The police were called out and Ruth was warned about her behaviour and told to get off home. In fact, she only left Tanza Road at 2 a.m. the next morning.

On Saturday, 9 April, Ruth again rang the Findlaters and once again the receiver was put down on her. At her request, Cussen drove her back to Tanza Road and parked while Ruth hid in a doorway, watching the Findlaters' house. She waited most of the day, and that evening her vigilence was rewarded when she saw a party in the flat. Then, at 10 p.m. she saw Blakely leave with an attractive woman on his arm. It was the final straw for Ruth Ellis.

On Sunday, 10 April, Carole Findlater ran out of cigarettes. She also needed more drinks for the flat as the party the night before had depleted their stocks. Blakely and another friend, Chris Gunnell, said that they would drive down to the Magdala, have a couple of drinks and then bring back the supplies. The two men then went down to South Hill Park, had a nice quiet drink or two in the Magdala, and made to leave at 9.30 p.m.

Blakely's car was parked directly outside the pub. As Chris Gunnell stood by the front passenger seat, waiting to be let in, Blakely walked around to the driver's side, fumbling for his keys. It was then that a blonde woman stepped forward and shouted one word: 'David!'

Blakely probably knew that the voice belonged to Ruth Ellis and so chose to ignore it. At that, Ruth reached into her handbag and drew out a .38 Smith and Wesson revolver. Once again she called his name and this time Blakely turned. Seeing the gun, Blakely tried to run around the back of his car, using it as some sort of barrier. Ruth fired twice at his fleeing form.

In all, Ruth fired six bullets. Four of those hit David Blakely, one missed completely and the sixth ricocheted off a wall and hit a passer-by, Mrs Gladys Yule, in her thumb. Then the gun clicked again and again on the empty chamber. That was to be Ruth's one regret, for she had intended saving the last bullet for herself.

Hearing the shots, a number of customers ran out of the Magdala to see what was going on. Seeing them, Ruth asked if one of them would please call for the police. There was no real need, for the man she spoke to was an off-duty policeman, Alan Thompson, and it was he who made the arrest.

Ruth Ellis appeared at the Old Bailey on 20 June. The two-day trial was presided over by Mr Justice Havers. One might have thought that having heard all the evidence of Blakely's treatment of her, Ruth might have escaped with a verdict of manslaughter, but she showed little interest in her own defence and it is said that one simple sentence sealed her fate. Mr Christmas Humphreys, who led for the prosecution, asked Ruth, 'Mrs Ellis, when you fired the revolver at close range into the body of David Blakely, what did you intend to do?' Ruth replied, 'It is obvious when I shot him I intended to kill him.' The jury were out for just fourteen minutes to decide that she was guilty of murder.

Ruth refused to enter an appeal against her death sentence. Waiting in the condemned cell, she wrote to Blakely's mother, apologising for what she had done and adding that she was happy to repay the debt she now owed.

On Wednesday, 13 July 1955 Ruth Ellis became the last woman to be executed in Britain when she was hanged at Holloway by Albert Pierrepoint. It is said that she walked bravely to her death after taking a small tot of brandy to fortify her.

Joseph Chrimes, 1959

On Wednesday, 31 December 1958, as the country was celebrating the birth of the New Year, 60-year-old Norah Summerfield was being battered to death in her bungalow in Harlington Road, Hillingdon. Her body wasn't found until 2 January. Fortunately for the police, someone had already been talking about the crime.

Joseph Chrimes had told a friend, Michael Ulrich, that he intended breaking into the old woman's bungalow and asked him if he wanted to join in with the plan. These two then met up with Ronald Hedley Charles Pritchard, close to the bungalow, and discussed how they were going to get in. At this point Ulrich said he wanted nothing to do with it and left. Once news of Norah's death became public knowledge, it was Ulrich who went to the police and told them about the other two men.

On 6 January, two early morning police raids netted Chrimes and Pritchard, and, under questioning, each admitted stealing, among other items, a clock, a cigarette case and some spoons. As for the murder of Norah Summerfield, each blamed the other.

According to Chrimes, they had entered the bungalow quietly but then Norah appeared and Pritchard began hitting her. Pritchard in his turn said that it had been Chrimes who battered the woman with a tyre lever. He had actually tried to stop Chrimes but had been pushed out of the way. The police were satisfied that both men were involved and so both were charged with capital murder.

It should be remembered that by this time, capital punishment had been the subject of much debate and the law had been changed. Now murderers could only be hanged for certain types of crime. One of these was a murder committed in the furtherance of theft, so Chrimes and Pritchard would be facing the noose.

The two men faced their trial at the Old Bailey before Mr Justice Donovan over two days, starting on 3 March. Both pleaded guilty to breaking and entering but not guilty to murder. At the beginning of the hearing the prosecution announced that they would offer no evidence against Pritchard, who then stepped into the witness box to give evidence.

The jury retired on the second day but returned to court after one hour to ask the judge why no evidence had been offered against Pritchard. It was explained to them that this had been because it would not have been consistent with the prosecution's case that it was Chrimes who struck the fatal blows. The jury retired again and eventually found Chrimes guilty as charged. Pritchard was sent to Borstal for his part in the robbery.

An appeal was dismissed on 10 April. Just over two weeks later, on Tuesday, 28 April, Chrimes was hanged at Pentonville by Harry Allen and Royston Rickard.

Ronald Henry Marwood, 1959

On Sunday, 14 December 1958, Ronald Marwood celebrated his wedding anniversary. That evening, his wife decided to stay at home in Huntingdon Street, Islington while Ronald went out for a few drinks with some friends, including Mick Boon. By the end of the evening, Marwood had consumed ten pints.

The group of friends ended up at Gray's Dancehall on Seven Sisters Road, Holloway, and it wasn't long before a group of youths made it plain that they wanted trouble. Words were exchanged, insults thrown and then a few scuffles broke out. One of the rival group produced a small axe which he swung at Marwood's head. Marwood fell down with a small wound but soon pulled himself to his feet. Not wishing to have anything further to do with the fracas, he held a handkerchief to his head and made to walk away. It was then that he noticed his friend, Mick Boon, being spoken to by a policeman.

Perhaps it was the alcohol he had consumed, or the blow he had received to his head, or a combination of both, but Marwood took this as a sign that Boon was being picked on or singled out. Marwood decided he had to interfere.

The police officer, 23-year-old Raymond Henry Summers, gently pushed Marwood away as he remonstrated with him. Marwood did not want to be ignored in this way, and lashed out at the officer. The policeman fell to the ground and Marwood ran off.

At 5 a.m. the next morning, Marwood was one of ten men interviewed by the police. Constable Summers had not been hit, he had been stabbed, and this was now a murder investigation. Further, because a policeman had been killed, it was capital murder. At this stage, though, the police did not have enough evidence to charge anyone and Marwood, along with all the others, was released after questioning.

The matter preyed heavily on Marwood's mind and at 8 p.m. on 22 January 1959, he walked into the police station and admitted that he was the man who had struck Constable Summers. Three hours later, he was charged with murder.

Twenty-five-year-old Marwood appeared before Mr Justice Gorman at the Old Bailey on 19 March. Here he claimed that at the time he had first gone across to the policeman, he had had his hands in his pockets. The officer had punched him and he had hit back. He had not even been aware that he had a knife in his hand at the time. There was certainly no intention to kill. Nevertheless, he was found guilty and sentenced to death.

Strenuous attempts were made to obtain a reprieve for Marwood. No less than 150 Members of Parliament signed an appeal for clemency. There was also a public petition signed by thousands of people and an attempt was made to obtain permission to appeal to the House of Lords.

None of this saved Marwood and he was hanged at Pentonville on Friday, 8 May by Harry Allen and Harry Robinson.

Guenther Fritz Erwin Podola, 1959

Guenther Podola was born in Germany and after the Second World War emigrated to Canada. It was there that he started a life of crime, which ended with him being deported in 1958. In May of the following year he came to London and lived as he had in Canada, committing petty burglaries. He was not a very successful thief and soon became known to the police.

An idea of how incompetent Podola was as a thief may be gathered from a robbery he committed early in the summer of 1959. He broke into a house and then telephoned the woman who lived there and threatened to blackmail her. So it was that on Monday, 13 July, two officers, Detective Sergeant Raymond William Purdy and Detective Sergeant John Sandford were sent to arrest him.

Podola was cautioned and then arrested but at that moment broke free and made a run for it. The two officers chased him and after some minutes, cornered their fugitive in a block of flats at 105 Onslow Square.

Podola was arrested for a second time and told to stand in a corner. Momentarily distracted, neither officer saw Podola reach into his pocket and produce a gun. A shot was fired and Sergeant Purdy fell. While Sergeant Sandford ministered to his colleague, Podola made good his escape as Sergeant Purdy breathed his last.

Two days later, on 15 July, Sergeant Purdy's widow contacted the police. By now her husband's belongings had been returned to her but among them was an address book that hadn't belonged to him. The book was collected and examined and it appeared that it belonged to the wanted man, Podola. It seemed that Purdy had taken the book after Podola had been arrested the first time. All the names and addresses in the book were checked out and this eventually led to one address: the Claremont House Hotel at 95 Queen's Gate, Kensington.

Officers visited the hotel on 16 July and determined that the occupant of room 15 was Podola. The police assembled outside the door and, at a given signal, the door was smashed open. Unfortunately, Podola was right behind that door and he received a very nasty bang on the head. Taken to hospital, it was 20 July before he was fit enough to be charged with the murder of Sergeant Purdy. Podola simply replied that he had no idea whatsoever of what the police were talking about.

This book is filled with people who claimed to have no recollection of committing a particular crime. Podola now claimed that as a direct result of his arrest, he had no memory of the crime he was alleged to have committed. That was why he, in effect, faced two trials.

The first trial took place on 10 September but this was merely to decide if Podola's memory loss was genuine. Medical opinion was divided; some thought it might be genuine, others decided that he was faking. It took the jury until 23 September to decide that Podola was faking.

The very next day, 24 September, the full trial started. Podola appeared at the Old Bailey, before Mr Justice Davies, and the hearing lasted for two days. Asked how he wished to plead, Podola persisted in claiming that he could not plead as he had no memory of the crime and so could offer no defence. A not guilty plea was entered and after the jury had heard all the evidence they took just ninety minutes to decide that the prisoner was guilty.

An appeal failed and on Thursday, 5 November Podola was hanged at Wandsworth by Harry Allen and Royston Rickard.

Norman James Harris & Francis Forsyth, 1960

Saturday, 25 June 1960 saw 23-year-old Alan Jee enjoying a great night out with his fiancée, Jacqueline Herbert. The young man walked Jacqueline home, made arrangements for their next meeting and then caught a bus to his own house at Hounslow.

The bus stopped and Alan alighted. His home was just a few streets away and on the way he took a short cut down a pathway at the bottom of James Street. Even as he took his first steps down the dark alley, he noticed a group of four youths at the far end.

When Alan reached the group they started to attack him for no reason whatsoever. He was punched to the ground and then kicked repeatedly with all four of the thugs joining in. His battered form was found later that night and rushed to hospital. Unfortunately, Alan Jee died from his injuries two days later on 27 June. The police believed that the fatal blow was a particularly vicious kick to the head.

After they had finished assaulting Alan, the four thugs ran off and passed Anthony Cowell who was standing at the other end of James Street. He was able to give the police excellent descriptions of the men and his testimony put the time of the attack at 11.17 p.m.

There were many young men interviewed in connection with the brutal, senseless crime, one of which was 23-year-old Norman Harris, who was spoken to on 29 June but at this stage, there was nothing to connect him, or indeed anyone else with the murder. The police had apparently come up against a brick wall. The badly needed breakthrough came on 17 July.

It was on that date that Kevin Cullinan came forward to say that a friend of his had been boasting about the attack. He was happy to give the name of that friend to the police: 18-year-old Francis Forsyth, who was known by the nickname Flossy. Cullinan was even more useful to the police because Flossy named all the others involved in the attack. The police now had all four names.

The four men were picked up on 19 July. All four finally made statements and as a result, Norman Harris, Christopher Louis Darby, Terence Lutt and Francis Forsyth were charged with murder. Further, since the killers had rifled through Alan Jee's pockets after attacking him and stolen what little money he had, the crime was capital murder.

The trial opened at the Old Bailey on 20 September before Mr Justice Winn and would last until 26 September. All four claimed that they had been nowhere near the alley on the night in question but this was soon shown to be a lie. Alan Jee's blood had been found on Forsyth's shoes and as the trial progressed, it became clear that Lutt had struck the first blow and Forsyth had done much of the kicking.

Throughout the trial, only Darby claimed not to have used any violence upon Alan Jee and in due course, the charge against him was reduced to one of non-capital murder.

Finally, after forty minutes of deliberation the jury announced that all four were guilty.

Darby was sentenced to life imprisonment. Lutt, who at 17 was too young to hang, was to be held at Her Majesty's pleasure. The other two were sentenced to death.

On Thursday, 10 November, Harris was hanged at Pentonville by Robert Leslie Stewart and Harry Robinson. At the same time, Forsyth was hanged at Wandsworth by Harry Allen and Royston Rickard.

In fact, this event was to lead, indirectly, to two more deaths. Victor John Terry had been a close friend of Francis Forsyth and, after hearing of his execution on the radio, Terry and others went on a raid at Lloyds Bank in Durrington, near Worthing. During that raid, John Henry Pull was shot dead. Terry would later claim that he had been very angry and upset upon hearing about Forsyth and that might have affected him at the time. As a result, Terry was hanged on the same gallows as Forsyth.

Edwin Albert Arthur Bush, 1961

On Thursday, 2 March 1961 a young man walked into the antique shop at 23 Cecil Court, off Charing Cross Road, and asked the owner, Louis Meier, the price of a large dress sword in the window. Told that the item cost £15, the young man said his thanks and then went into another shop across the road and asked the owner there, Mr Roberts, what he would pay for such a sword. He was told that in order to be given an accurate price, he would have to bring the item in with him.

The next day, Friday, the same young man was back in Meier's shop, where he was greeted by the assistant, 59-year-old Elsie May Batten. The young man then stabbed Elsie, hit her with a stone vase and then stabbed her again. Satisfied that she was no longer a threat to him, he helped himself to the

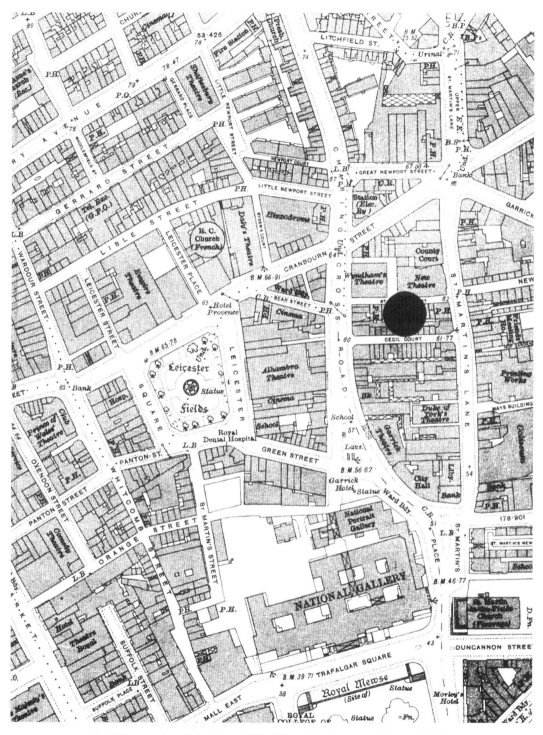

Cecil Court, where Edwin Bush killed Elsie May Batten on 3 March 1961.
(Reproduced with the permission of Alan Godfrey Maps)

dress sword and took it straight across to Mr Roberts's shop. The particular gentleman was out so the sword was left with his son, Paul Roberts, and the potential seller was told to return.

The killer, whoever he was, must have realised that if he did go back, the police would almost certainly be waiting for him. He never did return which meant that his crime had been totally without purpose. Nevertheless, he had stolen the sword after killing Elsie Batten so when he was captured, he would be facing a charge of capital murder.

Three people had seen the young man who had so covetted the sword and together they gave an excellent description to the police. The police then used a relatively new technique and formed what they called an Identikit picture of the wanted man. In fact, this was the very first time that the process was used in a murder case. So accurate was the likeness that it led rapidly to the arrest of the young man, Edwin Bush, a man of mixed race.

When he was interviewed, Bush initially denied any involvement in the murder of Elsie Batten. Faced with such evidence as his footprint in blood at the scene, his fingerprints on the sword and the fact that there was blood on his clothing, he finally admitted that he had lost his temper with Elsie after she had made some racist remark as they were haggling over the price of the sword.

Placed on trial at the Old Bailey from 12–13 May, Bush maintained that he had not intended to kill Elsie but was still found guilty. On Thursday, 6 July he earned his place in history by becoming the last man ever to be executed at Pentonville when he was hanged by Harry Allen and John Edward.

SOUTH LONDON

Ada Chard-Williams, 1900

In the early part of the twentieth century, a practice known as baby farming was quite widespread. The basic plan was simple. A woman, acting as intermediary, would find unfortunate young girls who found themselves pregnant but could not, for one reason or another, look after the child. The child would be handed over to the intermediary together with a financial consideration and the child would then be sold on to a woman who wanted a child, for even more money. The trade could be very lucrative but Ada Chard-Williams had discovered a way to make more money still.

Florence Jones was a young, unmarried woman who could just not take care of her baby daughter, whom she had named Selina Ellen. Just as it seemed that there was no way out of her predicament, she read a newspaper advertisement from someone seeking to adopt a child. Florence wrote off to the lady, a Mrs Hewetson, at the given address in Hammersmith.

In fact, the address given was not, as might be expected, a private house, but a newsagent's shop which people used as a mail drop. Further, Mrs Hewetson did not exist and the letter Florence sent was actually picked up by William Chard-Williams, Ada's husband.

A reply was sent to Florence Jones and on 31 August 1899, a meeting took place between her and 'Mrs Hewetson' who was, of course, actually Ada Chard-Williams. The meeting was at Charing Cross station and from there Florence was taken to a house in Hammersmith which Ada said was the house where baby Selina would be taken care of. Unfortunately, it was impossible to show her around now as there were workmen in there, making alterations to the place. Florence was allowed to make a note of the address and handed over £3 of the agreed £5 fee, Selina herself and some baby clothes.

Some time later, Florence Jones made the return trip to the house at Hammersmith to pay the remaining £2 but not only was there no trace of Mrs Hewetson or Selina, but no one there knew anything about the matter. Florence reported the situation to the police.

The first port of call for the police was the newsagent's where Florence's letter had been received. Here they determined the real identity of Mrs Hewetson, and that William Chard-Williams had apparently also been involved. A home address given by Ada proved to be false and it seemed that the investigation would be stalled but then, on 27 September, the body of a baby was washed up in the Thames at Battersea. The poor child was identified as Selina Jones and the date of death given as around Saturday, 23 September. Selina had been just 21 months old. She had been battered and strangled.

Eventually the Chard-Williams were traced to an address in Grove Road, Barnes, but upon arriving there, officers found the couple had moved on yet again, some time in October. However, on 5 December, the police received a letter from Ada herself. In this missive she said she had seen newspaper reports of Selina's death. She confirmed that she had been operating as a baby farmer but denied any knowledge of Selina's murder. The child had been passed on to a Mrs Smith of Croydon and it must have been her who had killed the child.

Further diligent work finally led to the tracing and arrest of Ada and her husband, William, and both were charged with murder. They appeared together at the Old Bailey before Mr Justice Ridley over two days, beginning on 16 February 1900.

Much of the evidence was circumstantial but one piece was most telling. The body of little Selina had been tied up in a parcel before being dumped into the river and that parcel was tied with string that had been knotted in a rather peculiar fashion. When Ada and William were finally arrested, their home was searched and many parcels of clothing were found. All of those parcels were tied with string knotted in the exact same unique fashion.

When the verdict came, it was that Ada was guilty of murder while William was found not guilty. The jury did add that they believed William was an accessory to murder but that charge was never subsequently persued by the police so he walked from court a free man.

On Tuesday, 6 March 1900, 24-year-old Ada Chard-Williams was hanged at Newgate by James Billington. She was executed for one murder but the authorities placed more at her door, for other children's bodies had been found in the Thames and they too had been tied in parcels where the string was knotted in a rather peculiar way.

George Henry Parker, 1901

Rhoda King took her seat in an empty third-class carriage of the 11.20 a.m. train from Southampton to London. She was travelling to the capital to visit her son in Battersea. His wife was sick and Rhoda thought she might be of some help. It was Thursday, 17 January 1901.

The train reached Eastleigh and a well-dressed young man, 23-year-old George Parker, climbed in. He sat in the corner, directly opposite Rhoda, with his back to the engine.

At Winchester, William Pearson, a 43-year-old farmer of 1 Christchurch Road, joined the train. William was heading up to London on business. For a few miles he read his newspaper, then he put it down onto his lap and allowed the gentle rhythm of the train to lull him to sleep.

In due course, the train reached Wimbledon. Rhoda King was looking out of the window at the passing houses when a loud report made her jump. Turning to look back into the carriage she saw, to her horror, that William Pearson had been shot in the head and Parker was now rifling through the man's pockets.

Looking around himself, Pearson saw that not only was there a witness in the carriage but she was now staring at him. He glared back and told her to be quiet or she would get some of the same. Whether Rhoda would have heeded the threat or not was irrelevant for as soon as the words left his lips, Parker fired at her, the bullet hitting Rhoda just underneath her left eye.

The train now pulled into Vauxhall station and Parker, seeing his chance to escape, opened the door and jumped down onto the platform. As he ran off, Rhoda King recovered a little from the shock of being wounded and followed the fleeing figure shouting, 'Stop that man!'

A number of porters and passengers gave chase and ran after Parker, towards Vauxhall Bridge. The group passed a policeman on point duty and he too joined in the chase. Finally, seeing that they were gaining on him, Parker turned into the gasworks where he was cornered and taken into custody.

Parker's trial for murder took place before Mr Justice Phillimore at the Old Bailey on 2 March. Rhoda King was the star witness. She had now made a full recovery from her own wound, though her flesh was still blackened and bruised, and the jury listened intently to her story.

Parker himself claimed that he had acted on the spur of the moment. The previous night he had been with his girlfriend, Elizabeth Rowland, in Southampton. He was unemployed and short of money so he had bought the gun with the intention of killing Elizabeth and then himself, but had been unable to go through with it. They had then travelled to Eastleigh together and he had then gone on to London, ostensibly to find work. It was on that journey, as he brooded on his lot, that he thought of robbing and killing Pearson. It was an act of impulse and no murder was intended.

The story did not move the jury and on Tuesday, 19 March, Parker was hanged at Wandsworth by James and William Billington.

Ernest Walter Wickham, 1901

Mr Edwards was in a deep sleep when a sharp cry woke him from his slumbers. Glancing across at the clock, he saw that it was 1.45 a.m. on Thursday, 27 June 1901.

Edwards got out of bed and walked to his window. Glancing down into Dalberg Road, Brixton, he saw nothing but then he turned slightly and saw a young woman appear from around the corner at Jelf Road. She was followed immediately by a man who stopped her, took out a razor and drew it across her throat. Edwards had just witnessed a murder and now ran down to the street to offer what assistance he could. It was too late; the woman was already dead and her assailant was nowhere to be seen.

At 2.15 a.m. that same morning, Ernest Wickham approached a coffee stall on the corner of Acre Lane and ordered a cup from the proprietor, Ernest Peachey. As he waited for his coffee, Wickham tried to light a cigarette but was apparently having little success. Peachey could see why there was a problem for Wickham's hands were covered in blood and this had stained and dampened the cigarettes. Naturally, Peachey asked Wickham what had happened. The bloodstained man replied that he had been fighting.

Back in Dalberg Road, the police had now identified the dead woman as 35-year-old Amy Eugenie Russell. Investigations also revealed that she had been seeing Ernest Wickham, who lived at 40 Santley Street, also in Brixton.

One other clue was a trail of blood spots, and these led diectly to the coffee stall in Acre Lane. A quick talk to Peachey gave officers the name of Ernest Wickham and confirmation that he had been heaviliy bloodstained. Officers now went directly to Wickham's lodgings in Santley Street and roused him from his bed. It was now 4 a.m. and Wickham's hands were still covered in blood. Further, his clothing and boots were also bloodstained as was a razor found nearby. Wickham was arrested and charged with murder.

The trial opened before Mr Justice Wills at the Old Bailey on 23 July. Asked how he wished to plead, Wickham replied, 'Anything you like' before his counsel formally entered a plea of not guilty.

The court was shown that Wickham and Amy had gone to the Raglan Beerhouse in Cornwall Road at midnight on 26 June. The couple argued in there and at one stage the landlord had asked Amy what the matter was. She had replied that she didn't know if life was worth living any longer, to which Wickham had retorted, 'If life is not worth living, then you will die tonight.'

The defence was that Wickham was so drunk that night that he could not form the intention to kill, but the jury did not accept that plea and he was found guilty as charged. Just over three weeks later, on Tuesday, 13 August, Wickham was hanged at Wandsworth by James and William Billington.

Charles Robert Earl, 1902

When the Pamphilon family first moved into 73 Second Avenue, Mortlake, they got on very well with their new neighbours. People were welcoming and friendly, no more so than Charles Earl, a retired baker who lived just a few doors away. Then, in the early part of 1901, for some reason all that changed.

In July of that year, Earl created a disturbance outside no. 73. So bad did things become that Mr Pamphilon had to go outside to remonstrate with Earl. A fight developed and Earl was knocked to the ground. Not one to be bested, Earl returned later and smashed all the front windows of the Pamphilon house. The police were called and Earl was arrested and charged with criminal damage and was fined at a later court appearance.

Soon after this, Earl bumped into Mrs Hibberd who lodged with the Pamphilons, and told her that he had not finished with the family yet. She tried to make the peace and suggested that Earl let the matter drop but he swore that he would have his revenge for the fine he had paid.

On the afternoon of Thursday, 6 March 1902, Earl purchased a revolver and some cartridges. That same evening he decided that the time for action had come.

Mrs Margaret Pamphilon worked in Kensington High Street and Earl was well aware of that. He visited the shop where she was an assistant and asked to see her but was told that she had gone home early that day. Earl said that he would call on her there.

That evening, the Pamphilons were entertaining friends when suddenly the doorbell rang. It was Margaret who went to the door to find that it was Earl. He asked if he could see Mr Pamphilon, but even before Margaret could reply, three quick shots rang out as Earl shouted, 'Take that!'

The rest of the family and their guests ran to the front door but Earl had already vanished. As for Margaret Pamphilon, she lay on the floor with two bullet wounds in her arm and one in her forehead. The latter bullet ensured that Margaret was quite dead.

Arrested a short time later, Earl admitted that he had shot Mrs Pamphilon and stated that the reason for it, and indeed all the trouble between them, was that he believed the Pamphilons were responsible for his wife having left him the year before. There was no truth in that belief.

Margaret Pamphilon worked in Kensington High Street at the time she was shot by Charles Earl.

Earl was tried before Mr Justice Grantham at the Old Bailey from 11–14 April. His defence was that he had been insane at the time of the shooting and so was not responsible for his actions. The jury, however, did not even bother to leave the box before announcing their guilty verdict.

Asked if he had anything to say, Earl replied, 'I shot the woman because she was twenty times worse than a common harlot and her husband knows it, and he is a bigger liar than her. I am guilty my Lord.' Just fifteen days later, on Tuesday, 29 April Earl was hanged at Wandsworth by William Billington and Henry Pierrepoint.

George William Hibbs, 1902

Miriam Jane Tye lived in Barmore Street, Battersea, and rented out rooms to working men. One of her lodgers was 40-year-old George Hibbs who moved in around the middle of 1899.

Hibbs was not the most patient of men and was known to have something of a temper. On 1 June 1902 he demonstrated this by attempting to stab Miriam after an argument. Lucky for Miriam, the blade merely passed through her clothing and did not wound her. Shocked perhaps at what he had nearly done, Hibbs apologised, was forgiven and was allowed to stay at Barmore Street.

Almost four weeks later, on Saturday, 28 June at around 11 a.m., Hibbs asked Miriam if she had a clean shirt for him. She was not perhaps in the best of moods and refused to give him a fresh shirt, claiming that he would only pawn it and spend the money on drink. Hibbs walked away, but it was plain that he was not pleased.

Later that same day, one of the other lodgers heard screams coming from the rooms Miriam occupied. Going to investigate, he found Miriam lying on the floor, bleeding copiously from a stab wound in her stomach. Close by lay a shoemaker's knife, and near that stood the form of George Hibbs, surveying what he had done.

Miriam was still alive and confirmed that it was Hibbs who had attacked her. The police and a doctor were called and as Miriam was rushed to hospital, Hibbs was taken into custody. He claimed that, despite what Miriam had said, he knew nothing about the attack upon her. He was still charged with attempted murder.

Two days after the attack, on Monday, 30 June, Miriam died from her wounds and the charge was amended to one of murder. Hibbs appeared to answer this charge at the Old Bailey on 24 July, before Mr Justice Lawrance.

Hibbs's defence was that he should only be guilty of manslaughter since he had had no intention to kill. It was an argument that had gotten out of hand, nothing more, and Miriam had been stabbed in the heat of the moment. To counter this, the prosecution gave details of the earlier attack on 1 June and it was plain that the crime was deliberate.

Sentenced to death, Hibbs continued to maintain that he had not intended to kill Miriam. However, while in the condemned cell, he did finally confess that he had stabbed Miriam deliberately because he loved her, was jealous and had been drinking. He was hanged at Wandsworth on Wednesday, 13 August 1902 by William Billington and Henry Pierrepoint.

William Brown, 1902

On a November evening in 1902, William Brown and his wife, Elizabeth, were seen drinking in two public houses in Mortlake. In the first, they seemed to be happy enough, chatting happily to each other, but in the second, they were seen arguing.

The next morning William went to a neighbour's house and told them that his wife was dead. Sure enough, when they checked, the neighbours found Elizabeth lying at the foor of her stairs, but this wasn't a simple accident for she had been very badly beaten. So terrible were her injuries that the neighbours called in the police and Brown was arrested and charged with murder. At first he denied any involvement and claimed that his wife had fallen down the stairs, but after some questioning, he admitted that he was responsible for her death.

Brown appeared before Mr Justice Bigham at the Old Bailey on 26 November. By now he had withdrawn his confession and said that his wife had been attacked by someone outside the house, had managed to drag herself inside her house and was probably trying to get upstairs to him when she died. This was soon shown to be pure invention by Brown.

A small boy named Cox testified that he had been playing in the street when he saw William Brown returning home from the pub. A couple of minutes later he heard the cry of, 'Murder!' from inside the house. Curious as to what was happening, the boy then looked into Brown's house and saw him kicking his wife at the foot of the stairs. Cox ran for help to a neighbour's house but when they returned they heard Elizabeth shout from within that she didn't need their help.

As if this wasn't enough to destroy Brown's story, medical evidence detailed her injuries, which included a broken breastbone, and stated that she could not have crawled anywhere after sustaining such injuries. In short, she was beaten and killed where she was found.

The jury took one hour to decide on Brown's guilt and he was hanged at Wandsworth on Tuesday, 16 December by Henry Pierrepoint and John Ellis.

Edgar Owen (Edwards), 1903

John William Darby ran a successful grocery business from 22 Wyndham Road, Camberwell, but it was time to move up in the world so he advertised the business for sale. He was delighted when he received a reply to his advertisement and an appointment was made to view the premises. The prospective buyer, Edgar Edwards, arranged to call on Monday, 1 December 1902.

The meeting went very well. Mr Edwards seemed to be very impressed with the business premises and set-up and in due course, asked to see the books. John Darby was more than happy to comply. He began to collect all the financial documents together while his wife, Beatrice, carrying their daughter, 10-week-old Ethel, continued to show Mr Edwards around the living area.

It was then, while he was alone with Beatrice, that Edgar Edwards took the opportunity to put his real plan into action. Taking a large window sash weight from a rolled-up newspaper he had been carrying, Edwards battered Beatrice Darby to death. He then calmly waited until John Darby appeared with the financial documents and then battered him too. Finally, he silenced the crying child by strangling her. In just a few minutes, Edgar Edwards had murdered three people.

The crime had been planned a couple of weeks before. Edwards had told his girlfriend, Sarah Summers, that he was going to buy a business for himself. He had also arranged with a friend named Goodwin for him and his wife to run the shop once he had acquired it. It was now time to put the rest of the plan into action.

The first thing to do was to hide the three bodies. These were placed, as a temporary measure, in an upstairs room, which Edwards then locked. He had already arranged to meet the Goodwins at the corner of Wyndham Road at 11.30 a.m. but was now running a little late. By the time Edwards did appear it was a few minutes after noon and he then escorted the Goodwins to the shop at no. 22. They were given their own tour of the premises but warned to stay out of the one locked room upstairs. Edwards explained this by saying that the previous owners had left some of their belongings there. The next step was to raise some money from at least some of the Darbys' possessions. A gold watch and chain were pawned, for which he received £7.

Edwards stayed with the Goodwins at 22 Wyndham Road until 10 December. Before this, he had put further plans into play. On Wednesday the 3rd he had visited an estate agent and gave a couple of false references, one of which was in the name of William Darby, and took a lease on 89 Church

Road, Leyton. That same day, the first possible problem appeared in the form of Mrs Baldwin, who was Beatrice Darby's sister. Edwards merely told her that the Darbys were staying with friends and he wasn't sure when they would be back.

Two days later, on Friday, 5 December, Edwards hired a pony and trap and began moving some of the Darbys' furniture to Church Road. Among the items he moved were some large sacks and a heavy trunk. Though no one could have guessed it at the time, they contained the bodies of the three people he had murdered. Five days after this, on 10 December, Edwards left Wyndham Road forever.

On 16 December, Edwards was seen digging a large hole in the garden of the house at 89 Church Road. By early the next morning the hole had been filled in and levelled off. It had all been so very easy. Perhaps it was time to try the whole thing again.

John Garland was also a grocer and he too had advertised his business for sale. Once again there was an interested buyer in the form of one Edgar Edwards. On 23 December, Garland was invited to Edwards's home at Church Road to discuss terms.

The discusion went well and after concluding their business, John Garland turned to leave. Immediately a heavy sash weight was brought crashing down upon his head. This was followed by more blows, but although he was badly hurt, Garland managed to stagger out into the street and escape the murderous onslaught. The alarm was raised and Edgar Edwards was arrested for assault.

The police searched the premises at Church Road and found something they simply could not understand. Garland had been battered with a sash weight but the police found two such weights, both stained with blood. This implied that there had been another, earlier attack upon someone else and it was simple inference to believe that perhaps the previous victim had not been as lucky as John Garland. The police began to investigate Edwards much more deeply.

The search at Church Road also revealed a number of pawn tickets and some of these were in the surname of Darby. Soon they were interviewing Darby's neighbours and Mrs Baldwin, who had called at Wyndham Road on 3 December. It was only a matter of time before the large hole in the garden at Church Road was mentioned and upon digging it up, the police found the three missing bodies. They had all been dismembered.

Charged with three murders, Edgar Edwards appeared at the Old Bailey before Mr Justice Wright over two days, from 12 February 1903. His only possible defence was one of insanity and he attempted to demonstrate this with his behaviour in court. He initially refused to plea and often burst into laughter as the evidence against him was detailed.

There was only one defence witness, an uncle who revealed that the prisoner's real name was actually Edgar Owen, and outlining a number of family members who had demonstrated mental health problems. It did nothing to save Edwards who was found guilty.

Asked if he had anything to say, Edwards continued with his erratic demonstrations by replying, 'No, get on with it, as quick as you like.' As the dreaded words of the death sentence were intoned, Edwards laughed and observed that it was just like being on the stage.

Just over two weeks later, on Tuesday, 3 March, Edgar Owen, also known as Edgar Edwards, was hanged at Wandsworth by William Billington and Henry Pierrepoint. His last words, spoken to the prison chaplain, were said to be, 'I've been looking forward to this.'

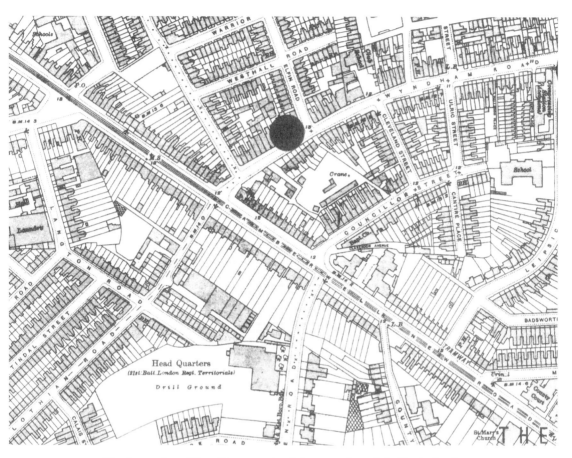

The house where Edgar Owen murdered three members of the Darby family.
(Reproduced with the permission of Alan Godfrey Maps)

William Joseph Tuffen, 1903

At around 10.30 p.m. on Thursday, 23 April 1903, William Tuffen and his wife, Caroline, were heard arguing as they walked from their local public house to their home at 12 Alexandra Road, Thames Ditton. The next morning, a visitor to Tuffen's house found him with the lodger, Mary Stone, sitting on his knee. Of Caroline, there was no sign.

On 5 May, Caroline's brother paid a visit to Alexandra Road. There was still no sign of Caroline and, not satisfied with the explanation from William Tuffen, the police were called in.

It was 7 May when the police called at Tuffen's home. There was no reply to their knocking so the door was forced open. There, in the front bedroom lay the battered body of Caroline Tuffen. She had been dead for some time, probably since she had last been seen on 23 April.

William Tuffen and Mary Stone were both missing from the house and descriptions of them were circulated. This led to their apprehension at Norbiton railway station. Both were questioned and

Mary claimed to know nothing of the murder. According to her, Tuffen had said that his wife had gone away. The police took no chances and both were now charged with murder and being an accessory after the fact.

The trial took place at Guildford on 22 July, before Mr Justice Darling. The proceedings began with an extensive discussion over just what charges should be heard. In due course, it was decided that all the charges should stand and both prisoners pleaded not guilty.

After listening to the evidence, the jury decided that Tuffen was guilty of murder while Mary Stone was guilty of being an accessory. The judge then pointed out that, according to the law, this meant that Mary was guilty of murder too and both were sentenced to death.

Eventually, Mary Stone's sentence was commuted to one of life imprisonment. Tuffen was not so lucky and was hanged at Wandsworth on Tuesday, 11 August by Henry Pierrepoint and John Ellis.

Edward Harrison, 1905

Edward Harrison was a violent man and often this violence manifested itself in attacks upon his long-suffering wife. Finally, in September 1904, she decided that the latest attack upon her was the last straw. She had him summonsed for assault and he was sentenced to pay 20s or face ten days in prison. Since Harrison was unable to pay, he was sent to jail.

Obviously this would not change Harrison and there could be little doubt that future assaults would follow once he was released. So it was that Harrison's married daughter, Elizabeth Jane Rickus, found fresh lodgings for her mother. If Harrison couldn't find her, he couldn't assault her anymore.

Upon his release, Harrison found employment as a potman at a pub in Deptford. Soon after this he called on Elizabeth and asked her if she knew where her mother was staying now. Elizabeth lied and said she had no idea. At that Harrison fell to his knees and rather melodramtically said that if he did not find her, there would be a murder.

On Thursday, 26 January 1905, Harrison again made threats towards his daughter and, when later that same day, Elizabeth's body was found in her kitchen, her throat cut so deeply that her head was almost severed, Harrison was the obvious suspect. He was arrested that evening and without being questioned, volunteered the information that he had killed Elizabeth and was pleased with what he had done.

Harrison's trial took place before Mr Justice Darling at the Old Bailey on 10 February, Harrison claiming that the crime was one of self-defence. He admitted he had gone to see his daughter again, they had argued and it had been her who had picked up a knife and rushed at him. They had grappled, the weapon had fallen to the floor and he saw that her throat had been accidentally slashed. The problem with this defence was that Harrison had been heard to issue threats more than once. Further, he had practically bragged about his crime to the police.

Found guilty, Harrison was hanged at Wandsworth on Tuesday, 28 February by John Billington and Henry Pierrepoint. His last words, as the trap was sprung, were, 'I did it'.

Alfred Stratton & Albert Ernest Stratton, 1905

William Jones arrived for work at the paint store at 34 High Street, Deptford, as usual on the morning of Monday, 27 March 1905, but was surprised to find the premises still securely locked. A resourceful soul, William then went for Mr Chapman who actually owned the building and told him that he couldn't raise Thomas Farrow, who ran the shop, or his wife Ann.

Taking his own keys, Mr Chapman opened up no. 34 and found that Thomas Farrow lay in the back room and had been battered to death. His wife was upstairs in the bedroom. She too had been battered but was still alive. Medical help and the police were immediately summoned.

It was plain that the motive for the crime had been one of robbery. A cash box had been forced open and the contents stolen. The thief had left a clue, though, a clear bloody fingerprint on one side of the broken box. At this time, fingerprinting was still a relatively new science and the evidence it provided had never been tested in a murder case.

An appeal for witnesses brought some interesting information. Ellen Stanton had seen two men running down Deptford High Street at 7.15 a.m. and was able to give excellent descriptions to the police. These descriptions matched ones given by Henry Littlefield who said he had seen two men behaving strangely near the shop. Furthermore, he was able to name the two men as brothers Alfred and Albert Stratton.

A check on the addresses used by the two brothers showed that they had left their lodgings and gone to ground. The police did, however, trace Alfred's girlfriend, Mary Cromerty, who lived at 23 Brookmill Road. She confirmed that Alfred had left the house early on the morning of the murder and when he returned had told her that if anyone asked, she was to say he had been home all night.

When Albert's landlady was interviewed, she could only tell the police that she had once seen two silk stockings cut down to make masks. Two such masks had been found at the murder scene. The evidence against the Strattons was mouting up.

On Friday, 31 March, Ann Farrow died from her injuries, making this a double murder investigation. Four days later, on 3 April, Alfred was arrested in a public house. The next day, 4 April, his brother Albert was picked up in Stepney. Both were now fingerprinted and the bloody print found on the cash box was shown to match Alfred's right thumb.

The Stratton brothers appeared before Mr Justice Channell at the Old Bailey over two days, commencing on 5 May. Both pleaded not guilty but the fingerprint evidence was overwhelming. Consequently, on Tuesday, 23 May, the Strattons were hanged together at Wandsworth by John Billington, Henry Pierrepoint and John Ellis.

Alfred John Heal, 1905

In 1905, Alfred Heal lived at 83 Westmacott Street, Camerberwell, and he fell head over heels in love with Ellen Maria Goodspeed who lived next door at no. 81. The relationship between them developed rapidly and by April, an engagement had been announced. The couple were due to wed on Easter Monday. Unfortunately, soon after this Heal lost his job and the wedding had to be postponed.

There was one other problem for Heal to worry about. Before Ellen had started walking out with him, she had been seeing a gentleman named Wyndham Homes and wherever Heal and Ellen went, Homes seemed to be there too. In the pub, in the park, even walking down the street, there were constant sightings of Homes. This began to tell on an already worried Heal who began to think that not only had Ellen and Homes been friends, but that they had been much more. Indeed, Heal convinced himself that Ellen had given her virginity to Homes.

This jealousy caused more than one argument and these came to a head on Thursday, 27 April. Heal went out alone at 8 p.m. leaving Ellen with his father, mother and sister. He did not return until after 9 p.m.

At 9.30 p.m. Heal's father, William, retired to bed. At 10 p.m. he was followed by his wife, Ellen Heal and after another half hour, Heal's sister, Nellie, also went up to her room. This left Heal and Ellen Goodspeed alone downstairs at no. 81.

At 11 p.m., the entire household was roused by a blood-curdling scream. Even before Mr and Mrs Heal could rouse themselves from their bed, Ellen ran into their room, blood pouring from a deep wound in her throat. She was rushed to hospital but died from her injuries on Sunday, 7 May. Heal, previously charged with attempted murder, now faced the hangman's noose.

Heal faced his trial at the Old Bailey before Mr Justice Grantham on 31 May. Here it was shown that poor Ellen would not have lived into old age whatever happened. She had been suffering from a kidney disease and would have died within ten years. Further evidence showed that the crime had been totally uneccessary as Ellen was also still a virgin.

Sentenced to death for murder, 22-year-old Heal was hanged at Wandsworth on Tuesday, 20 June by John Billington and John Ellis.

Frederick Reynolds, 1906

Frederick Reynolds had been seeing Sophie Lovell for around eighteen months but Sophie's mother did not approve of her choice of this man. She knew he was a very jealous man and felt he would get her daughter into trouble. Even when Mrs Lovell died in August 1906, her last request had been that Sophie give up Reynolds.

Soon after this, Sophie decided to honour her mother's wishes, especially as she also had her own doubts about the relationship. At first, Reynolds wasn't too upset. It was surely just a matter of time before Sophie came to her senses and started seeing him again. Then, to his dismay, Sophie met Henry Lambourne.

The two met on Saturday, 8 September 1906 and there was an instant attraction between them. When Henry asked if he might see Sophie again the next day, she readily agreed. That meeting also went swimmingly and arrangements were made to meet up the next night too.

At 9.30 p.m. on Monday the 10th, Henry and Sophie were enjoying a quiet stroll down Willow Walk in Bermondsey when they noticed that someone was following them. Although Henry did not recognise

Mr Justice Laurence, who sentenced Frederick Reynolds to death for the murder of Sophie Lovell.

the man, Sophie did; it was Reynolds. She told Henry who he was and suggested they ignore him, but it was clear that Reynolds was spoiling for some sort of confrontation. Then, just as the young couple turned their backs to walk away, Reynolds sprang forward and struck Sophie on the back of her head.

As Sophie turned back, two more blows hit home and she fell to the ground. Reynolds was then upon her, drawing a knife from his pocket. Even before Henry Lambourne could assist, Sophie's throat had been cut.

Henry called out for assistance and two men nearby, Thomas Jones and William Fisher, moved forward to help but Reynolds managed to escape. He was not arrested until 10.15 p.m. when he gave himself up and made a full confession to what he had done.

The trial took place before Mr Justice Lawrence at the Old Bailey on 25 October, where Reynolds pleaded guilty. Given time to consider his plea, Reynolds returned to court to say that he was guilty of killing Sophie but had not intended murder and was only guilty of manslaughter. Nevertheless, it took the jury just two minutes to decide that this was murder and on Tuesday, 13 November, Reynolds was hanged at Wandsworth by Henry Pierrepoint and John Ellis.

Richard Clifford Brinkley, 1907

In early 1907, there were four people living at 32 Churchill Road, Croydon. Fifty-five-year-old Richard Beck was the head of the family and he lived with his wife, Anne Elizabeth and their two daughters, 21-year-old Daisy Kathleen and 19-year-old Hilda May. Then, on Friday, 5 April, the family took in a lodger, Reginald Parker. Things were fine until the evening of Saturday, 20 April.

The Beck family had all been out that evening and it was quite late by the time they all sat together in the front room, where Daisy noticed two bottles of ale and one of stout on the table. Some supper was made and afterwards, Hilda retired for the night. It was then that Richard Beck poured some of the stout into two glasses, one for himself and one for his wife. Daisy too was offered a sip, from her father's glass. Immediately it became clear that there was something very wrong.

Anne ran into the kitchen, groaning loudly. Daisy collapsed onto the settee, fighting for breath. At first Richard seemed to be unaffected but after a minute or two, he too began gasping for air. Their cries for help brought Hilda rushing back downstairs. She ran for a neighbour who called the doctor but by the early hours of the next morning, Richard and Anne Beck were dead. Daisy had to be taken to hospital and eventually made a full recovery, finally being discharged on 24 April.

The cause of the tragedy was soon determined. Dr William Dempster suspected some form of poisoning and examined the three bottles on the table. The two bottles of ale appeared to be fine but the third one, the stout, smelled strongly of bitter almonds, the tell-tale aroma of cyanide. The police were now investigating a double murder.

Two facts immediately came to light. The room where the bottles had been placed was actually occupied by the lodger, Parker, and curiously, he had arranged to spend that particular evening elsewhere. So, in the early hours of 21 April, officers called at 269 Brighton Road, where Parker had slept on the fateful night. He in turn told officers about a man who might be responsible for the poisoning: Richard Brinkley.

According to Parker, he and Brinkley were business associates and had known each other for about three years. A few days ago, Brinkley had asked Parker if he might find a guard dog for him and so, at around 8 p.m. on 20 April, Parker had taken a vicious looking bulldog back to Churchill Road. Around an hour later Brinkley called, carrying with him a bottle of Oatmeal Stout. Parker had thought this rather strange at the time since Brinkley was a life-long teetotaller.

A glass was produced and Brinkley drank down some of the stout before pouring some more for Parker. At that point Brinkley had asked for a glass of water and Parker briefly left the room to fetch one. Later still, the two men went for a walk and Brinkley agreed to buy the bulldog for £5.

The inference of this story was that it had been Brinkley who had poisoned the bottle of stout while Parker was out of the room. No motive for this could be suggested as yet but it was decided to arrest Brinkley on suspicion of murder. He was picked up at around midnight on 21 April and charged with murder the following day.

Brinkley appeared before Mr Justice Bigham at Guildford on 22 July, the case lasting until 25 July, and now, finally, a possible motive was outlined.

Brinkley, it seemed, had become rather close to a widow, Johanna Maria Louisa Blume, and she had argued with her family and wanted to leave all her property to him. According to Parker, Brinkley had, towards the end of 1906, asked him to sign a piece of paper that was something to do with an outing Brinkley was planning and, rather naively, Parker signed it without reading through it. The suggestion was that Brinkley had forged the will and obtained Parker's signature upon it as a witness by deception. Mrs Blume had since died and the relatives were contesting the will. If Parker were spoken to about the matter, the deception would come to light, so therefore Parker had to be eliminated. He had been the intended victim and the Beck family had been poisoned by accident.

The case against Brinkley appeared to be strong. It was shown that he had access to Prussic acid, a man fitting his description had been seen buying the stout, a handwriting expert said that he thought Mrs Blume's signature on the will did not appear to be genuine, and he now seemed to have a motive for killing Parker. There were, however, problems with this 'cast-iron' case.

Brinkley said that Parker had not been deceived into signing the will and had been offered £100 for doing so, once the old woman died. Parker denied this but his own wife testified that he had told her that he was due £100 for a document he had witnessed.

The beer-shop assistant who identified Brinkley as the purchaser of the stout was John Holden, who added that there were two other customers in the shop at the time. These two customers were traced and both denied seeing Brinkley, thought they did remember each other.

Despite these contradictions, the jury found that there was a strong enough case and Brinkley was sentenced to death. He was hanged at Wandsworth on Tuesday, 13 August by Henry Pierrepoint and John Ellis.

Julius Wammer, 1909

Benjamin Vanderluis had had a good night. Business at his fish and chip shop on Waterloo Road had been brisk and now, yet again, there were customers waiting to be served. Even as the shop emptied, there was but a few moments delay before a man and three women entered and Benjamin recognised one of the women as 24-year-old Cissie Archer, a regular customer.

Cissie was looking at a display of crabs when suddenly, the man who had come in with her drew out a revolver and shot her. Cissie was badly hurt but managed to run out of the shop. She reached the corner of Waterloo Road and Stamford Street before she collapsed and died. Her assailant, meanwhile, had aimed his gun at one of the other women but his shot missed her and struck Benjamin in his hand. A third shot was attempted but the gun jammed and at this point the man was jumped upon by John Lush and held until the police arrived.

The shooter was identified as Julius Wammer and he expressed regret over shooting Benjamin Vanderluis. He showed no remorse, though, over killing Cissie claiming that she and the other woman had stolen a gold chain from his lodgings at the Trafalgar Hotel in York Road.

Wammer appeared at the Old Bailey before the Lord Chief Justice, Lord Alverstone, on 21 July, his defence being that he had been drinking so much that the alcohol had affected his mind and he could not have formed the intention to kill. The jury did not accept his explanation and on Tuesday, 10 August, Wammer was hanged at Wandsworth by Henry Pierrepoint and William Willis.

The corner of Waterloo Road and Stamford Street where Cissie Archer died after being shot by Julius Wammer.

Thomas William Jesshope, 1910

On Sunday, 27 March 1910, Edward John Mills started work at the Empire Music Hall on Coldharbour Lane, Camberwell. The following day, Monday the 28th, Mills, who still did not know his way around the premises, was being shown how to lock the building up by John Healey, a carpenter and stagehand. At one point, Mills was a few feet behind Healey so he did not see the hidden figure leap out of the shadows and plunge a knife deep into Healey's left side.

Healey called out, 'Help me Charlie, he's stabbed me!' Charles Gray, the hall keeper, rushed to his aid. As Gray went to fetch a glass of water, he noticed, near the stage door, a face he recognised: Thomas Jesshope, a fireman who had recently been sacked. Asked if he had anything to do with the stabbing, Jesshope replied, 'Yes' and then to emphasise his words, he drew out a knife and added, 'This is the blade I've done it with.'

The Empire Music Hall, where Thomas Jesshope murdered John Healey on 27 March 1910.

Sergeant Thomas Curtis was on duty in Coldharbour Lane when Charles Gray approached him and told him what had happened. Going to the theatre, Curtis saw that Jesshope had made no attempt to escape and was simply standing at the stage door, waiting to be arrested. He was taken into custody and charged with murder.

The trial took place on 29 April before Mr Justice Lawrence at the Old Bailey, where Jesshope's defence was that he had been insane at the time of the attack. Here it was explaind that Jesshope had worked at the Hall for about a year and often turned up for work suffering from the effects of drink.

On Friday, 25 March, William Nutt, the stage manager, had warned him because he appeared to be tipsy. Jeshope ignored that warning because by 10.20 p.m. that same night he was incapable through drink and the matter was reported to Percy Ford, the manager. When, the next night, Jesshope was again found drunk, he was dismissed on the spot.

The next day, at 11 a.m., Jesshope was outside the Hall when Charles Gray turned up for work. Jesshope asked after Healey and was told that he was inside, cleaning the stage. Jesshope replied that he would wait for him one night instead. This seemed to show that the crime was totally premeditated and so the jury returned a guilty verdict.

A subsequent appeal was dismissed and on Wednesday, 25 May, Jesshope was hanged at Wandsworth by Henry Pierrepoint and William Willis.

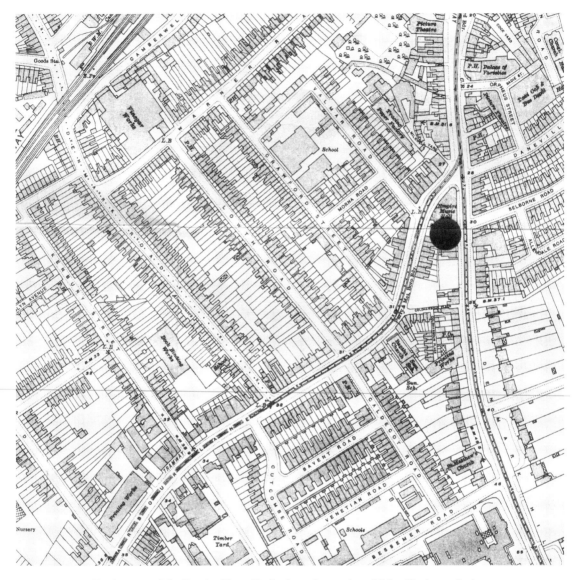

The location of the Empire Music Hall where the murder of John Healey took place.
(Reproduced with the permission of Alan Godfrey Maps)

Frederick Henry Thomas, 1911

At the close of the Edwardian era, ladies in Britain were expected to behave in a certain rather demure way. This was certainly not true of Harriett Ann Eckhardt. She liked men and men liked her. By 1907 she had married for a second time, her new husband being Ernest Eckhardt who worked on board a ship and spent a good deal of time away from the family home at Rothbury Terrace, Azof Street, Greenwich. Harriett saw an opportunity and, while still married to Ernest, took a lover in the form of Frederick Thomas.

It didn't take Ernest long to find out that his wife was seeing another man and on his return from a voyage in April 1911, he told her that she had to stop seeing Thomas. Harriett agreed readily but just as soon as Ernest was back on his ship, Thomas was calling at the house again. Once again Ernest found out the truth; that Harriett had ignored his instructions. It was time for more drastic action if this affair was to be stopped.

Ernest had a good friend named Bruno Koch who lived in Limehouse. On Wednesday, 16 August, Koch was invited to spend the evening with Ernest and Harriett. Later that night, when Ernest returned to his ship, he left Koch at home with Harriett and even suggested that he take her to the Elephant and Castle Theatre.

It is possible that Ernest believed that he could trust Koch and that nothing would develop between him and Harriett. If that was the case then he was very much mistaken for that night, Koch shared Harriett's bed. Ernest had apparently only succeeded in replacing one lover with another.

Koch stayed with Harriett for the next two nights too but now there was a problem. Frederick Thomas was due to call on Harriett and she couldn't allow this so she sent him a note in which she wrote that Ernest had not gone away after all and he shouldn't call at the house. Thomas was immediately suspicious. He knew Harriett very well and suspected that she might have found herself another lover. He decided to visit the house anyway and see for himself.

At some time between 1 a.m. and 2 a.m. on Saturday, 19 August, there was a knock on the front door of Harriett's house. Koch hid in the kitchen while Harriett went to see who it was. Koch heard the visitor, whom he could tell was male, running through various rooms of the house. Finally it went quiet and Koch waited for Harriett to come and get him.

It was 7 a.m. before Koch gathered the courage to venture from his hiding place. He found Harriett's body at the foot of the stairs, her throat cut and a postcard near the body mentioning him and Harriett.

The police found Ernest Eckhardt on board his ship and told him of the death of his wife. He in turn suggested the name of a possible suspect: Frederick Thomas. When Thomas was interviewed, he readily admitted that he had killed Harriett. He even told the police to go to his home at 245 Brunswick Road, Poplar, where they would find a full explanation. Sure enough, officers found two letters. The first was the note from Harriett saying her husband had not gone away and the other was a full written confession to her murder.

Arrested and placed in the police cells, Thomas then calmly drew a razor from his boot and slashed his own throat. He was rushed to hospital where prompt medical treatment saved his life.

At his trial before Mr Justice Scrutton at the Old Bailey on 16 October, Thomas pleaded not guilty by reason of insanity but the jury still found him guilty as charged.

On Wednesday, 15 November Thomas was hanged at Wandsworth by John Ellis and Thomas Pierrepoint.

Sargent Philp, 1912

Rose Philp had been married to her husband, Sargent for eleven years and had borne him six children. They were a happy enough family until Philp lost his right eye in an accident at work. Employees had little legal protection in those days and as a result, Sargent was dismissed. The family now found themselves in financial trouble.

So bad did things become that in June 1912, Rose was forced to move in with her sister, Alice Hawkins, at 31 Morby Road, Old Kent Road. She took the youngest child with her, leaving the rest with Philp.

Things did not improve and on 8 July, Rose took out a separation order. Philp tried desperately to get her to return to him but it was no use. As far as Rose was concerned, the relationship was finally over. Exactly one week later, on 15 July, Philp appeared at Alice Hawkins's house and left the other children with his wife.

On 25 July, Philp was back again. Rose wasn't in at the time but Alice Hawkins and her mother, Mrs Keighley, were there and they heard Philp say that he would rather swing than pay any money under the separation order.

The next day, Friday, 26 July, Philp returned to Morby Road and this time Rose was in the house. Philp was excited and announced that he had found himself a new job and was due to start on the following Monday. Surely Rose would return to him now and they could be happy again. Rose simply replied that she would only think of returning when he had a house for them. That was the final blow for Philp. He drew a knife and stabbed Rose.

Rose was hurt but she managed to push past Philp and ran to Mary Hollis's house at no. 31. It was there, in the kitchen, that Philp caught up with her and cut her throat.

Seeing what he had done, Philp turned the knife upon himself and was about to slash his own throat but two other neighbours, Thomas John Langridge from no. 40 and John Reeves from no. 29, stopped him and took the knife from him.

Philp appeared before Mr Justice Lush at the Old Bailey on 12 September. It was a short hearing and Philp was soon adjudged to be guilty. Just nineteen days later, on Tuesday, 1 October, Sargent Philp was hanged at Wandsworth by John Ellis and Thomas Pierrepoint.

George Marshall, 1915

The house at 70 Mina Road, Walworth, was owned by Thomas Warner and he had taken in a number of lodgers. The latest to arrive, in the summer of 1914, was George Marshall.

Marshall had been introduced to Thomas by yet another lodger, Alice Anderson. She was a friendly woman and even cooked Marshall's meals for him and kept his room clean. Unfortunately, Marshall took these simple acts of kindness as meaning that Alice belonged to him.

On the evening of Saturday, 3 July 1915, Warner visited the Duke of York pub in Bagshot Street. Marshall worked there as a barman and as he served Warner, he asked if he had seen Alice at all. Warner replied that he had not, finished his drink, returned home and retired to his bed at 10.20 p.m.

Warner was having problems getting off to sleep so he was still awake at 11 p.m. when he heard Marshall come in. Just ten minutes later Warner heard Marshall shout, 'Mr Warner, I want you up here a minute!'

Sighing heavily, Warner pulled on his slippers and went up to Marshall's room. At that moment, Alice walked in and Marshall pointed out two depressions in his bed and claimed that while he had been out working, Alice had been entertaining someone in his room. Warner said that it was nothing to do with him, and returned to his own room.

Ten minutes later a loud thumping noise rang through the house. Warner again got up to investigate and this time found Alice Anderson at the foot of the stairs, her throat cut from ear to ear.

The police were called and Constable Frederick Butler duly attended. Asked if he had anything to do with the death of Alice, Marshall replied, 'I 'ain't half give her a gash. I meant to do it, the wicked cow. I'll give her make this place a knocking shop.'

Charged with murder, Marshall appeared before Mr Justice Avory at the Old Bailey on 20 July, where he pleaded provocation, saying that he had killed Alice during the heat of an argument. This was discounted by the prosecution who showed that Alice had been relaxing on her own bed when she had been attacked.

Found guilty, Marshall was hanged at Wandsworth on Tuesday, 17 August by John Ellis and George Brown.

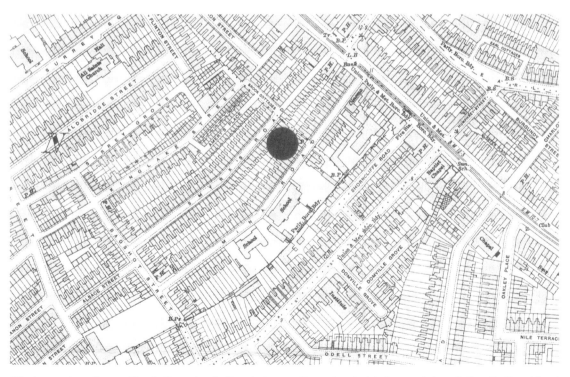

The house where George Marshall murdered Alice Anderson. (Reproduced with the permission of Alan Godfrey Maps)

Arthur Harold Victor Stamrowsky, 1918

On the night of Monday, 12 November 1917, the Tighe family retired to their beds at Winkfield Lodge, Parkside, Wimbledon at 11.30 p.m. The head of the house, Captain Edward Kenrick Bunbury Tighe suffered from asthma so he slept in a separate bedroom to his wife.

The next morning, the maid was passing Captain Tighe's room when she heard a groaning noise from within. Going to investigate, she found that the captain had been brutally battered with a poker.

Police investigations showed that someone had gained entry to Winkfield Lodge by using an open window at the back. The poker had been taken from a fire-set belonging to the house. As for any missing items, all that had been taken was an old oxidised watch and a mackintosh. It was surmised that a thief had gained entrance, been disturbed by the captain, had struck out with the poker and then taken the coat to hide some bloodstains.

Five days after the attack, on 17 November, Captain Tighe died from his injuries. This was now a case of murder.

Almost one month later, on 11 December, a pawnbroker contacted the police to say that he had had a customer who had wanted to pawn some items that might well be stolen property. The police staked out the premises and waited. Later the same day the man returned and was found to be carrying some £200 worth of silver plate that had been stolen from a house in Streatham. He was arrested and identified himself as Arthur de Stamir, whose real name was Stamrowsky.

A routine search of Stamrowsky's rooms revealed other stolen items and among them was an old oxidised watch and a raincoat. These were shown to have been taken from Winkfield Lodge and so a charge of murder was added to those of robbery and burglary.

Stamrowsky appeared before Mr Justice Darling at the Old Bailey on 10 January 1918 and the defence was that it had been another man who had attacked and killed Captain Tighe.

According to Stamrowsky, he had met a man named Reginald Fisher, an Australian soldier, on 7 November. The two men had discussed and planned a robbery and had gone to Winkfield Lodge on the 12th. After searching the ground floor rooms, Fisher had picked up a poker to force any doors open. They had then gone upstairs into Tighe's room but he had woken. Scared that he might raise the alarm, Fisher had lashed out with the poker.

The prosecution doubted that Fisher even existed but even if he had, the two men had gone to commit a robbery together and a man had been killed. In the eyes of the law both men would be equally guilty of murder. The jury agreed and Stamrowsky was duly sentenced to death.

On Tuesday, 12 February, 26-year-old Stamrowsky was hanged at Wandsworth by John Ellis and George Brown.

Joseph Jones, 1918

On Thursday, 8 November 1917, a Canadian soldier, John Mackinlay, met up with a countryman, Oliver Gilbert Imlay, at the YMCA on Waterloo Road. The two men went for a drink together where

Parkside, Wimbledon, where Captain Tighe was battered to death by Arthur Stamrowsky.

they fell into conversation with an Australian soldier. The three men later left the pub together and close to Waterloo Bridge, the Australian spotted another couple of friends.

In due course, all five men began talking and the Canadians told them where they were staying. The Australians told them they knew of somewhere much better and volunteered to show them. The group walked off together but then, passing down an alley-way called Valentine Place, off the Blackfriars Road, Mackinlay heard a thump. Turning around, he saw that Imlay was on the ground. Before he could find out what was wrong, Mackinlay was suddenly attacked and rendered unconscious.

Both Mackinlay and Imlay were badly hurt but while Mackinlay would recover from his injuries, Imlay was not as fortunate and died three days later, on 11 November. The search was on for the two Australian soldiers.

The first to be picked up was Ernest Edward Sharp who was arrested as a deserter on 23 November. When questioned about going AWOL, he said he wished to make a statement about something else and went on to say that in October he had met up with two men, Thomas Vincent Maguire and Joseph Jones. On 8 November he had been talking to Maguire and Jones on Waterloo Bridge. There were two Canadian soldiers there and Jones had told them about some place they might be able to stay.

When they reached Blackfriars Road, Jones had battered one of the soldiers, Imlay, with a trucheon and then rifled through his pockets. Meanwhile, it had been Maguire who attacked the other soldier. The other two were now traced and then all three men were arrested and charged with murder.

The trial opened before Mr Justice Darling at the Old Bailey on 14 January 1918 and lasted for two days. At the very beginning it was announced that Sharp would give evidence against the other two and as a consequence, no evidence was given against him on the murder charge. Instead, he pleaded guilty to robbery for which he received seven years' imprisonment.

The other two men claimed that they had acted in self-defence but Sharp's testimony meant that both were found guilty of robbery with violence and Jones was also found guilty of murder. Maguire received a term of ten years' imprisonment and Jones was sentenced to death.

At his appeal, Jones claimed that since he had been convicted on the evidence of accomplices who had been sent to jail, his conviction was unsafe. The appeal court disagreed and the sentence was confirmed. As a result, on Thursday, 21 February, Jones was hanged at Wandsworth by John Ellis and William Willis.

Marks Goodmacher, 1920

Marks Goodmacher adored his daughter, Fanny. When she married and changed her surname to Zetoun, he welcomed her and her new husband back to his home and for some time, the arrangement worked perfectly. Eventually, though, Goodmacher took to interfering rather too much, telling his daughter how a good Jewish home should be run and finding fault with much of what she did. Finally, Fanny said she had had enough and announced that she and her husband were moving out to a place of their own.

Goodmacher tried hard, perhaps too hard, to get Fanny to move back in with him and this only served to widen the rift between them. Still, the Day of Atonement was fast approaching and Goodmacher was absolutely sure that Fanny would take the opportunity of that holy day to fix things between them.

The Day of Atonement passed and Fanny did not even contact her father, let alone apologise for any slight nor to try to mend things. Goodmacher decided that more drastic action was now called for.

On Thursday, 23 September, Mr Zetoun returned home from work to find that there was no sign of his wife. Going upstairs to their bedroom, he found Fanny lying dead across the bed, a gaping wound in her throat. The culprit was easy to determine for there lay Marks Goodmacher, spread-eagled across his daughter, his own throat having also been cut.

Goodmacher recovered from his self-inflicted wound and was able to appear before Mr Justice Darling at the Old Bailey on 18 November. The verdict was a formality and on 30 December, Goodmacher was hanged at Pentonville by William Willis and Robert Baxter.

Frederick William Maximillian Jesse, 1923

Mabel Edmunds had not been seen for some days. Mabel ran a boarding house at 156 York Road, Lambeth, and some of her guests were now growing a little concerned for her. They even asked one of the residents, Frederick Jesse, who also happened to be Mabel's nephew, if he knew anything. His explanation that Mabel had gone to visit friends in Sheerness did not seem to ring true.

On 23 July 1923, a policeman patrolling his beat found an envelope floating in the Thames. It was found to contain Mabel's marriage certificate and a letter. Some of the lodgers, including Jesse, were now interviewed but no new information was forthcoming.

Five days later, on 28 July, a handwritten note was pushed through the letterbox at York Road. This note purported to be from Mabel's estranged husband and was a full confession to Mabel's murder. Apparently, her husband had killed her, and then drowned himself in the Thames. The note was passed on to the police who decided that it was time to search 156 York Road.

Th search took place on 30 July and there, in one of the rooms upstairs, officers found Mabel's body. She had been strangled and lay on her bed but her killer had then cut off her legs and left them on a table nearby. All the occupants of the house were questioned again and when it came to Jesse's turn, he admitted that he was the killer.

Jesse claimed that he owed his aunt some money and she was constantly nagging him to repay it. On Saturday, 21 July she had nagged him again. To escape this, he had gone to his own room but she had followed him there and struck out at him. She had even thrown some caustic soda over him and he had lashed out in self-defence. They had struggled and fell on the bed together.

At that point, Jesse's mind went blank and he had no recollection of actually strangling her. Scared for his own safety, he decided to cut up the body before dumping it but lost his nerve after he had taken the legs off.

Jesse faced his trial at the Old Bailey before Mr Justice Swift over two days, commencing on 17 September. The jury took just thirty-five minutes to decide that Jesse had known full well what he was doing and he was sentenced to death. An appeal was entered and dismissed and on Thursday, 1 November, Jesse was hanged at Wandsworth by John Ellis and Robert Baxter.

Frederick Stephen Fuller & James Murphy, 1927

Forty-two-year-old James Staunton was a night watchman employed to guard a building site in Brancaster Lane, Sanderstead, Purley. On the night of Saturday, 14 May 1927, someone raided the yard and stole a quantity of lead and brass. More importantly, the thief or thieves battered Staunton and left him unconscious.

The police appealed for witnesses and very soon people came forward who reported seeing a grey Ford van, registration KX 871, close by the yard. This van was traced to three men: Joseph Torch, James Cornelius Pearson and Hedley Albert McCormack. These three were picked up and all charged with robbery and assault but it soon became clear that all had alibis and the van had nothing to do with the robbery. All three were then released.

On 17 May, James Staunton died from his injuries and by now enquiries had shifted to a young labourer from the building site who had not turn up for work after the attack. Frederick Fuller was married, with six children and another on the way. He was now missing from home. Eventually he was traced to Doncaster where, on 2 May, he was picked up with a friend of his, James Murphy, at the Bridge Hotel.

Brought back to London, both men were now questioned about the robbery and murder. Both agreed that they had attacked Staunton but denied murder. They said that they had gone to the yard, where a fight took place between them and Staunton, who fell back and hit his head. They then rifled his pockets and took what money he had.

Fuller and Murphy appeared before Mr Justice Rowlatt at the Old Bailey on 5 July, where it was explained to the jury that if the two prisoners had gone to the yard intending to steal and had killed Staunton in the process, then they were guilty of murder. If, however, the robbery had followed a clean fist-fight, then they could be found guilty of manslaughter.

In the event, the jury decided that the robbery came first and so the two were guilty of murder. An appeal also failed and on Wednesday, 3 August, Fuller and Murphy were hanged side by side at Wandsworth by Robert Baxter and three assistants: Lionel Mann, Henry Pollard and Thomas Phillips. While he had been waiting in the condemned cell, Fuller's wife had given birth to their seventh child, a girl.

Sidney Bernard Goulter, 1928

Charles Hicks worked as a park-keeper in Richmond. On the morning of Wednesday, 5 October 1927, he was walking through the grounds when he spotted a bundle beneath some bushes, close by the Robin Hood gate. Hicks's first thought was that someone had dumped some rubbish illegally but closer inspection revealed that the bundle was the battered and strangled body of a woman.

A police search of the surrounding area revealed a handbag and this led to the name Constance Gertrude Oliver of Falcon Grove, Battersea. There were signs of a struggle close to where the body had been found, along with an umbrella broken into four pieces. There were also signs that the killer had tried to burn the body.

Constance's parents confirmed that she had left home at 7.30 p.m. on Sunday, 2 October to meet Sidney Goulter. They were also able to give an address for Goulter: 24 Bockhampton Road, Kingston-upon-Thames. A visit to that address revealed that Goulter had not been at home since 1 October.

By coincidence, Goulter visited his parents' house again that same day, 5 October, only to be told that the police wished to speak to him. He made no comment and left the house to catch a bus. The police were waiting outside and Goulter was arrested.

When he was interviewed, Goulter explained that he had started work as an assistant at a coffee stall in Falcon Road, Battersea, in August. Constance had worked nearby and they had become friendly and agreed to meet up on Sunday, 2 October. They met as arranged and caught a bus to Richmond Park where they sat down together on a bench.

They talked for a time and Goulter suggested they meet again the following Monday. Constance explained that she couldn't make that date as she had agreed to go to the Lyceum with a girlfriend and two men. This caused Goulter to lose his temper and he took Constance's umbrella from her and hit her with it. She fought back and struck him with her handbag, whereupon he put his hands around her throat and strangled her into unconsciousness. Later he had lit a cigarette and thrown away the match. He did not notice that it had landed on her body. He had not deliberately tried to burn her.

Placed on trial before Mr Justice Horridge at the Old Bailey on 5 December, Goulter tried to maintain that the killing had been accidental. At one stage Goulter had tied strips from Constance's clothing around her throat and it was held that her throat had swelled, causing the strips to tighten. The prosecution showed that the strips must have been tied tightly to begin with and were the direct cause of Constance's death.

The jury took only seven minutes to decide on Goulter's guilt and he was hanged at Wandsworth on Friday, 6 January 1928 by Robert Baxter and Henry Pollard.

Frederick Lock, 1928

In February 1928, Frederick Lock's behaviour began to alter. A widower with four children, Lock had lived with Florence Alice Kitching for nearly four years, usually in quite a happy state, but this changed on 4 February.

It was on this date that Lock and Florence visited her aunt, Florence Nicholls, at 19 Hardington Street off the Edgware Road. Without warning, Lock picked up a knife and threatened to stab his paramour. Luckily, Mrs Nicholls managed to take the knife from him but Lock then retaliated by hitting Florence Kitching in the face. There was something obviously wrong here so it was no surprise that Florence wrote to her mother in Cornwall and asked if she might stay with her.

As it happened, Florence's stepfather was rather ill at the time. The letter had therefore come at a most opportune moment and Florence's mother, Mrs O'Neill, travelled to London with the intention of bringing her daughter back to Cornwall with her. She made her journey on Wednesday, 8 February.

By arrangement, Mrs O'Neill, her sister, Mrs Nicholls, Lock and Florence all met in the Lord Nelson pub. The conversation seemed to be quite amicable, so Florence expressed no concern when Lock suggested the two of them return to their home at 28 Cooper's Road, off the Old Kent Road, to see to the children's evening meal.

It was 1.45 p.m. when Lock returned but now he was alone. He suggested that Mrs O'Neill return with him when she would see why Florence could no longer make the trip to Cornwall. Mrs O'Neill and her sister then accompanied Lock back to Cooper's Road where they found Florence on the kitchen floor with her throat cut.

Put on trial for murder, Lock appeared before Mr Justice Humphreys at the Old Bailey on 1 March. His defence was one of insanity and Dr Reginald Hearn did testify that in his opinion Lock had not known what he was doing at the time he killed Florence. He also stated that Lock, although only 39 years of age, was in the early stages of dementia and would eventually become certifiable. Despite this testimony, the jury took just ten minutes to decide that Lock was sane and therefore guilty of murder.

On Thursday, 12 April, Lock was hanged at Wandsworth by Robert Baxter and Lionel Mann.

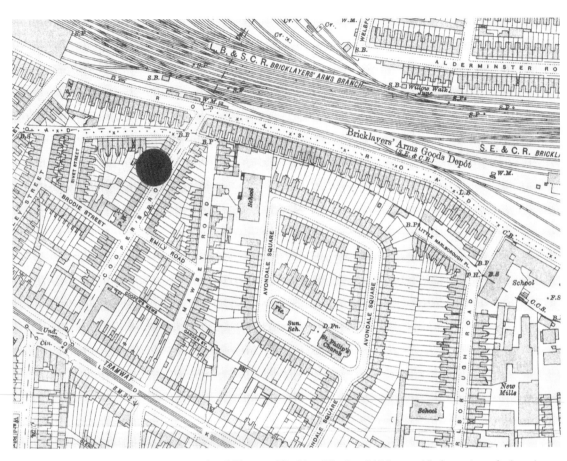

The house where Frederick Lock murdered Florence Kitching. The Lord Nelson public house is at the junction with Brodie Street. (Reproduced with the permission of Alan Godfrey Maps)

William Harold Goddard, 1932

On 30 November 1931, William Goddard walked into the police station in his home town of Ipswich and confessed to a murder.

Goddard explained that he had been working on the barge *Speranza*, berthed at the North Woolwich causeway in London. On Friday, 27 November he had asked his skipper, Charles William Lambert, if there was any mail for him. Lambert replied that there were two letters for Goddard, one of which was from his fiancée. Unfortunately, Lambert had used a different, rather derogatory word to describe Goddard's bride-to-be. And so Goddard had lashed out and struck Lambert on the jaw. Lambert fell down some steps and Goddard followed him down to make sure that he was all right. Lambert was indeed fine and held a heavy coal hammer in his hand. The two men had then fought. At one stage Goddard received a heavy blow to the back of his neck but had finally managed to wrestle the hammer from Lambert and hit him with it, rendering him unconscious.

Continuing his story, Goddard then detailed how he had gone for a walk to cool off. He returned to the barge at 5 p.m. only to find that Lambert had not moved. Checking for a pulse, Goddard found to his horror that Lambert was dead. He then took a watch and chain to make it look like a robbery. Now he felt it was better if he came clean and told the truth.

There was, however, an important omission in Goddard's narrative. He had not mentioned that there was a rope around Lambert's neck and the post-mortem would show that he had been partly strangled. Goddard tried to explain this by saying that his first thought was to dump the body overboard and he intended to drag him by the neck but found he could not manage it.

Goddard appeared before Mr Justice Finlay at the Old Bailey over two days, starting on 19 January 1932. The case turned on one single phrase.

According to the police, when Goddard had first made his statement in Ipswich he had said that Lambert was making so much noise after he hit him with the hammer that he had to, 'finish him off'. Goddard denied ever saying those words and still maintained that this was a case of manslaughter, not murder.

In the event, the jury chose to believe the police version of events and as a result, Goddard was hanged at Pentonville on Tuesday, 23 February by Robert Baxter and Thomas Phillips.

Raymond Henry Bousquet, 1935

Raymond Bousquet, a Canadian, had once been a boxer, fighting under the name of Del Fontaine. A married man, he nevertheless enjoyed the admiration of his female fans and one of those fans was Hilda Meek, whom he met at a dance hall in Streatham, in 1932.

At the time they met, Hilda told Bousquet that she was 18. This was still rather young for him as he was 27, but he would have been more dismayed to learn that Hilda was actually only 16.

A relationship began and continued for two years until Bousquet returned to his native Winnipeg. Hilda sent him letter after letter, telling him how much she loved him and missed him and eventually Bousquet decided to return to England. Unfortunately, not long after his return, Bousquet discovered that Hilda had been unfaithful to him.

On the evening of Wednesday, 10 July 1935, Bousquet met Hilda at the Redcap pub at Camberwell at 7 p.m. As they left that pub, Bousquet handed her a letter which she placed in her pocket, saying she would read it later. The couple then moved on to the Cleve Hall Hotel at Denmark Hill where Hilda read the note and was dismayed to find that it contained a threat to shoot her if she continued seeing the other man. After this, they returned to the Redcap before moving on yet again, to the Surry where Hilda walked out, saying she was going to fetch her mother so that she could join them in a drink.

Bousquet waited for twenty minutes and then went to look for Hilda. The door at Aldred Road, Kennington, was locked but luckily Hilda had given him a key. As he let himself in, Bousquet saw that Alice, Hilda's mother, was busily applying make-up prior to going to the Surry. As for Hilda, she was on the telephone arranging to meet someone at 10 p.m.

Bousquet knew that Hilda was going to meet the other man in her life. In a rage, he snatched the receiver from her and screamed into it that she wouldn't be coming after all. Hilda calmly took it back and told the person at the other end that indeed she would, as arranged. A major argument then broke out which brought Alice Meek into the room to try to calm things down. She did not succeed for finally, deciding enough was enough, Bousquet drew out a gun and began firing indiscriminately. Screaming, both women rushed out into the street only to be followed by Bousquet who then shot them both.

Alice Meek was not Bousquet's target and he left her lying where she was. He walked over to Hilda, bent down, picked her up and carried her back inside her house. Alice would recover from her injuries but Hilda was already dead.

Bousquet offered no resistance when arrested. Placed on trial for murder, he appeared before Mr Justice Porter at the Old Bailey between 10 and 16 September, where he pleaded not guilty to murder, claiming that the crime was one of manslaughter. Two witnesses, William Henry McGuiness, who lived above the Meeks, and Cecil William Slade, who lived at 62 Aldred Road and had been outside his house at the time, testified that Bousquet appeared to know exactly what he was doing at the time he shot both women.

Found guilty, Bousquet was hanged at Wandsworth on Tuesday, 29 October by Robert Baxter and Thomas Phillips.

Frederick Herbert Charles Field, 1936

Frederick Field, an aircraftman at Hendon, went AWOL on 24 March 1936. His first port of call was the home of a female acquaintance of his, Florence Elizabeth McGregor, who lived in Tooting, but he only stayed with her for one night. From there he moved to an allotment at Wimbledon, where he stayed in a hut for a few nights until, on Saturday, 4 April, he met a good Samaritan at a coffee stall.

Forty-eight-year-old Beatrice Vilna Sutton lived at Elmhurst Mansions, Edgeley Road, in Clapham and after listening to Field's story, she offered him a bed at her home. Field accepted her kind offer but then, once they were alone, he repaid her by strangling her. He left her flat at 11.30 p.m. that same night.

On the Sunday, Field was arrested for desertion. On Monday, 6 April, he was interviewed by Detective Inspector Brown in regard to some missing cheques, which had been traced to him. It was then that he confessed to killing Beatrice and backed up his story by giving a detailed description of the flat.

Further evidence soon built up against Field. The coffee stall owner, John Hennesey, confirmed Field's meeting with Beatrice and that they had left together. Two women were found who testified that they had seen a man matching Field's description close to the murder house on the night in question. It was then that Field withdrew his highly detailed confession.

A new story was now put forward. Field claimed that he had slept in a cupboard in Elmhurst Mansions and on 4 April he had heard a quarrel and saw a man running out of the building. He had then found Beatrice's body and, since he wished to commit suicide, he then made a careful note of everything so that his false confession would be believed.

On 13 May, Field appeared before Mr Justice Charles at the Old Bailey. The jury listened to both stories and decided that they believed the original confession. Only now was it revealed that on 2 October 1931, a lady named Norah Upchurch had been found strangled in a building in Shaftesbury Avenue. A year later, Field had confessed to the crime but later withdrawn that confession and as a result, had never been charged with the crime.

Having possibly escaped the noose once, Field was not so fortunate the second time. He was hanged at Wandsworth on Tuesday, 30 June by Alfred Allen and Stanley Cross.

Wallace Jenden, 1936

Thirty-eight-year-old Alice Whye was separated from her husband and, in 1936, was living with her two children and her mother at Cuthbert Road, Croydon. Since 1935 she had been seeing 57-year-old Wallace Jenden.

In early April of that year, Jenden began to show that he had a very jealous streak. He once told Alice's sister to tell her to '…come here tonight or she will know about it. If I can't have her, no one else will.'

For a time things settled down, until the evening of Saturday 23 May. On that night, Alice and Jenden left her house together and went to visit a local public house. They were seen leaving the bar at 9.45 p.m. but Alice did not return home that night.

The next morning, at 6 a.m., Alice's mother went to the hut on Stubbs Mead Allotments at Croydon, where Jenden lived, to see if he had any news of Alice. There was no reply to her knocking. She returned later but again there was no one home. At 8 a.m., Alice's daughter, Eileen, also went to the allotment. This time Jenden was there but he said he had not seen Alice since they had parted company the previous night.

The police were informed about Alice's disappearance and that afternoon, Sergeant Scott went along to see Jenden. He found him lying on the pathway close to the hut and he appeared to be very drunk. Jenden was asked about Alice and again claimed to have no knowledge of her whereabouts. Sergeant Scott was far from satisfied and decided to keep watch.

After a few minutes, Jenden unlocked the door to his hut and, seeing his opportunity, Sergeant Scott rushed forward and into the hut, just in time to stop Jenden from cutting his own throat. The reason for this intended course of action was plain to see, for there, on the hut floor, lay Alice Whye. She had been stabbed and her throat had been cut.

Charged with murder, Jenden appeared before Mr Justice Hilbery at the Old Bailey on 3 July, where he claimed that he had been so drunk that he had not known what he was doing. The jury did not agree and consequently, on Wednesday, 5 August, Jenden was hanged at Wandsworth by Thomas Pierrepoint and Robert Wilson.

George Brain, 1938

On the morning of Thursday, 14 July 1938, a motorist driving through Somerset Road in Wimbledon saw a woman's body lying in the road in front of him. He immediately called the police.

At first glance it appeared that the woman had been the victim of a hit and run, but upon closer inspection, police found that the woman had been battered and stabbed and then dumped where she lay. Further, her killer had then run over her body in an attempt to make it look like an accident. The tyre tracks showed that the car was either a Morris Minor or an Austin Seven. It didn't take long to identify the dead woman. She was 30-year-old Rose Muriel Atkins, a prostitute who was better known as Irish Rose.

The search for the car was narrowed down a little when a witness came forward and said he had seen Rose getting into a green van on 13 July. The witness also believed that the van was a Morris.

Two days after the discovery of Rose's body, on Saturday, 16 July, a shoe repair company, G. Hart & Sons, contacted the police on another matter. One of their employees, 27-year-old George Brain had vanished with £32 of the company's cash and was now mising from his home at 18 St James Cottages, Richmond. More importantly perhaps, Brain had been a driver for the firm and the vehicle he drove was a van; a green Morris van.

The van was kept at a garage on Whitfield Place and when the vehicle was searched the police found bloodstains, a knife and Rose's missing handbag. Further, there was a clear thumbprint on that handbag and it was surmised that as the print did not belong to Rose, it most likely belonged to her killer.

On 25 July, the police at Sheerness received a report that a man had been spotted sleeping rough close to the cliffs. A routine patrol was sent out and they found a rather scruffy, dishevelled man whose description they recognised as one circulated by their colleagues in Wimbledon. George Brain had been found.

Brain confessed that he had killed Rose but claimed that he had not known what he was doing. He admitted that he had picked her up at around 11.30 p.m. on 13 July and said that they had argued over money. The argument developed into a struggle during which Rose bit Brain's finger. This incensed him and he hit her. This was not enough to satisfy his rage, though, for he then took a starting handle, which he used to batter her until finally he came to his senses. He was, then, only guilty of manslaughter.

Brain's trial took place before Mr Justice Wrottesley at the Old Bailey, commencing on 19 September and lasting two days. The prosecution pointed out that in his own description of events, Brain had made no mention of the fact that he had also stabbed Rose and driven off over her body. This was hardly consistent with his story of suddenly realising what he had done and coming to his senses. The jury agreed and Brain was sentenced to death.

On Tuesday, 1 November, Brain was hanged at Wandsworth by Thomas Pierrepoint and two assistants: Stanley Cross and Herbert Morris.

The Old Bailey, where George Brain, and so many others mentioned in this book, were placed on trial and eventually sentenced to death.

Harry Armstrong, 1939

The morning of Monday, 2 January 1939 was cold and crisp as Kathleen Lawrence began her duties. Kathleen worked as a chambermaid at a hotel situated at 22 York Road, Lambeth. She was getting through her work quite well this particular morning and then the time came to clean room 6.

Kathleen knocked on the door but received no reply. She would need the master key in order to get in so she went downstairs and explained this to the manager, Richard Vaughan Jones. Richard went back up to room 6 with Kathleen and opened the door. It was time to call the police. There, in the bed, lay the strangled body of a woman, the same one who had checked in with her husband, Harry Armstrong, only the night before.

Detective Inspector William Fury was in charge of the investigation and it didn't take him long to determine that the woman was not Mrs Armstrong but 17-year-old Peggy Irene Violet Pentecost who lived in Brighton. She and Armstrong, who lived in Seaford, were not actually married but had become engaged on New Year's Eve. A description of 38-year-old Armstrong was then circulated, and he was picked up by an alert officer in Baker Street that same afternoon and charged with murder.

Armstrong appeared before Mr Justice Humphreys at the Old Bailey on 1 March. The proceedings lasted for two days during which Armstrong pleaded not guilty. During the trial it would become clear that the entire case was one of timing.

Dr Keith Simpson, the pathologist, had placed the time of Peggy's death at between 9 p.m. and 11 p.m. on 1 January. Armstrong, however, claimed that he had left the hotel much earlier than 9 p.m. and had gone to a café in Westminster Bridge Road. It was here that he had met a woman, Rose Kirby, at just after 10 p.m. They fell into conversation and left at 11 p.m. to check into a hotel in Paddington. This story was confirmed in every detail by Rose Kirby.

The timings had been checked by the police and this alibi meant that if Armstrong were indeed the killer, then Peggy would have been murdered at 9.30 p.m. This did, of course, fit in with the findings of Dr Simpson but another piece of evidence seemed to contradict this. The hotel manager, Richard Jones, testified that he heard a door click shut in the hotel on 1 January, and he believed that this was the room in which Peggy's body was later found. Unfortunately for the prosecution, this sound was heard at 11.30 p.m., by which time Armstrong was in another hotel with Rose Kirby.

It was, perhaps, one final piece of evidence which swayed the collective mind of the jury. When Armstrong was arrested, the police had found a postcard on him. Addressed to Peggy's mother in Brighton, it read, 'This is the best way out. Love Harry.' Armstrong said that this was just a card to say he couldn't go through with the wedding but the prosecution suggested that it meant he was going to kill Peggy.

Found guilty, Armstrong made a speech to the jury in which he swore again that he was not guilty of murder. He was then sentenced to death. He did not appeal against that sentence, preferring to rely on a petition for a reprieve. This avenue failed and on Tuesday, 21 March Armstrong was hanged at Wandsworth by Thomas Phillips and Albert Pierrepoint.

Wiliam Thomas Butler, 1939

Dr Day was puzzled. The man in front of him, who had given his name as Charles Jackson, said that he had injured his hands on a wood-cutting machine, but the wounds were simply not consistent with such an accident. They looked more like injuries that would have been caused by a knife or a dagger.

There was one other factor that made the doctor suspicious. Dr Day had earlier that same day, Saturday, 24 December 1938, examined the body of 64-year-old Ernest Percival Key, who had been rushed to hospital from his jeweller's shop at 74 Victoria Road, Surbiton. Mr Key had been stabbed thirty times during an attempted robbery. Was it possible that the two sets of injuries were connected? To be on the safe side, Dr Day passed the information on to the police.

When Charles Jackson was questioned, it soon became clear that he had given the doctor a false name and was in fact 29-year-old William Butler, a known housebreaker. He certainly deserved closer scrutiny.

Victoria Road, Surbiton, where Ernest Percival Key had his jeweller's shop and where he was murdered by William Butler on Christmas Eve, 1938.

The killer of Ernest Key had, in his haste to escape from the shop, left behind a bowler hat. This was scientifically examined and in turn gave officers details of the colour and length of the owner's hair. It was noted that Butler's hair was an exact match. By 17 January 1939, the police felt that they had enough to charge Butler.

The trial opened before Mr Justice Singleton at the Old Bailey on 15 February, and lasted for two days. Knowing that his hat put him at the scene of the crime, Butler had by now admitted that he had been there and even admitted to stealing some jewellery, but said that he had stabbed Ernest Key only when he had attacked him. The prosecution then pointed out that Key was twice the age of Butler and the severity of the attack hardly suggested a simple case of self-defence.

Found guilty and condemned to death, Butler was hanged at Wandsworth on Wednesday, 29 March by Thomas Pierrepoint and Thomas Phillips.

Ernest Edmund Hamerton, 1940

There were three people living at 93 Inville Road, Walworth. The house was owned by Phyllis Rebecca Bridgen who lived there with her 8-year-old son, Philip Thomas. There was also a lodger, 28-year-old Elsie May Ellington.

In July 1939, Elsie received a visitor in the form of her boyfriend, Ernest Hamerton. He was even allowed to stay over for the weekend though, of course, in a separate room. The visit seemed to go very well and when Hamerton came on another visit, on 8 Jaury 1940, he was allowed to stay again, this time for even longer.

On the evening of Wednesday, 15 January, Hamerton asked Elsie if she would go to the pictures with him. She said she did not want to so Hamerton went by himself. Later, Elise went out by herself. Phyllis Bridgen was ill at the time and retired early. As she lay in bed she heard Elsie and Hamerton return to the house, separately.

The next morning, Phyllis was still feeling rather sick so she called for her son and asked him if he would go into Elsie's room and ask her to make a cup of tea. Philip did as he was asked and as a result, at around 8.40 a.m., Elsie brought the tea in to Phyllis. Elsie then went downstairs to make Philip some cocoa.

Philip sat in the kitchen, watching Elsie busy herself, and at one stage he saw her go into the small scullery. Almost immediately, Hamerton followed Elsie in and then closed the door behind him. Philip could see nothing of what was going on inside the scullery but he did hear a loud thump followed by a scream. He ran upstairs and told his mother what he had witnessed.

Despite her illness, Phyllis went downstairs to investigate. By now the scullery door was open and Hamerton was standing nearby. Asked what he had done, Hamerton admitted that he had struck Elsie and was now going to fetch a doctor for her. As he left the house, Phyllis checked inside the scullery and found Elsie lying on the floor. She had been stabbed twenty-four times and the knife still lay embedded in her heart.

The police were called and a search was launched for Hamerton. It was known that he was a native of Manchester so officers arranged to meet the London train in that city. Hamerton was indeed on the train and was duly arrested by Constable John Reston Calder.

Sent back to London, Hamerton appeared before Mr Justice Wrottesley at the Old Bailey on 8 February. Here it was revealed that on the journey back to London, Hamerton made a full confession and claimed that he had killed Elsie because she had promised to marry him but had then changed her mind.

That confession sealed Hamerton's fate and on Wednesday, 27 March he was hanged at Wandsworth by Thomas Phillips and Alexander Riley.

Stanley Edward Cole, 1940

Gordon Edward Girl and his wife, Doris Eugenia, were a happy enough couple. They had married in 1931 and now had an 8-year-old daughter, Sybil. The entire family lived at 77 Hartfield Crescent, Wimbledon with their lodger, Louise Bolton.

In about April 1940, Doris had become friendly with 23-year-old Stanley Cole and he had started spending a good deal of time at Hartfield Crescent. He had even been known to spend the occasional night there, sleeping on the settee.

On Thursday, 22 August, Louise Bolton returned home to her lodgings to find the house empty. Knowing that Doris liked to visit the Crooked Billet pub, she walked down there and found Sybil standing outside. The young girl explained that her mother was inside, with Cole. Louise did not want to interfere so she took Sybil home with her. She later noted that it was around 10 p.m. before Doris and Cole returned to Hartfield Crescent.

It was obvious that Cole was in some sort of mood. He turned to Sybil and said, 'Why let that bloody cow bring you home?' Louise was incensed and said that she was thinking of reporting his behaviour to the police. Some five minutes later, Cole went up to Louise's room and apologised for what he had said. The house then settled down for the night.

At 12.40 a.m. the next morning, Cole walked into Wimbledon police station, announced that he had just killed a woman, and then burst into tears. He explained what he had done, and upon checking at no. 77, officers found Doris's body with a knife still embedded in her back.

Cole claimed that he could not explain why he had done this terrible thing. He told officers about their visit to the pub the previous night and of later being left alone with Doris downstairs. They had had some more drinks and at one stage Doris had bent forward to pick something up off the floor. He had simply picked the knife up off the table and stabbed her for no reason.

Cole appeared before Mr Justice Hallett at the Old Bailey on 10 September, the proceedings lasting for three days. Here Cole was totally uncooperative and refused to go into the witness box to explain what had happened. The jury retired to consider their verdict and after thirty-five minutes had to return to court and ask the judge for further guidance. Eventually, however, they managed to agree that Cole was guilty as charged.

On Thursday, 31 October, Cole was hanged at Wandsworth by Thomas Pierrepoint and three assistants: Herbert Morris, Harry Kirk and Henry Critchell.

John Ernest Smith, 1941

There could be no doubt about it. John Smith and Christina Rose Dicksee were in love and did their very best to prove it to each other. Smith would regularly write as many as nine letters per day to Christina and once sent her thirteen! As for Christina, she also wrote to him many times. So it was no surprise when marriage was discussed and a formal engagement announced in April 1941.

Christina's parents certainly approved of Smith and had not the slightest objection to the relationship, but they did have just one concern. Christina was 24 and Smith just 21 so Mr and Mrs Dicksee suggested that it might possibly be a good idea if they didn't rush into marriage and waited until they were a little older.

Christina saw the sense in this and agreed readily but Smith, for some reason, saw it as an affront. He managed to convice himself that Mr and Mrs Dicksee did not approve of him and were actively trying to split him and Christina up. He thought about this constantly and as the days passed, brooded more and more about the problem.

On Wednesday, 29 October, Christina visited Smith at his parents' house on the Old Kent Road. The young lovers were alone in Smith's room when suddenly a blood-curdling scream rang out. Smith's stepfather went to investigate and found Christina lying dead on the floor. Smith had killed the object of his love by stabbing her thirty-four times.

Smith appeared before Mr Justice Hilbery at the Old Bailey on 14 November. The defence was one of insanity, but after the attack, Smith had made a full confession to the police stating that he had made up his mind on the Tuesday before the attack to kill Christina.

This proved that the crime was premeditated and so, as a result, Smith was found guilty and was hanged at Wandsworth on Wednesday, 3 December by Albert Pierrepoint and Harry Allen.

Patrick William Kingston, 1942

At 8.20 p.m. on Wednesday, 15 July 1942, 11-year-old Sheila Margaret Wilson went home for her supper. Normally, this would mean that the girl was in for the night but as she ate, she told her mother that she had been given 2*d* to run an errand later. Edith Wilson, Shiela's mother, assumed that one of the neighbours had asked her to fetch a newspaper, so gave her permission. At 8.33 p.m., Shiela was off out again to do as she had been asked.

The minutes passed and turned into hours and still Sheila did not come home. Margaret and her other children went out looking for her, and during their search, knocked on the doors of their neighbours in Leahurst Road, Lewisham. One of those doors was at no. 19 but Rose Ryder, who lived there, hadn't seen Sheila. Neither had Rose's lodger, Patrick Kingston.

In due course the police were called in and a full-scale search organised. Five days later, on 20 July, enquiries led back to no. 19 and the room occupied by Kingston. The room was searched and there, underneath the floorboards, officers found the strangled body of Sheila Wilson, a cord still knotted tightly around her neck. Unfortunately, by this time, Patrick Kingston had vanished.

The newspapers of the day were keen to help. They published a full description of the wanted man, including the details that he had been injured in a bomb blast in November 1940 and as a result, walked with a limp and had a deformed left hand. On 23 July, they even published a photograph of Kingston and this led to his arrest the same day.

Kingston appeared before Mr Justice Hallett at the Old Bailey on 14 September. He pleaded guilty to the charge, though he was at a loss to explain why he had killed the girl. The entire proceedings lasted just five minutes.

On Tuesday, 6 October, 38-year-old Kingston was hanged at Wandsworth by Albert Pierrepoint and Herbert Morris.

Herbert Hiram Bounds, 1942

Herbert Bounds and his wife, Elizabeth married in 1923 and by 1942, they had had five children. Unfortunately four of these had died, leaving just a 9-year-old daughter. The family lived at 113 Gloucester Road, Croydon. There was one other problem: Herbert and Elizabeth just didn't get on together.

Herbert was a total hypochondriac and was always 'coming down' with something. By the autumn of 1942, he had not worked for a year and had visited his long-suffering doctor, Ansel Fry, many times. Elizabeth had no time for all this nonsense and showed little sympathy to Herbert's many complaints of illness. This in turn made him believe that her constant nagging to sort himself out meant that she was actively making him sick.

On the morning of Friday, 21 August, yet another argument broke out between Herbert and Elizabeth. She had certainly had enough, for at one stage she grabbed a knife and shouted, 'I'll cut your throat you bastard if you don't get out soon and do something!' At that, Herbert took out his razor and drew it across his wife's throat.

Seeing all this, Herbert's daughter ran screaming from the house. This caused Herbert to come to his senses somewhat, for he then walked to a police box in Windmill Road where he gave himself up to Special Constable Harry Harding, who happened to be standing there.

Herbert Bounds faced his trial at the Old Bailey on 16 September before Mr Justice Hallett, his plea being that he had acted in self-defence when Elizabeth had first attacked him. This was greatly weakened when the prosecution pointed out that the razor he had used belonged to Elizabeth. Herbert had gone to her cabinet and removed it, implying that his attack was premeditated and planned.

Found guilty, Herbert Bounds was hanged at Wandsworth on Friday, 6 November by Thomas Pierrepoint and Henry Critchell.

Harry Dobkin, 1943

On 17 July 1942 workmen were demolishing the burnt-out Vauxhall Baptist Chapel in Kennington Lane when they lifted a large stone slab. Beneath that slab, in a small cavity, lay a skeleton. The matter was reported to the local police.

The remains were examined by Dr Keith Simpson, who was able to glean a good deal of information from them. To begin with, he found the remains of a dried-up womb, showing that the skelteon was female and that she had died within the last eighteen months. This put the earliest possible date of death at January 1941. The skelton also enabled Simpson to deduce that the woman had been very slightly over 5ft tall in life and she had brown hair, greying slightly, probably putting her age at somewhere between 40 and 50. With this information, officers trawled the missing person's list and one name leapt out at them.

Rachel Dobkin had vanished on Friday, 11 April 1941, which happened to be Good Friday. She had been 47 years old and her height and hair colouring matched. Even more interesting, her husband, Harry Dobkin, had been employed as a firewatcher at the very church where the body had been found.

Still, the police had not finished checking out the information they had. Rachel's sister supplied a photograph of the missing woman and this was now superimposed upon an X-ray of the skull from the church. The bone structures matched exactly. Finally, Rachel's dentist was traced and he identified the fillings in the remaining teeth. It was now certain: the body was that of Rachel Dobkin.

The marriage between Rachel and Harry Dobkin had been a disasterous one. They had married in September 1920 but separated after just three days! Rachel, though, was pregnant and the resulting child meant that Harry had to pay maintainance. These payments were irregular and Harry had even spent time in prison as a result. Could this have been a motive for her murder?

Harry Dobkin was arrested and charged with murder. He appeared at the Old Bailey on 18 November 1942, the proceedings lasting until 23 November.

The only possible escape was for the defence to challenge the identification of the skeletal remains. Dr Simpson had given the height of the woman as very close to 5ft, but on the original missing person's notice, Rachel Dobkin had been described as being 5ft 3in tall.

That height had been given by Rachel's sister when she first reported her missing. Now, in court, she testified that Rachel had been the same height as herself and someone writing down the description had written this as 5ft 3in. A tape measure was produced in court and Rachel's sister was shown to be fractionally under 5ft tall.

It was enough for the jury, who were now convinced that the body was Rachel's and the man responsible for her death was Harry Dobkin. As a result, Dobkin was found guilty and hanged at Wandsworth on Wednesday, 27 January 1943 by Albert Pierrepoint and Herbert Morris.

Dudley George Rayner, 1943

It should have been a perfect marriage. In August 1942, a beautiful woman, Josephine Colalucia, serving in the ATS, married Dudley Rayner, a Burmese sergeant in the Pioneer Corp. The couple were devoted to each other and Dudley was completely besotted with his attractive new wife. Shortly after the wedding, in November 1942, Josephine Rayner was sent to join her unit and for a short time she and Dudley lost touch with each other. He was devastated.

In was a very short separation and Josephine was soon in touch with her husband again, but the matter caused a change in Dudley. The separation began to prey upon his mind. Even after they had obtained their first home together, in Weighton Road, Anerley, he began to brood on what life would be like without his adored Josephine.

There were other separations. After all, Britain was at war and both the Rayners were serving in the forces. Still, they always returned to spend time together at Weighton Road and cherished their brief periods with each other. Yet Dudley still thought of life without his wife and one day, those thoughts proved to be too much to bear.

Both the Rayners were on leave in early February 1943. On the morning of Monday, 8 February, they enjoyed breakfast together. Dudley then happily polished his wife's shoes for her until they gleamed. It was while he was performing that task that he noticed a hammer lying on the floor. Without any warning, Dudley Rayner picked up that hammer and used it to batter his wife to death. Josephine was just 19 years old.

Dudley Rayner faced Mr Justice Oliver at the Old Bailey on 12 March and made no attempt to avoid the consequences of his actions. He pleaded guilty to the charge and was sentenced to death within nine minutes. Further, he refused to appeal against that sentence or allow any attempt to be made to obtain a reprieve.

On Wednesday, 31 March, 26-year-old Dudley was hanged at Wandsworth by Albert Pierrepoint and Stephen Wade. It was less than two months since he had murdered the wife he loved so much.

Terence Casey, 1943

At close to 11.25 p.m. on Tuesday, 13 July, John Walton, an air-raid warden on his beat, heard strange noises coming from the front garden of 8 Gwendolen Street, Putney. Going to investigate, Walton shone his torch into the darkness and saw a partly clothed woman and a soldier. This was not an ordinary courting couple however, for the woman was being strangled to death. Walton drew a whistle and summoned the police.

The dead woman was identified as Bridget Nora Mitton and her assailant, who had been caught red-handed, was 22-year-old Terence Casey, a private in the Royal Army Medical Corp. The events of that night were then pieced together.

Casey had been drinking in a pub on Quill Lane and Freda Gibbons, the barmaid there, said that he had been rather fresh with her and she had told him in no uncertain terms to go away. Casey had not been easily disuaded and said he would wait outside for her. Later that evening, Bridget Mitton came into the pub to buy a bottle of stout. Soon afterwards, Freda left to go home and had seen Bridget talking to a friend. She had also seen Casey, waiting on the corner and noticed that as Bridget walked off, Casey had followed her. It seemed that Casey, determined to get some female company for himself, had simply decided to attack the first woman he saw.

Casey appeared before Mr Justice Singleton at the Old Bailey on 22 September. The proceedings lasted for three days, during which Casey claimed that he was not responsible for his actions.

Casey said he had no memory of what happened after he left the pub. He was examined by Dr Nelson Hill who stated that he had detected abnormal patterns in the electrical activity in Casey's brain. It might well be that drink could cause him to have episodes where he would remember nothing, but the jury were not convinced and after deliberating for forty-five minutes, found Casey guilty.

An appeal was entered but subsequently dismissed and Casey was hanged at Wandsworth on Friday, 19 November by Albert Pierrepoint and Henry Critchell.

Ernest James Harman Kemp, 1944

For Arthur Belcher, Tuesday, 15 February 1944 was an ordinary day. After enjoying a nice breakfast, Belcher decided to walk down to his allotment at Sherard Road, Eltham. It was then that his day changed, for upon arriving there he found the body of a young woman, a knotted scarf tied tightly around her throat.

The police were called and upon checking the dead woman's identity discs, determined that she was 21-year-old Iris Miriam Deeley, a leading airccraftwoman in the WAAF. Further, it was easy to determine that Iris had had a pass from Kidbrooke Camp where she was based and had arranged to meet her fiancé, William Quill. That gentleman was now interviewed and he was able to say that he and Iris had gone to Charing Cross station, only to find that Iris had missed the train back to Kidbrooke. She had then decided to catch one to Lewisham at 11.25 p.m., and walk to her base from there.

Other witnesses came forward to confirm Quill's story. Iris had been seen walking down Lewisham High Street where she fell in company with a soldier. They then walked on together, towards the allotments. The police now knew that the killer was almost certainly this second serviceman.

The case was finally solved by a very alert railway policeman. On 22 February, an army sergeant was kissing a WAAF, presumably his girlfriend, at St Pancras, when the railway policeman noticed that the medal ribbons he was displaying upon his chest did not ring true. The policeman informed his colleagues and the sergeant was taken in to explain the discrepancy.

The sergeant was searched and among his belongings were some clothing coupons in the name of W. Quill. This linked the sergeant to the murder of Iris Deeley and he was now questioned on this matter. The sergeant turned out to be a deserter named Ernest Kemp. Under questioning, he admitted being in Lewisham on the night of the murder and even to being the soldier seen in Iris's company, but claimed that she had been alive and well when they parted near the railway bridge. He had never been on the allotments with her.

It was now that the police revealed their final clue. Close by Iris's body, they had found some size 11 footprints. Kemp's shoes were checked and these were shown to match those prints. Kemp now finally admitted that he had killed Iris, but told the police it was an accident. He had touched her breasts and she resisted, so he forced her to the ground and began undressing her. They struggled and he grabbed her scarf to restrain her. The more she struggled, the more the scarf tightened and before he knew what he was doing, she was dead.

The trial took place before Mr Justice Cassels at the Old Bailey on 18 April, with Kemp pleading guilty to manslaughter. The jury, though, took just fifteen minutes to decide that this was a case of murder.

Twenty-one-year-old Kemp was hanged at Wandsworth on D-Day, Tuesday, 6 June 1944 by Albert Pierrepoint and Herbert Morris.

Arthur Clegg, 1946

On 6 November 1945, a tragic bundle washed up onto the banks of the River Thames. The bundle was the body of a baby girl, just a few days old. There was one clue to the child's identity, for on her wrist was a hospital name band with the words, 'Baby Clegg' written on it. The cause of death was drowning.

It didn't take long for the police to trace the child. Jill Clegg had been born on 19 October to Joan Clegg, a 20-year-old unmarried mother. Joan was now interviewed and explained that she had kept the pregnancy secret from her mother but had explained to her father, Arthur Clegg, about her condition. Arthur said he would stand by her and would find someone to adopt the child once it was born.

Ten days after Jill was born, Monday, 29 October, Joan Clegg left hospital but the baby stayed behind. The hospital staff knew of Joan's intention not to keep the child and they had found a family who were interested in taking her, but it was to be to no avail. The next day, 30 October, Arthur Clegg picked up Jill at 4.45 p.m. When he arrived home, however, he was alone and Jill Clegg was never seen alive again.

Arthur was now interviewed and claimed that he had intended to take the baby to an adoption agency he knew of, but just as he was entering the premises, he saw a woman on the stairs who said she was looking to adopt. She gave her name as Clarke and Arthur had handed the child over. It must have been Mrs Clarke who had killed the child.

Arthur Clegg appeared before Mr Justice Croom-Johnson at the Old Bailey on 7 February 1945, the hearing lasting for two days. The jury chose not to believe in the existence of 'Mrs Clarke' and decided that Clegg had simply disposed of Jill as she was an incumbrance. Indeed, there was even the suggestion that Clegg himself may have been the real father.

Sentenced to death, Clegg was hanged at Wandsworth on Tuesday, 19 March by Albert Pierrepoint and Herbert Morris.

David Baillie Mason, 1946

In the early hours of Wednesday, 29 May 1946, Dr Taylor was called out to 12a Haslemere Close, Wallington, by 39-year-old David Mason. Apparently, Mason's wife, Dorothy Louisa Mildred, had been taken ill and had collapsed.

Dr Taylor found that he was too late and Dorothy was dead. Even as he turned to leave, the doctor was asked by Mason if he would also mind taking a look at David John, Mason's son. The doctor found that the child too was dead and wasted no time in calling in the police.

Post-mortems were carried out on both bodies and it transpired that Dorothy had been strangled and David John had died from asphyxiation. It appeared to be a double murder. Questioned about the matter, Mason said that he recalled he and his wife arguing on the Tuesday night and at one stage he was leaning over her while she was on the bed. That was the last he remembered and when he woke, Dorothy was dead.

This story did not really ring true so Mason amended it somewhat. He now claimed that when Dorothy came home from work, he told her that their son was in bed but not asleep. Dorothy had roared, 'I will make the little brat sleep!' and had gone up to the child's bedroom. Mason followed her to find that she was smothering the boy.

Dorothy immediately turned her attentions to her husband and attacked him. In the struggle that followed, Mason had put his hands around her throat and must have strangled her accidentally. In short, Dorothy had murdered their son and Mason himself was only guilty of manslaughter.

Mason appeared before Mr Justice Cassels at the Old Bailey from 22–25 July. One of the key witnesses was Dorothy's brother, William Richard Frederick Rogers, who swore that Mason was always devoted to his son whereas Dorothy treated the child with indifference. This seemed to back up the story Mason was telling, but the jury could not understand why Mason had lied in the first place, especially when the explanation he gave was that he had done so to protect his wife's memory.

Found guilty, Mason was hanged at Wandsworth on Friday, 6 September by Albert Pierrepoint. Since this was a double execution – with Sydney John Smith also being hanged for a murder at Hastings – Pierrepoint had two assistants: Harry Allen and Henry Critchell.

Frank Josiah Freiyer, 1946

Frank Freiyer had an excellent war record. He had enlisted in the RAF as a volunteer at the age of 19, had served with the 8th Army and had even fought at El Alamein. Freiyer was certainly a strong, confident man but there was one problem he did not seem able to overcome.

For some weeks, Freiyer had been seeing Joyce Brierley but now had grown tired of her and ideally wanted to end the relationship, but for some reason didn't seem able to do so, even when given the opportunity.

Joyce was fully aware that Freiyer was unhappy in the relationship and on 2 September 1946, she wrote to him to say that if he wanted to end it, he could do so and she wouldn't cause him any problems. Freiyer did not take this way out and even though it was obvious that neither of them were happy, he and Joyce even took a brief holiday on Canvey Island with his mother. They returned to their homes on 14 September. Joyce now wrote Freiyer a second letter again saying that he could finish with her if he wished. Again he did not take her up on the offer.

At 10.30 p.m. on Friday, 20 September, Freiyer walked in to Woolwich police station and said that he had just killed a woman in Maryon Park, Charlton. He went on to make a full written statement in which he explained that he and Joyce had gone to the park at 8.30 p.m. and had gone to a shelter, close to the bandstand.

They had talked of their troubles for a little while and then, at 10.15 p.m. they decided to go home, he to 2 Liffler Road and she to 99 Brewery Road. As they kissed goodnight, he suddenly placed his hands around her throat and began to strangle her. Joyce fought back and even managed to bite Freiyer's nose, but he was too strong and soon she fell limp in his arms.

In fact, the police found two people who had actually witnessed the murder. Jack Norton Hazeldine and his girlfriend, Miss Beecroft had also wanted to use the shelter, but they had seen Freiyer with his hands around Joyce's throat and had assumed that they were just a courting couple.

Freiyer appeared before Mr Justice Stable at the Old Bailey on 25 October. With his own statement, and the evidence of Jack Hazeldine and his girlfriend, the verdict was but a formality.

On Wednesday, 13 November, Freiyer, who was by now 26, was hanged at Wandsworth by Albert Pierrepoint and Harry Kirk.

David John Williams, 1947

It was the old story of a marriage gone wrong. In early 1947, Margaret Williams left her husband, David, and took lodgings with Mrs Lynch at 16 Parkleigh Road, Merton. David tried to persuade his wife to return to him but she was adamant; the relationship was over.

On the morning of Thursday, 6 February, Margaret left her lodgings to go to work. She had gone but a few steps when David approached her. Words were exchanged and then David produced a hammer and hit his wife once, on the back of the head.

Margaret fell to the ground but David hadn't finished with her yet. He now crouched down and smashed her head repeatedly into the concrete. Satisfied that he had done what he intended, David then covered his wife with his coat and waited. Margaret was rushed to hospital but died in the ambulance on the way. David was now charged with murder.

David Williams faced his trial before Mr Justice Byrne at the Old Bailey on 7 March. Here he claimed that although they had been separated, he and Margaret had been meeting in secret and sometimes had sex. This had continued until he discovered that she might have been two-timing him with another man. That had caused him to make his mind up to kill her.

On the morning of the attack he had hidden and waited for Margaret to appear. When she did, he asked her if she would return to him and when she refused, he drew out the hammer and battered her with it. His defence now was that he had been insane at the time.

Details of his family history were given, along with confirmation that David had tried to gas himself on Sunday, 2 February. All this was countered by the testimony of Dr Hugh Grierson, who testified that the prisoner was perfectly sane.

Found guilty and condemned to death, David Williams was hanged at Wandsworth by Albert Pierrepoint and Harry Kirk on Tuesday, 15 April.

Albert Price, 1950

On Wednesday, 7 June 1950, Walter Laurence Blunden walked across some wasteland in Fish Lane, Bognor Regis, on his way to a local café. Halfway across he noticed a handle poking out from some bushes. Going over to investigate, Blunden found that it was a maroon-coloured pushchair with two children inside, both apparently asleep. It was only when Blunden looked more carefully that he saw that both children were dead.

On the same day that the two bodies were found, another drama was unfolding at 20 Grange Close, New Malden. A neighbour, Joan Edith Doe had noticed that the milk on the doorstep was not being collected. Looking into no. 20 through the window, she saw the shape of a body. The police were called and when they forced an entry they discovered Doris Price. She had been battered to death. Her two young children and her husband, Albert Price, were all missing.

It wasn't very long before the two finds were connected and the two children in Bognor were identified as 3-year-old Jennifer Valerie Price and her 10-month-old sister, Maureen Ann. These were the two missing children of Doris Price and it now became even more urgent that Albert Price be traced and interviewed.

A description of Price was circulated but it was not until the early hours of 13 June that Constable Adams and Constable Fisher spotted him in Green Park, London. He was arrested and taken to Cannon Row police station where he was interviewed and charged with murder.

Price appeared at the Old Bailey before Mr Justice Parker on 12 July, with the defence claiming that Price had been insane at the time of the murders. It was, perhaps, Price's own statement to the police which did most to convict him.

In this document Price explained that he had incurred a gambling debt in 1948. This, along with other regular payments for rent, furniture and such meant that he was now getting deeper and deeper into debt. He borrowed money to make ends meet and ended up being sued for that debt. The payments the court ordered him to make meant that financially, things got worse and worse.

By April 1950, Price was being threatened with bailffs and this stress caused his wife to become ill. Then, finally, on Saturday, 3 June he had received a letter from Malden Council giving him and his family notice to quit. This was the final straw. He went up to his bedroom and battered his wife to death with an axe.

The next morning, 4 June, he took the children down to Bognor and gave both girls some milk into which he had dissolved sleeping pills. Once they were unconscious, he had smothered them both before returning to London. His intention had been to kill himself but his nerve failed him.

In the event, the jury took just forty minutes to decide that Price was sane and therefore guilty of murder. An appeal failed on 31 July and on Wednesday, 16 August, Price was hanged at Wandsworth by Albert Pierrepoint and Harry Allen.

Frank Burgess, 1952

Twenty-two-year-old Johanna Hallahan had worked at the Elgin Court Hotel on Elgin Road, East Croydon for just five weeks. She was a most attractive girl and very popular with staff and guests alike. Further, she was a happy girl and had recently become engaged to Charles Patrick Hughes.

On Monday, 21 April, Charles and Johanna parted at 3.15 p.m., having first arranged to meet up later that same day. Johanna failed to keep that appointment but Charles was not unduly concerned and believed that work at the hotel might have held her up.

The next day, Tuesday the 22nd, was Johanna's day off so no one expected to see her at work. Wednesday was a different matter, though. Johanna was a most diligent employee and when she didn't appear at work, the hotel owner, Mr Peel, decided to investigate.

Johanna lived on the premises and when Mr Peel received no reply to his knock on her door, his first thought was that she might have been taken ill or had an accident of some kind. Rather than simply burst into the room, however, Mr Peel went around the back to look in at Johanna's window. He saw a pair of woman's legs lying on the floor. Something was wrong and now Peel did take his pass key and opened Johanna's door. She was beyond all aid, having been strangled. The motive for the crime appeared to be robbery for the gas meter had been forced open and the contents taken.

The police soon discovered that another hotel employee had also not turned up for work that day. Like Johanna, Frank Burgess had also been entitled to the Monday off but had not appeared on the Tuesday. Further, when his room was checked, there was no sign of him but the gas meter in his room had also been forced open.

It appeared that Burgess had killed Johanna and then taken money from both meters and escaped. This seemed to be confirmed by letters found in Burgess's room. Burgess was actually on probabtion for an attack upon a taxi driver earlier in the year and the letters were addressed to his probation officer, Frank Arthur Hepworth. In them Burgess apologised for what he had done and also included a chilling confession to the murder of Johanna Hallahan. At the end he had written, 'I found it was in quite a fit of laughter that I killed her.'

It didn't take the police long to find Burgess and he again admitted responsibility for Johanna's death. He now added that he had asked her if he might borrow some money to go out with. She had lent him £1, whereupon he had killed her, though he could give no reason for his actions.

A motive is not necessary for a charge of murder, and at the trial, which took place before Mr Justice Streatfeild at the Old Bailey on 30 June, the jury had little trouble in finding Burgess guilty. He was hanged at Wandsworth on Tuesday, 22 July by Albert Pierrepoint and Syd Dernley.

John Kenneth Livesey, 1952

The house at Blackheath Hill could hardly be described as a happy one. Two families, related by marriage, shared the house and were at daggers with each other. On one side was John Livesey and his wife. On the other was Harry Small, his wife, Stephanie Marie and their 13-year-old daughter ,Patricia. The main protagonists in this hateful situation were John Livesey and Stephanie Small, his mother-in-law.

On 15 July 1952, the atmosphere worsened even more and a full-scale fight took place. Stephanie assaulted Livesey's wife, and Livesey intervened by punching Harry Small. Livesey was told that he and his wife would have to move out. They ignored the request.

Eleven days later, on Saturday, 26 July, most of the family were at a neighbour's house watching television, still something of a rarity at the time. John Livesey and Stepanie Small were left alone. It was a recipe for disaster.

One can assume that there was yet another argument but the truth of that will never be known. What is a fact is that at some time that afternoon, Livesey took a knife and stabbed his mother-in-law in the back twenty-four times. He then vanished from the house.

Livesey was picked up in due course and while he admitted the many arguments and fights with Stephanie and the other members of his extended family, he denied killing Stephanie. Nevertheless, he was charged with murder.

The trial opened before Mr Justice Hilbery at the Old Bailey on 24 October. Here Livesey again said that he did not kill Stephanie, but had merely found her body. As for trying to run away afterwards he said that once the family history became known, he would be an obvious suspect and had thought it better to escape.

Found guilty and sentenced to death, Livesey's appeal was heard and dismissed on 1 December. As a result, he was hanged at Wandsworth on Wednesday, 17 December by Albert Pierrepoint and Syd Dernley.

It is likely that it was this execution which ended Dernley's career as an assistant hangman. Once Livesey's body had been taken down from the scaffold, Dernley observed that the dead man had a magnificent set of 'vital parts'. This gratuitous and ignorant comment found its way back to the authorities and, apart from one more execution for which he had already been commissioned, Dernley was never asked to officiate again.

Derek William Bentley, 1953

It was 9.15 p.m. on Sunday, 2 November 1952 and Edith Alice Ware was upstairs at 74 Tamworth Road, Croydon, tucking her daughter into bed. Glancing out of the bedroom window towards Barlow and Parkers warehouse, which was almost directly opposite, Edith saw a young man climbing over the gates. He was with another man who glanced around and then followed his companion over the gates. It looked like there was a break-in about to take place. Edith told her husband, John what she had seen and he dashed to a telephone box and rang for the police.

The first two officers on the scene were Detective Constable Frederick Fairfax and Constable Norman Harrison. Climbing over the gates himself, Fairfax saw signs that someone had shinned up a drainpipe and got onto the roof. He followed and was the first policeman to reach the roof of the warehouse.

Fairfax saw that there were two young men already up there, and as he watched, they both dashed behind a lift shaft. Fairfax approached them and announced, 'I am a police officer, come out from behind that stack.' An abusive reply followed but Fairfax moved forward and managed to grab one of the two intruders and pull him to the opposite side of the lift stack.

Fairfax had grabbed 19-year-old Derek Bentley, the taller of the two men. Meanwhile, his partner, 16-year-old Christopher Craig, was armed with a pistol and for the next thirty minutes or so he fired indiscriminately at the police as other officers joined Fairfax on the roof. At one stage, the door to the staircase burst open and a uniformed officer, Constable Sydney Miles, dashed out. A shot was fired in his direction and Miles fell dead. The stand-off continued for a time until Craig finally ran out of ammunition and threw himself off the roof into a nearby greenhouse. Both Craig and Bentley were then arrested and charged with murder.

Christopher Craig and Derek Bentley appeared at the Old Bailey before the Lord Chief Justice, Lord Goddard, on 9 December, the proceedings lasting for three days. Most of the witnesses were serving police officers.

Detective Constable Fairfax confirmed that after he had seized Bentley he had searched him in case he too was armed. There was no gun but Bentley did have a knuckleduster in his right-hand coat pocket. There was also a knife in his right-hand breast pocket.

After some time, Fairfax heard a fellow officer shout out for help in climbing the drainpipe. He then assisted Constable James Christie McDonald up and both officers then returned to where Fairfax had left Bentley. Soon afterwards, the door to the stairs burst open and Constable Miles was shot. Moments later, Constable Harrison came out of the stairwell and joined them. Later, after Bentley had been taken downstairs, Fairfax rushed at Craig and saw him jump over the edge of the roof. During this time, Fairfax was also shot in the shoulder, and received treatment for this at the same hospital that Craig was taken to.

Constable McDonald confirmed that he had arrived at the scene in the same car as the dead officer, Constable Miles. As he was climbing the drainpipe, he heard a man whom he now knew to be Derek Bentley, shout, 'Let him have it Chris!' After being assisted onto the roof, McDonald saw Miles being shot dead. Shortly afterwards they were joined by Constable Jaggs, who had also climbed up the drainpipe.

Perhaps the most telling phrase, and one which was used by the prosecution to establish Derek Bentley's guilt, was his shout, 'Let him have it Chris!' This was heard by Fairfax and McDonald and other officers, including Constable Norman Harrison. This was taken as Bentley inciting Craig to shoot and made him equally responsible for Constable Miles's death. The jury agreed and took seventy-five minutes to decide that both defendents were guilty. Craig was too young to hang and so was sentenced to be detained during Her Majsty's pleasure, but Derek Bentley was sentenced to hang.

On 13 January 1953 an appeal was dismissed and, on Wednesday, 28 January, Derek Bentley was hanged at Wandsworth by Albert Pierrepoint and Harry Allen. The case, however, was far from over for other evidence was not revealed at the time.

At the same time that Fairfax, McDonald and Harrison all heard Bentley shout, 'Let him have it Chris!', there was another officer on the roof. Constable Claude Pain travelled in the same police car as Constable Fairfax and as the latter climbed the drainpipe, Pain found a ladder and reached the roof before the very first shot was fired. Pain was on that roof all the time, right up to the point where Craig leapt off it and swore that Bentley never said those five fateful words. Indeed, once Miles had been shot, Bentley spent most of the time crying. Curiously, the three officers who claimed to have heard the phrase were all decorated for bravery. Pain was never even mentioned in the evidence and received nothing.

Even if one puts this to one side, there is still doubt. If the fateful words were spoken, they could just as easily have been a request for Craig to hand over the weapon, but even if Bentley had intended him to shoot the police, he should still not have been hanged. Medical evidence showed that Bentley was epileptic and had an Intelligent Quotient in the mid-60s and a reading age of just $4\frac{1}{2}$.

There was also the matter of the weapons found on Derek Bentley. Much importance was given to these at the trial but it must be remembered that both the knuckleduster and the knife were found in his right-hand pockets. Derek Bentley was left-handed.

The State, as always with miscarriages of justice, dragged its feet for years. In the early 1990s it admitted, somewhat reluctantly, that Bentley should not have been hanged due to his mental subnormalities but ruled that he was still guilty of murder. It was not until 1998 that a full pardon was finally granted.

For Derek William Bentley, unlawfully hanged by an immovable State bent on pure revenge, it was forty-five years too late.

John Francis Wilkinson, 1953

The house in Boundaries Road, Balham, was certainly a full one. On 14 July 1953, Hermann Schrieber married Charlotte Gray and moved into the house with Charlotte's 5-year-old daughter, Miriam Susan.

In addition, there were also three lodgers living in the house, one of whom was 24-year-old John Wilkinson.

Exactly one month later, on Friday, 14 August, at around 8 p.m., little Miriam fell asleep on a divan settee. When the rest of the household retired, Miriam was left where she was. All remained well until 1 a.m. on Saturday, 15 August.

It was at that hour that Hermann Schrieber was woken by a loud bang. Thinking that it may well have come from outside, he simply rolled over and went back to sleep. Two hours later, at 3 a.m., Charlotte was also woken, this time by the sound of breaking glass. She too took no notice and went back to sleep. Still the disturbances continued and at 5.45 a.m. the front door was slammed. Despite all these noises, it was not until 6.30 a.m. that Charlotte and Hermann finally rose from their bed.

They were shocked, to say the least. The downstairs of the house was full of smoke and it appeared that someone had started a small fire on the kitchen floor. The first priority was to put the flames out and only then was it discovered that Miriam was dead. The child was examined by Dr Philip Chandler. He was able to say that Miriam had not died as a result of the fire or smoke. She had been struck on the head three times with some blunt instrument and there had even been an attempt at rape.

The police determined that the only person missing from the house was one of the lodgers, John Wilkinson. His description was circulated and so accurate was this that he was arrested at Hinchley Wood in the early hours of 16 August. His only comment was, 'I'm glad you picked me up.'

Wilkinson readily admitted his part in the death of Miriam Gray. He stated that he had taken a bottle of vermouth and one of beer and drank them both in his room. Then he had broken a chair, which was probably the loud thud Hermann had heard, and wrapped one of the legs in a piece of torn blanket. He had then gone downstairs, battered Miriam with the chair leg, removed her pyjama bottoms and tried to have sex with her. He had then started the fire on the floor before leaving the house.

The trial took place at the Old Bailey before Mr Justice Hilbery over two days, commencing on 2 November, and an attempt was made to show that Wilkinson was insane. Evidence was given that four of his siblings suffered from fits and that other relatives had been in asylums. Dr Desmond Curran, however, had examined Wilkinson and while he did describe the prisoner as abnormal with a psychotic personality, he was, nevertheless, sane.

The jury took forty-five minutes to find Wilkinson guilty and consequently, he was hanged at Wandsworth on Friday, 18 December by Stephen Wade and Royston Rickard.

Alfred Charles Whiteway, 1953

On Sunday, 31 May 1953, 16-year-old Barbara Songhurst and her close friend, 18-year-old Christine Reed, went for a cycle ride on the Thames towpath. They were seen together between 11 p.m. and 11.30 p.m. but when they did not arrive home, were reported as missing persons.

On 1 June, Barbara's body was found in the river near Richmond. She had been battered to death, stabbed and raped before death. Five days after this, on 6 June, Christine was also found at Richmond. She too had been stabbed to death. The police were looking for a double killer.

Towards the end of June, an arrest was made in an unconnected case. Alfred Whiteway was accused of assualting two women, one of whom he had raped. Three things immediately linked Whiteway to the murders of Barbara and Christine. First, a rape had been a factor in both cases; second, Whiteway lived in the area of Teddington where Christine and Barbara had been attacked and finally, Whiteway was known to cycle around the area and the attack had been on a cycle path. Whiteway was now questioned about the two murders.

At first he denied any knowledge of the attacks, saying that although they were separated, he had been with his wife at the time. It was when an officer was cleaning out the car used to arrest Whiteway that an interesting discovery was made. There, hidden underneath one of the seats was an axe. This was forensically examined and shown to have inflicted some of the injuries on Barbara Songhurst. Faced with this evidence, Whiteway confessed to both murders.

According to Whiteway's statement, he had gone out with the intention of committing a rape. At first he had only seen one of the two girls so her hit her over the head and rendered her unconscious. Only now did he see that she had a companion with her and she was now screaming. He ran over to hit her and knock her out too and only now did he realise that the first girl knew him. He had no choice. He had to kill them both in order to avoid detection and arrest.

Whiteway's trial took place before Mr Justice Hilbery at the Old Bailey from 26–30 October, where he pleaded not guilty, claiming that he had never admitted to any of it and that the police had manufactured his confession.

Having listened to the evidence, the jury took less than an hour to return their guilty verdict and Whiteway was hanged at Wandsworth on Tuesday, 22 December by Albert Pierrepoint and John Broadbent.

Rupert Geoffrey Wells, 1954

Nellie Officer was scared and the object of that fear was her boyfriend. In 1952 she had met Rupert Wells and he had moved in with her at 5 Eton Road, Kingston-upon-Thames at Christmastime 1953. At first things were fine but now Nellie discovered that Rupert was rather too fond of drink and when he had had too much, he became violent.

On the evening of Saturday, 8 May 1954 Nellie was working at the Old Crown Hotel. It was a relatively quiet night and at one stage she got talking to one of the customers. By coincidence, his surname too was Wells, though he was no relation to Rupert.

Sidney George Wells listened carefully as Nellie outlined her concerns over Rupert. She told him that she was nervous about going home and Sidney, concerned for her safety, said that he would go back with her and make sure that she was all right.

Nellie finished work and Sidney went back with her to Eton Road. There was no sign of Rupert but to be on the safe side, Sidney searched the house from top to bottom. Finally, as Nellie retired to her room, Sidney made himself comfortable in the living room, in case Rupert came home drunk and started causing trouble.

The night passed without incident and at 9 a.m. on Sunday, 9 May Sidney left the house. Just five minutes later, Mary Theresa Tuffen, who lived next door at no. 7, heard some terrible screams coming from Nellie Officer's house.

At 12.20 p.m. that same day, Rupert Wells walked into the Borough Arms pub on Park Road and told the landlord, Henry McDermott, that he had killed Nellie. Henry listened to Rupert's story and then called in the police. In due course, Constable Low arrived and he, Henry McDermott and Rupert then all made their way back to Eton Road. There they found Nellie, sitting in an armchair. She had been strangled.

Rupert Wells appeared before Mr Justice Jones at Lewes on 26 July, with the proceedings lasting for three days. The defence was really in two parts. First, Wells claimed that he had drunk so much alcohol that he did not know what he was doing and so could not form the intention to kill. The second part of the defence was that Wells was also taking Phenergan, a hypnotic sedative, and one of its side effects could possibly be disorientation.

The jury did not accept either argument and found Wells guilty after deliberating for less than an hour. An appeal was entered and dismissed and on Wednesday, 1 September Wells was hanged at Wandsworth by Albert Pierrepoint and Robert Leslie Stewart.

Sydney Joseph Clarke, 1955

Early on the morning of Thursday, 10 February 1955, the brutalised body of Rose Elizabeth Fairhurst was found on a bombsite at the junction of Loman Street and Great Suffolk Street, Southwark. Rose had been battered and strangled. Her clothing had been almost torn from her body and there was evidence that she had been raped.

The first thing for the police to do was piece together Rose's movements the previous evening. It was soon determined that she had been drinking in the Alfred's Head pub with a friend, Ruby Johnstone. When Ruby was spoken to she detailed an encounter in the pub with Sydney Clarke, who had apparently offered Rose 10s for sex and they had left the bar together at 9.30 p.m.

In due course, Clarke was traced to Rowton House, a hostel for men. When interviewed, he claimed he had been in Bristol on Wednesday the 9th, the night of the murder. The porter at Rowton House, Brindley Thomas Pedrick, confirmed that Clarke had arrived there just before midnight on the 9th and had said at the time that he had just travelled from Bristol, but that hardly proved that he was telling the truth. The testimony of Ruby Johnstone placed him firmly in the Alfred's Head and this testimony was strengthened by the blood evidence.

Clarke was a group AB secretor and tests on the semen found on Rose's body showed that her killer had the same characteristic. Further, such a blood type covered only about two per cent of the population. Faced with this, Clarke made a statement admitting his part in Rose's death.

Clarke confirmed that he had been drinking heavily and had approached Rose for sex. From the pub they walked to the bombsite where he found an old mattress for them to lie on but she refused, saying that it was too filthy. They had argued and he had 'gone mad' and attacked her. He remembered nothing else until he came to his senses in a café near Waterloo Bridge. In short, he was laying the ground for a plea of insanity.

The trial took place at the Old Bailey on 23 March, where guilty but insane was indeed the plea. This was largely discounted by Dr Matheson, who testified that Clarke was a sadist but was not insane.

Found guilty, Clarke was hanged at Wandsworth on Thursday, 14 April by Albert Pierrepoint and Robert Leslie Stewart.

3

SUMMARY OF EXECUTIONS IN LONDON FOR MURDERS COMMITTED OUTSIDE THE CAPITAL

At Pentonville

1904: John Sullivan, executed on Tuesday, 12 July for the murder of Dennis Lowthian, at sea

1911: Francisco Carlos Godhino, executed on Tuesday, 17 October for the murder of Alice Emily Brewster, at sea

1926: Johannes Josephus Cornelius Mommers, executed on Tuesday, 27 July for the murder of Augusta Viletta Pionbini at Thundersley, Essex

1926: Hashankhan Samander, executed on Tuesday, 2 November for the murder of Khanmar Jung Baz at Tilbury Docks

1928: Frederick Guy Browne, executed on Thursday, 31 May for the murder of Constable George William Gutteridge at Howe Green, Essex (See Wandsworth – William Kennedy)

1933: Robert James Kirby, executed on Wednesday, 11 October for the murder of his girlfriend, Grace Ivy Newing, at Chadwell Heath

1937: Leslie George Stone, executed on Friday, 13 August for the murder of his ex-girlfriend, Ruby Ann Keen at Leighton Buzzard

1937: John Thomas Rodgers, executed on Thursday, 18 November for the murder of Lilian Maud Chamberlain at Northwood, Middlesex

1943: William Henry Turner, executed on Wednesday, 24 March for the murder of Ann Elizabeth Wade at Audley Road, Colchester

1945: Joachim Palme-Goltz, Joseph Mertins, Heinz Breuling, Erich Koenig and Kurt Zuchlsdorff, all executed on Saturday, 6 October for the murder of a fellow PoW, Wolfgang Rosterg at the Comrie Prison Camp in Perthshire

1945: Armin Kuehne and Emil Schmittendorff, both executed on Friday, 16 November for the murder of a fellow PoW, Gerhardt Rettig, near Sheffield

1945: James McNicol, executed on Friday, 21 December for the murder of Donald Alfred Richard Kirkaldie at Thorpe Bay

1945: John Riley Young, executed on Friday, 21 December for the murder of Frederick Benjamin Lucas and Cissie Clara Lucas at Leigh-on-Sea

1949: William Claude Hodson Jones, executed on Wednesday, 28 September for the murder of Waltraut Lehman in woods in Germany in July 1945

1953: George James Newland, executed on Wednesday, 23 December for the murder of Henry John Tandy in Orsett, Essex

At Wandsworth

1921: Jack Alfred Field and William Thomas Gray, executed on Friday, 4 February for the murder of Irene Violet Munro on the Crumbles beach at Eastbourne

1924: Jean Pierre Vacquier, executed on Tuesday, 12 August for the murder of Alfred George Poynter Jones at the Blue Anchor Hotel, Byfleet

1924: Patrick Herbert Mahon, executed on Wednesday, 3 September for the murder of his lover, Emily Beilby Kaye in the Officer's House on the Crumbles beach at Eastbourne

1925: John Norman Holmes Thorne, executed on Wednesday, 22 April for the murder of his girlfriend Elsie Emily Cameron at Crowborough

1928: James Gillon, executed on Tuesday, 31 January for the murder of his sister Annie Gillon, at Lower Beeding

1928: William Kennedy, executed on Thursday, 31 May for the murder of Constable George William Gutteridge at Howe Green, Essex (See Pentonville – Frederick Guy Browne)

1928: William Charles Benson, executed on Tuesday, 20 November for the murder of his girlfriend, Charlotte Alice Harber near Coulsdon, Surrey

1930: Albert Edward Marjoram, executed on Wednesday, 11 June for the murder of Edith May Parker at Dartford Heath

1934: Albert Parker and Frederick William Probert, executed on Friday, 4 May for the murder of Joseph Bedford at Portslade near Brighton

1935: Leonard Albert Brigstock, executed on Tuesday, 2 April for the murder of Hubert Sidney Deggan at Chatham Docks

1935: Percy Charles Anderson, executed on Tuesday, 16 April for the murder of his girlfriend, Edith Constance Drew-Bear at Brighton

1936: George Arthur Bryant, executed on Tuesday, 14 July for the murder of his girlfriend, Ellen Margaret Mary Whiting at Dover

1938: Alfred Ernest Richards, executed on Tuesday, 12 July for the murder of his wife, Kathleen Richards at Welling, Kent

1938: William James Graves, executed on Tuesday, 19 July for the murder of his 14-month-old son, Tony Ruffle, in Dover

1939: Stanley Ernest Boon and Arthur John Smith, hanged on Wednesday, 25 October and Thursday, 26 October respectively for the murder of Mabel Maud Bundy at Hindhead

1940: William Charles Cowell, executed on Wednesday, 24 April for the murder of Anne Farrow Cook in woods near Hurstpierpoint

1942: Cyril Johnson, executed on Wednesday, 15 April for the murder of Maggie Smail at Ashford

1943: August Sangret, executed on Thursday, 29 April for the murder of his girlfriend, Joan Pearl Wolfe near Godalming in 1942

1943: Charles Arthur Raymond, executed on Saturday, 10 July for the murder of Marguerite Beatrice Burge near Goodwood

1943: Charles Eugene Gauthier, executed on Friday, 24 September for the murder of his lover, Annette Elizabeth Frederika Christina Pepper at Portslade near Brighton

1943: John Joseph Dorgan, executed on Wednesday, 22 December for the murder of his wife, Florence Elizabeth Agnes Dorgan, in Brighton

1945: Horace Beresford Gordon, executed on Tuesday, 9 January for the murder of Dorothy May Hillman, near Horsham

1945: Andrew Brown, executed on Tuesday, 30 January for the murder of Amelia Elizabeth Ann Knowles at Arundel

1946: Michal Niescior, executed on Thursday, 31 January for the murder of Charles Elphick, at Portslade near Brighton

1946: Sydney John Smith, executed on Friday, 6 September for the murder of John Whatman at Hastings

1947: Harold Hagger, executed on Tuesday, 18 March for the murder of Dagmar Petrzywalkski, at Wrotham Hill in Kent

1949: William John Davies, executed on Tuesday, 16 August for the murder of his girlfriend, Lucy Wilson inside Campbell's Restaurant in Eastbourne

1949: Ernest Soper Couzins, executed on Friday, 30 December for the murder of Victor Desmond Elias, in Canterbury

1951: Joseph Brown and Edward Charles Smith, executed on Wednesday, 25 April for the murder of Frederick Gosling at Chertsey

1951: James Virrels, executed on Thursday, 26 April for the murder of Alice Kate Roberts at Worthing

1953: John James Alcott, executed on Friday, 2 January for the murder of Geoffrey Charles 'Dixie' Dean at Ash Vale station near Aldershot

1954: James Reginald Doohan, executed on Wednesday, 14 April for the murder of Herbert Victor Ketley at Rushenden

1954: William Sanchez De Pina Hepper, executed on Wednesday, 11 August for the murder of 11-year-old Margaret Rose Louise Spevick at Hove

1961: Victor John Terry, executed on Thursday, 25 May for the murder of John Henry Pull during a bank raid at Durrington near Worthing

1961: Henryk Niemasz, executed on Friday, 8 September for the murder of his lover, Alice Buxton and her husband, Hubert Roderick Twells Buxton, at Aldington

4

SUMMARY OF EXECUTIONS IN LONDON FOR CRIMES OTHER THAN MURDER

Executed for Spying

1914: Carl Hans Lody, shot at the Tower on Friday, 6 November

1915: Carl Frederick Muller, shot at the Tower on Wednesday, 23 June

1915: Robert Rosenthal, hanged at Wandsworth on Thursday, 15 July

1915: Haicke Marinus Petrius Janssen and Willem Johannes Roos, both shot at the Tower on Friday, 30 July

1915: Ernest Waldemar Melin, shot at the Tower on Friday, 10 September

1915: Augusto Alfredo Roggen, shot at the Tower on Friday, 17 September

1915: Fernando Buschman, shot at the Tower on Tuesday, 19 October

1915: George T Breeckow, shot at the Tower on Tuesday, 26 October

1915: Irving Guy Ries, shot at the Tower on Wednesday, 27 October

1915: Albert Meyer, shot at the Tower on Saturday, 27 November

1916: Ludovico Hurwitz y Zender, shot at the Tower on Tuesday, 11 April

1940: Jose Waldeburg and Carl Meier, hanged at Pentonville on Tuesday, 10 December

1940: Charles Albert Van Dem Kieboom, hanged at Pentonville on Tuesday, 17 December

1941: George Johnson Armstrong, hanged at Wandsworth on Wednesday, 9 July

1941: Karl Theodore Drucke and Werner Henrich Walti, hanged at Wandsworth on 6 August

1941: Josef Jakobs, shot at the Tower on Thursday, 14 August

1941: Karel Richard Richter, hanged at Wandsworth on Wednesday, 10 December

1942: Jose Estella Key and Alphonse Louis Eugene Timmerman, hanged at Wandsworth on Tuesday, 7 July

1942: Duncan Alexander Croall Scott-Ford, hanged at Wandsworth on Tuesday, 3 November

1942: Johannes Marinus Dronkers, hanged at Wandsworth on Thursday, 31 December

1943: Franciscus Johannes Winter, hanged at Wandsworth on Tuesday, 26 January

1944: Oswald John Job, hanged at Pentonville on Thursday, 16 March

1944: Pierre Richard Charles Neukermans, hanged at Pentonville on Friday, 23 June

1944: Joseph Jan Van Hove, hanged at Pentonville on Wednesday, 12 July

Executed for Treason

1916: Roger Casement, hanged at Pentonville on Thursday, 3 August

1945: John Amery, hanged at Wandsworth on Wednesday, 19 December

1946: William Joyce, hanged at Wandsworth on Thursday, 3 January

1946: Theodore William John Schurch, hanged at Pentonville on Friday, 4 January

Summary of Executions

Prison	Executions
Newgate	9
Holloway	5
Tower of London	12
Pentonville	120
Wandsworth	117
Chelmsford	4
Maidstone	1
TOTAL	268